THE
ENERGY ILLUSION
AND
ECONOMIC STABILITY

Quantum Causality

HUI-LIANG TSAI

PRAEGER

New York
Westport, Connecticut
London

Library of Congress Cataloging-in-Publication Data

Tsai, Hui-Liang.
   The energy illusion and economic stability : quantum causality /
Hui-Liang Tsai.
      p.   cm.
   Bibliography: p.
   Includes index.
   ISBN 0-275-93191-9 (alk. paper)
   1. Power resources—Economic aspects.   2. Economic
stabilization.   3. Petroleum products—Prices.   4. Petroleum industry
and trade—Political aspects—Middle East.   5. Energy policy.
6. Economic policy.   I. Title.
HD9502.A2T77   1989
333.79—dc19   88-27097

Copyright © 1989 by Hui-Liang Tsai

Library of Congress Catalog Card Number: 88–27097
ISBN: 0-275–93191–9

First published in 1989

Praeger Publishers, One Madison Avenue, New York, NY 10010
A division of Greenwood Press, Inc.

Printed in the United States of America

The paper used in this book complies with the
Permanent Paper Standard issued by the National
Information Standards Organization (Z39.48-1984).

10 9 8 7 6 5 4 3 2 1

Contents

Figures

Tables

Preface

This book provides a systematic analysis of the problems of economic growth and stability presented by the changing role of energy in modern economics. As such, it provides a logical framework within which the key problems of the world energy issue may be analyzed. The theme is that energy does matter and that any interpretation of short-term movements in economic activity is likely to be seriously at fault if it neglects energy supply changes and repercussions.

The material is accessible to the general reader while at the same time sufficiently sophisticated to satisfy the experts who are engaged in, or would like to be engaged in, energy-policy analysis and forecasting. It is also organized for use in the classroom. First, it provides an overview of the nature and the roots of the energy "crisis," as well as economic aspects of complex contemporary energy issues and problems. Second, it provides an introduction to the technological characteristics of energy and future prospects of energy supply. Third, it contains a synopsis of the key elements of U.S. energy legislation and past public measures. Fourth, it presents the theoretical and empirical underpinnings of the energy-economy interactions. And, finally, it describes the established theories and techniques of microeconomics that can be applied to the analysis of energy resources as scarce inputs to production processes. With the knowledge gained from this book, one should be able to face the future with an ability to choose energy policies and make economic judgments concerning energy issues.

I am indebted to all those authors whose work I have referenced very freely. I am grateful for the encouragement and the guidance provided me on various occasions by Professor George Macesich of the Center for Yugoslav-American

Studies, Research, and Exchanges at Florida State University. My special thanks to Professor Jacob De Rooy of Penn State Harrisburg for his special interest in my research and his assistance in locating the reference materials needed for my work.

1

Economics, Politics, and the Energy Crisis

Ability to carry out stabilization policies successfully depends in good part on ability to react successfully to external shocks to which the economy is subjected. Monetary policy, as well as fiscal policy, must take such shocks into account, regardless of the sources of the shocks. They share equal responsibility for the long-run state of the economy.

The sudden and dramatic shocks in the form of a rise in the relative price of energy in the 1970s have significantly affected the world economic stability and productive capacity as they have that of other countries. Never before has energy played such a decisive role in international relations. A number of factors have made the nonoil-producing countries, especially those with industrial economies, vulnerable to an energy shock.

Indeed, of all events of importance to the global economy in this century, the oil price revolution of the 1970s has had by far the most far-reaching effect. The oil price increases have brought about major changes in the international economic, monetary, and financial systems, triggering large-scale alterations in world capital flows, with actual transfers of major resources between countries and regions, and causing world payments imbalances. They have also provoked much public discussion and disagreement about the problems that these changes will pose for the international economy. The economic, political, and psychological repercussions of what became known as the "energy crisis" have dominated much of the discussion on U. S. economic policies since 1973 and caused widespread questioning of the capacity of the world economy to adjust to the new situation at a tolerable cost. To say the least, the 1973–74 oil price increases have brought into existence a totally new balance of economic and political power, which instituted international economic relationships that are still evolving.

There continues to be a great deal of skepticism as to the true nature of the so-called "energy crisis." Whether the crisis is the direct result of international politics, nationalism, past domestic public policies, unchecked growth, individual wastefulness, conspiracy, or corporate greed, is uncertain. The certainty is that a crisis did exist, directly affecting the world economy in general and the national economies in particular.

ENERGY IN THE WORLD CONTEXT

The world energy situation is embedded in a larger political and economic context. Within this context, there are two strong historical currents running through the four decades since the end of World War II: the deepening world-wide growth of economic interdependence and the rapid development of nationalism among the nonindustrial countries. Nationalism has stalled the further development of a world economy, but economic interdependence has gone so far that the major countries are unable to extricate themselves. Conflict between them was, in fact, one of the main causes of the energy crisis in the 1970s.[1]

Economic Interdependence

The post–World War II era had brought the deepening growth of economic interdependence to the economies of nations, with oil playing a leading role both in promoting economic growth and in creating economic insecurity. Not only had interdependence led to, and resulted from, rapid recovery from the war's devastation and a long period of much-desired economic growth, it had also generated insecurity as nations lost control of their particular economic destinies.[2]

The restoration of war-shattered industry and subsequent rapid industrialization in Western Europe and Japan after World War II contributed strongly to a surging demand for petroleum, which led to the development of the oil industry in the Middle East. Fields that had been discovered before the war were brought into production quickly and cheaply, and intensive exploration soon uncovered large new oil reservoirs.

As a result, low-priced energy supplies had become relatively abundant in order to induce many nations to begin the development of energy-intensive economies. Industrial countries such as Great Britain, France, and Germany, which were once largely self-sufficient in their energy resources because of their domestic coal production, became increasingly dependent on cheaper, cleaner, and more-convenient-to-use imported oil. Other industrial countries such as Italy and Japan, that were deficient in domestic energy resources and relied heavily on imported oil for their energy resource needs, greatly increased the magnitude of that dependence as their economies advanced and their energy demands grew. Even the United States, which was largely self-sufficient in the past because of its vast oil reserves and abundant domestic coal production, became one of the world's largest importers in the 1970s, bringing in nearly half of the oil it consumed. With these increasing demands for imported oil, the Middle East share of imports rose from less than 15 percent in 1973 to about 33 percent by the late 1970s.

As these nations became heavily dependent upon oil from the Middle East to fill their energy needs, petroleum has become one of the most important commodities in international trade. In 1974, for example, trade in petroleum exceeded $100 billion, amounting to about 15 percent of the non-Communist world's trade. A growing dependence on oil was caused both by rates of economic growth much higher than achieved in prior decades and by a shift to oil from coal and other sources, largely on account of lower relative prices for oil right up to 1973.

The special importance of oil trade was further reinforced by the Arab oil embargo in late 1973 and early 1974, but it also posed by far "the most traumatic challenge to economic interdependence in the post–World War II period." In all countries heavily dependent on oil imports, the Arab oil embargo drove home the point that "the lifeblood of their national economies was under foreign control." Interdependence in oil thus led to profound economic insecurity throughout much of the non-Communist world.[3]

The oil embargo was brought on by the Arab-Israeli conflict of October 1973. Notwithstanding the cessation of open warfare and the subsequent conclusion of the Egyptian-Israeli treaty in 1979, tensions continue to exist in the region. In particular, control over world oil exports is inherently oligopolistic, and oil exports are potentially volatile and uncertain. Two-thirds of world oil exports originate in six countries that have a combined population of less than 60 million and are situated in a region of chronic internal tension and long-standing great power confrontation. Since demand for Middle East oil will in all likelihood continue strong throughout the 1980s and well into the 1990s, political developments there will inevitably have a substantial impact on the energy supply-demand balance of the world.[4]

More important, oil amounts to about one-fifth of the value of all imports for the developing countries with oil deficits, which contain the predominant portion of population in the developing world. The economic prospects of these countries are usually constrained by the availability of cheap external oil supplies and foreign exchanges. In particular, these countries were at the beginning of a period of intensive industrialization, modernization of transport systems, and a shift from traditional fuels like firewood and animal and vegetable waste to commercial sources of energy. Undoubtedly, the sudden recurrence of large increase in oil prices would lead not only to domestic economic crisis in these countries but also serious disruption of the international economic system.

Indeed, the shocks and repercussions produced by sharp increases in international oil prices and the manipulation of supplies had caused an unprece-

dented upheaval in the world economy in the 1970s and contributed to major
international economic crises in the 1980s. Harsher external conditions exacerbated the consequences of various policy-induced distortions in many oil-
importing developed, as well as nonoil developing, countries. Nations whose
industrial economic activities are closely linked to a reliable supply of imported
oil at reasonable prices were hard hit by inflation when supplies became uncertain and prices were abruptly increased. The oil shock itself, however, did not
have its effect through serious shortages. Rather it worked by reducing pur-
chasing power in the oil-importing countries.[5]

The historic significance of this event goes far beyond changes in the picture
of the world energy situation and questions about the stability of the Organization of the Petroleum Exporting Countries (OPEC). The oil price increases
in late 1974, for example, had transferred $75 billion to the oil-exporting coun-
tries, or about 2 percent of the total output of the oil-importing nations. This
large capital flow added measurably to cost-push pressures in a world already
suffering from inflation. Since most of this sudden, huge income transfer initially took the form of financial assets rather than current imports of goods and
services, it had a depressing effect on demand, output, and employment in the
industrial countries and brought about unprecedentedly large deficits in their
international payments. Intrinsically, or rather, paradoxically, the seeming
weakness of corrective forces made doubts about the economic future even
more bleak.[6]

The major concerns were whether the world financial system could safely
handle such large payments imbalances, regardless of their source, and whether
individual countries would always have access to the necessary financing. The
worries were amplified because no one was sure which institutions would handle the financing. Under such circumstances, assuring an individual country the
capacity to finance its oil-import needs is of crucial importance not only to the
country concerned but also to the efficient functioning of the international economic system as a whole. Failure to achieve an appropriate distribution would
involve at best a misallocation of resources and at worst a major slump or acute
liquidity shortages.

At the same time, both developed and nonoil developing countries acquired
very large deficits. They needed the oil money in amounts that would cover
their trade deficits. Some countries used these funds to invest in infrastructure
which ultimately reduced their dependence on oil and/or generated an income
stream sufficient to help pay their debts. Others, because of their less developed
nature, were unable to do this and found themselves getting deeper and deeper
in debt, eventually leading to the ''debt crisis'' of the 1980s.

Hence, while the Arab oil embargo had caused widespread feelings of insecurity in an evolving world economy, the quadrupled oil price increases imposed over that period by the Organization of the Petroleum Exporting Countries placed severe strains on the international financial institutions that were
designed to make economic interdependence workable. The integration of world

financial markets, brought upon by the economic interdependence, has eroded the effectiveness of government monetary policy as a means of controlling national economies. Not only could business firms undercut government monetary policies by private borrowing or lending activities in the Eurocurrency markets, also integrated multinational enterprises could circumvent capital restrictions and profit limitations by the prices they charged for sales between their different corporate subsidiaries.[7]

Explicably, the energy sector has exemplified the growth of economic interdependence during the post–World War II period. The international oil supply and demand situation generally, and the role of the oil companies in the Middle East in particular, have changed dramatically over the past decades. They will continue to change.

The irony, however, is that the collapse of oil prices in 1986, and again in 1987, has created an urgent need to reappraise the energy policies of producing and consuming nations. Producing countries now face uncertain prospects regarding their future incomes while consuming countries confront the risk of market disruptions and accompanying economic losses.

Even so, global energy developments are intrinsically interwoven with the functioning of the international economic order. The events of the 1970s served only as a reminder that "in a world of politically independent nation-states, too much economic interdependence may lead to insecurity in particular nations and thus to instability in the international system as a whole." In particular, "mismanagement of the energy crisis could rip apart the complex web of international institutions that have facilitated economic growth through interdependence since World War II."[8] The main problems the oil-importing countries face are how to maintain their economic growth, how to pay for high-priced imported oil, how to increase the security of foreign sources of supply, and how to develop more indigenous energy resources.

Nationalism

The rapid growth of nationalism in the new nations in general, and in the Middle East in particular, was perhaps the most important political factor influencing global energy developments during the past four decades. Immediately after World War II, the decolonization process engulfed many regions of the world. For a new nation carved out of a colonial empire or for an old nation riddled with foreign concessions, freedom of action meant, first and foremost, expropriating foreign interests and regaining unfettered sovereignty over its natural resources.[9]

This process was further exacerbated by serious insensitivity of the major oil corporations[10] to local sentiment and aspirations, which ultimately resulted in a severe setback for not only these companies and their long-range plans but also the entire world, which had sunk into a dependence on oil nurtured by the expectation of uninterrupted, low-cost supplies.[11]

The original concession agreements for oil exploration and production in the Middle East were entered into during the late 1920s and 1930s at times when the average wellhead value of crude oil in Texas, with which Middle East oil would have to compete in European markets, was falling. Despite the combination of depressed prices and unknown eventual costs of finding and producing new oil in difficult areas far removed from major markets, these concession agreements provided that the companies would pay the governments land rents and fixed payments for each barrel of oil produced—irrespective of the overall profitability of a venture.[12]

These agreements, however, granted foreign corporations with more or less complete ownership over the mineral rights on vast tracts of land in exchange for royalty payments which represented a fixed amount per barrel of oil produced. Foreign corporations determined the rate of development and amount of production from their concessions, and they set the price.

Nonetheless, the system of pricing followed by the oil majors had elements of irrationality, and a preponderance of self-interest. In the period preceding World War II, royalties were generally 20-to-25 cents a barrel.[13] The implications of a fixed royalty in an era of increasing prices were that producing countries suffered a worsening of their terms of trade when, paradoxically, oil prices were increasing in the international market. The royalty arrangement was widely resented by oil-exporting countries, but they lacked the will and strength to change it.

In particular, as oil companies wielded considerable power in the decision-making structures of many Middle East countries, the governments of these oil-exporting countries found it difficult to accept not only the unfavorable economic impact of oil operations but also the exclusion of the know-how for managing their own oil-producing assets. This conflict was further compounded by the post–World War II quest of the new nations for freedom of action and participation in the international system on a more equal footing. A vital commodity such as oil could not be insulated from the upsurge of nationalism. In effect, it became a major instrument in the diplomatic revolution instigated by the Third World nations.[14]

The oil price revolution was first initiated in the mid-1940s by the government of Venezuela, which imposed a tax on income earned by oil companies operating in that country. This tax was gradually increased, resulting in payments of 75 cents a barrel to the government. The significance of Venezuela's action was its impact on the rest of the oil-producing countries outside the United States. More importantly, Venezuela vigorously promoted the 50–50 concept, which allowed host governments to earn 50 percent of total production profits in the forms of taxes.[15]

The Venezuelan action incited nationalist elements in Iran during the late 1940s and early 1950s to further challenge the old concessionary system. From the nationalist viewpoint, the system was inseparable from Western political control and influence. Even in countries like Saudi Arabia, where it had not been imposed by a colonial power, the oil concessionary system was increasingly viewed as an unpalatable contradiction to sovereign control over natural resources.

As a commonality of interest and a desire to coordinate oil policies grew quickly, communications among oil-producing countries increased. These countries, the Arab nations in particular, saw a potential for greater control of the oil market. Subsequently, in 1959 the Arab League convened the first Arab Petroleum Congress, setting the stage for the formation of an organization of oil-producing countries. The establishment of this organization might have been delayed in "procedural tangles and the inertia of negotiations," had it not been for a unilateral step taken by the oil companies in 1959 and again in 1960 to protect themselves from a profit squeeze, due to a glut, with consumption lagging significantly behind production in the oil market. The oil companies cut the posted price[16] approximately 6 percent without discussing it with the producer countries, which stood to lose large amounts of revenues.[17] This unilateral cut of posted prices by the oil majors provided a strong impetus to the formation of the Organization of Petroleum Exporting Countries (OPEC) in the latter year.

On September 14, 1960, representatives of Saudi Arabia, Venezuela, Iran, Iraq, and Kuwait, meeting in Baghdad, adopted two principal resolutions. The first stated that the five countries could "no longer be indifferent to the attitude adopted by the oil companies in effecting (posted) price modifications." The resolution demanded that the oil companies "maintain their prices steady and free from all unnecessary fluctuations" and declared the countries' intention to "study and formulate a system to ensure the stabilization of prices by, among other means, the regulation of production . . ."

The second resolution advised that the "Conference decides to form a permanent organization called the Organization of the Petroleum Exporting Countries. . . . The principal aim of the organization shall be the unification of petroleum policies for the member countries and the determination of the best means for safeguarding the interests of member countries, individually and collectively."

With approval of the resolutions later that year by each of the governments, OPEC officially came into being. In little more than 10 years, OPEC expanded its membership to 13, of which six are Middle Eastern states.[18]

An uncooperative oil industry might have quashed the collusive efforts, but a happenstance of international politics ensured industrial cooperation with the OPEC governments. The new nations began in the 1960s, following legal independence, to seek ways to maximize their freedom of action in world affairs. They found that freedom from external political constraints would not only serve to enhance national prestige abroad but also help enhance economic security and build a sense of national identity at home. Therefore, nationalism was deemed necessary for the centralization of government authority and the development of a political infrastructure for economic development. Particularly, nationalization of foreign concessions was good politics. At home, such moves were generally highly popular. Abroad, the nationalizing governments would gain stature in the Third World, and losses in its relations with the United States could be offset by gains with the Soviet Union.[19]

To say the least, the upsurge of nationalism and the newly found freedom of the small nations had effectually provided a driving force for many of the new nations such as Algeria, Libya, Iraq, and Iran, to pursue the path of complete nationalization of foreign oil operations. In alleged retaliation for the British government's purported role in permitting Iran to occupy three Arab islands in the Gulf, the revolutionary government of Libya nationalized British Petroleum's 50 percent interest in the Sarir field in December 1971. Further nationalizations followed in Libya and in Iraq. Iran, the second largest oil exporter, also chose this path in 1973, though legal sovereignty over its resources had been regained much earlier, and assumed full operational conrol of the producing areas that it had owned since 1974 but which had been operated by the consortium.

Unflatteringly, incremental nationalization by these new, small nations was taking away the upstream assets and privilege and chipping away at the profits of the giant multinational oil corporations. The weakness of the corporate bargaining positions was made clear when governments in Algeria, Libya, Iraq, Iran, and elsewhere demonstrated that they could wrest control of oil operations from the multinational companies. By refusing to compensate the companies fully or push nationalization to completion immediately, the producer governments held open the possibility of better treatment and satisfactory agreements in the post-nationalization phase of relationship in exchange for the companies' cooperation with OPEC pricing. Having thus lost control of oil operations and lacking political support from the industrial governments as well, the multinationals capitulated to OPEC, enforcing its price policies, collecting its taxes, and selling its refined petroleum worldwide. These episodes demonstrated that the invincibility of the oil companies was but a myth.[20]

Not surprisingly, the participation levels by producing governments were renegotiated. After lengthy negotiations, a General Participation Agreement was reached in December 1972 by the oil companies with representatives of the governments of Saudi Arabia, Abu Dhabi, and Qatar. It provided for an immediate 25 percent participation interest by the producing governments, with additional shares each year thereafter, leading to 51 percent government participation by 1982. The agreement also provided for the companies to purchase a portion of the governments' share of the oil produced at a price reached by mutual agreement. The agreement further stated that the companies would be compensated for unrecovered investments, "with due allowance for inflation that has occurred since the investments were made." Kuwait did not ratify this agreement and instead held out for a larger ownership share.[21]

By the fall of 1973, however, the Gulf members of OPEC had became dissatisfied with not only the 1971 Tehran and Tripoli price and tax agreements, but also the modification of the 1971 agreements by the Geneva Agreement of January 1972 and June 1973, which raised the posted price of oil by 20 percent and 15 percent, respectively, to reflect currency changes and inflation. These countries regarded these gains as inadequate. They sought to revise the 1971 agreements by negotiations. When these proved inconclusive, the countries acted unilaterally. On October 16, 1973, they decreed an increase of about 70 percent in the posted prices of their crude oil. Since then, the OPEC governments have established oil prices and production policies in negotiations among themselves and have become the major force in revolutionizing contractual relationships with the international oil companies.

The rapidly changing events of the 1970s were mirrored in the fragility of these participation agreements. The OPEC countries were quick to take advantage of their new bargaining strength vis-à-vis the major oil companies. Participation levels called for in the 1972 agreement were deemed unsatisfactory less than a year later, and were escalated so that most of the other Gulf states joined Kuwait in achieving 60 percent ownership effective January 1974. In mid-1974, Kuwait obtained 60 percent, retroactive to January 1974. Saudi Arabia followed suit. In mid-1970s, Saudi Arabia insisted on 100 percent control.

These dramatic changes in oil pricing occurred roughly at the same time when the Arab-Israeli conflict broke out on October 6, 1973. They also coincided with the subsequent embargo of oil shipments from the Arab oil-producing states to the United States and the Netherlands, and a general Arab production cutback that affected all the major consuming countries, as a result of a series of political actions and production decisions by Iraq, Libya, and Kuwait. These actions had led to convulsive change in the global oil market and influenced the energy policies of nations around the world, resulting in some disruption in oil movements and uncertainties about future consequences for oil market. OPEC countries not only quadrupled their crude oil prices, but also accelerated the nationalization of oil operations. These changes give OPEC control over and responsibility for producing enough oil to balance the world demand for non-OPEC supply of energy.

The world oil market, which had been a buyer's market for more than a decade, was rapidly transformed into a seller's market, which enabled the oil-producing countries and the national oil companies of these countries to secure greater control over their markets. Not only did OPEC countries increase taxes during these early years of the 1970s, but they also increased their participation in their domestic petroleum operations.[22]

Importing countries must now adjust their energy consumption to levels consistent with oil volumes that OPEC makes available and at prices that it sets. These events marked the first instance that OPEC took the pricing function completely into its own hands. They also marked the end of a long struggle between the oil-producing countries and the major multinational oil companies.

In any event, the movement to gain government control over the production end of the worldwide oil industry has been on firm political ground, though not irreversible. In large measure, "the success of the movement was due to the strength of nationalism as a driving force in world politics."[23] It has brought about fundamental changes in the relationships between oil-producing countries, the international oil companies, and the consuming countries. These changes are still going on. More importantly, the decision of OPEC to interrupt supplies to the West for political reasons has demonstrated how the simple idea of price increases and production cuts could simultaneously be implemented across the market of great complexity.

ENERGY IN THE DOMESTIC CONTEXT: THE AMERICAN EXPERIENCE

The scarcity of solid information generated skepticism as to the true nature of the U.S. energy crisis during the 1970s. Some wondered if the crisis was a false issue raised by the major oil corporations to eliminate competition and raise profits. Perhaps, with this view in mind, critics charged that the crisis was in effect manipulated by the public relations department of the major oil corporations, which created, or at least, exacerbated, the situation as a means of securing economic advantage. Others believed that the country was simply experiencing a shortage of oil, and that other alternative energy sources had to be developed to meet our national energy growth.

A third prominent view was that the shortage of oil was a function of the failure of the United States to manage the international affairs of the country and to deal effectively with the oil-exporting developing countries. It was the disaster of U.S. policy in the international politics.

Another opinion was that the energy crisis was only a regional phenomenon. This view focuses on the regional shortages of gasoline and heating oil experienced between 1969 and 1974 and attributed the "shortage" to the bottleneck that had developed at the refinery step in domestic oil production. According to this view, the bottleneck developed because refinery capacity was not sufficient to meet the increasing demand for petroleum products.

Taken as a whole, these different beliefs indicate three things: (a) petroleum figured prominently in the U.S. energy picture, (b) no one, except oil industry officials, seemed to know much about how U.S. oil was produced, distributed, or priced, and (c) there was no clear consensus concerning the true nature of U.S. energy problems and as to what national energy goals should be established, what priority each should have, and what types of administrative machinery should be employed to meet them.

Nature and Roots of the U.S. Energy Crisis

The causes of the U.S. energy crisis have not yet been completely understood. To some extent, however, there are three distinctive views that can be identified as the nature and roots of the U.S. energy crisis. These include the "conspiracy" theory, the "lump of energy" concept, and the "market-failure" hypothesis. A brief review of these three views is provided below.

The "Conspiracy" Theory

The conspiracy theory had received widespread acceptance in the explanations of the U.S. energy crisis during the winter of 1973 even though there was no one person or organization sponsoring the theory. The conspiracy theorists suggested that the energy crisis was the result of a conspiracy by the major oil corporations to eliminate competition and raise profits.

The argument was that, to effectively sew up the U.S. gasoline market, the major oil corporations used the embargo as a smoke screen to cut off the supply of gasoline to independent and franchise gasoline dealers, as well as the independent oil refineries, and redirect it to retail outlets owned by the majors. Proponents of this theory charged that the majors had engaged in a "systematic and deliberate" course of action designed to eliminate price competition. They contended that there was no shortage of gasoline and that the majors were producing just as much gasoline as they had the previous year. They also believed that the Arab oil embargo had not affected gasoline supplies at all in this country. While the validity of this argument had not been proven, the information upon which this theory rested seemed compelling.[24]

First of all, over the years, the major oil corporations have parlayed their unique status into control of the domestic oil market. Twenty oil corporations, through their many subsidiary operations, almost completely control the flow of oil to and within this country. In 1970, for example, the 20 corporations controlled 94 percent of all domestic crude oil sources, 86 percent of the nation's refinery capacity, 69 percent of all pipeline facilities regulated by the Interstate Commerce Commission, and 79 percent of all retail gasoline outlets in America.[25]

Secondly, the supply relationship developed between the major oil companies and the independents over the years was characterized by more than adequate refinery capacities, relatively fewer and more economical automobiles, and filling station gas wars, trading stamps, and give-aways. But by 1973, according to the conspiracy theory, the market for gasoline had changed, though refinery capacities were being fully utilized at every location.

The proponents of the conspiracy theory contended that the majors used the Arab oil embargo of October 1973 as an excuse to discontinue supplying gasoline to their independent customers that they could now sell themselves. They also claimed that the independents were not the only retail gasoline dealers who had been forced out of business during the crisis. In many instances the operators of franchised major branded dealerships were denied the opportunity to renew their franchise agreements with the majors when their contracts expired, even though some of these stations had been in business for many years and sold large quantities of gasoline. After the station closed, the major would reopen the station with company personnel and continue business as usual, it was contended. As a result, independent and franchised gasoline dealers were going out of business at the rate of 200 closings per week in early 1974 because they could not get gasoline to sell despite the fact that existing refineries were run at full tilt. In most cases the independents had obtained their supply of gasoline from the majors prior to the embargo.[26]

Thirdly, the spiraling profit figures reported by the major oil corporations further fueled the controversy as to the true nature of the U.S. energy crisis. As the price of gasoline steadily climbed, and more and more retail dealers closed their doors, charges of "collusion" and price fixing were directed at the major oil corporations.

These charges were taken up not only by the attorneys general of the states of Connecticut, Maine, Michigan, New Jersey, and New York, but also by the Federal Trade Commission. With supports from 29 states in the prosecution of complaints against the major oil corporations, the Federal Trade Commission accused the "big eight" oil companies (Exxon, Shell, Mobil, Texaco, Gulf, Standard Oil of California, Standard Oil of Indiana, and Arco) of various illegal practices, including a "common course of action" which was said to have raised prices, generated excessive profits, and driven independent refiners out of business or prevented new competitors from entering the crude oil refining business.

Finally, the critics said that the energy crisis was a weapon used by energy companies to counter success of the popular movement for a better environment, which began in the mid-1960s and reached fruition in a series of federal and state laws passed in the late 1960s and early 1970s. Public concern with pollution had imposed costs on energy production that the energy corporations found burdensome. Refiners, for example, had to stop polluting the air. Coal operators occasionally had to restore the lands they ravaged. Nuclear power stations could no longer discharge hot water into a nearby river or vent radioactive iodine into the atmosphere. Indeed, implementation of such legislations as the National Environmental Policy Act of 1969, the Clean Air Act, the Federal Water Pollution Control Act, and the Solid Waste Disposal Act, had began to hurt the energy companies, thus creating a backlash. Since the environmentalists' weapon was political, the response also had to be political.[27]

To summarize, though as compelling as it seemed to be, the "conspiracy" theory could not be substantiated or refuted for lack of reliable information regarding the supply and demand of energy in the United States at the time of the Arab oil embargo.

The "Lump of Energy" Concept

The "lump of energy" view is the most widely accepted. It is the uncritical acceptance of the "lump of energy." It focuses on a growing imbalance between the absolute quantity of energy demanded and supplied. Thus, to some extent, this conception of the energy crisis is that of "an inexorable emergence and worsening of an energy gap manifested as shortages of gasoline in 1974 and of heating oil and natural gas in late 1976.''[28]

The proponents of this view pointed out that in 1973 the 6 percent of the world's population that lived in the United States consumed about 33 percent of the total world output of energy. Not only was too much energy used, but also decisions regarding the use and production of energy had not always considered the long-term effect on world needs because energy had always been cheap and plentiful.

Indeed, while United States energy consumption had grown at a rate of 4 percent per year between 1950 and 1965, and at a rate of about 5 percent per year between 1966 and 1974, U.S. energy production grew at only about 3 percent per year between 1950 and 1970. However, there was no significant growth in domestic energy production from 1970 to 1974. In effect, in 1970 the United States was using almost 50 percent more energy than it used in 1960, but during the same 10-year period the nation's ability to produce energy increased by less than 30 percent. Oil production peaked in 1969, natural gas production around 1967, and coal production around 1944.[29]

As the demand for energy grew, imported oil was called upon to make up the national energy deficit. During the 1950s imported oil accounted for about 10 percent of U.S. national oil consumption, and by 1973 this figure had risen to about 35 percent. This reliance on imported oil was a function of the disparity between energy consumption and production in this country and has been a subject of concern for many years.

The ''lump of energy'' view projects a continuing increase in the demand for energy while the amount of oil and natural gas supplied diminish.[30] Accordingly, projections are made estimating the length of the ''grace period'' during which alternative energy plans must be made. Depending upon the projection of the growth rate of oil demand, some estimates of recoverable oil resources show that the grace period will end sometime before the year 2020 when the world's presently estimated recoverable oil resources will be exhausted.

The policy measures of the ''lump of energy'' view are straightforward at best. These include mandated conservation and the pursuit of energy efficiency during transition to alternative energy sources. These alternative sources include such renewable and inexhaustible energy sources as solar and wind energy and viable nuclear fusion technology. The transition period is to be facilitated by an appropriate mix of policies including subsidies, tax credits, taxes, and incentive pricing for new oil and natural gas and coal conversion.

To enforce conservation as a means of resolving the ''energy crisis,'' argued the proponents, the power of the government must be used. Most of these arguments, however, are based on naive definitions of conservation, meaning ''use less'' or ''save energy'' as if all other resources were of zero value. Concepts of this kind are found repeatedly in the Energy Policy Project Report of the Ford Foundation.[31]

The "Market-Failure" Hypothesis

Rejecting the "lump of energy" concept, the "market view" diagnoses the problem as deterioration in capacity of the energy market to adjust to man-made and nature-induced shocks. To such extent, the nature of the energy problem, argue the proponents, is instrinsically the "inadequate capacity" of the energy market to adjust to unexpected shocks, such as the Arab oil embargo in 1973–74 and nature-induced severe weather conditons. This view holds that the origin of the U.S. energy crisis is in the past public policy actions that have supplanted market competition by political manipulation designed to shelter some segments of the energy industry from the rigors of market competition.[32]

Despite its importance, energy is simply another commodity or service which competes for a share of limited budgets. The amounts of energy supplied and demanded are both determined by "laws of economics" that govern producers and consumer behavior. The higher the price the smaller the quantity demanded, other things equal. The longer the adjustment period, the more substitutes will become available. A greated quantity of energy will be supplied as prices rise not only by existing supplies but also by new high-cost supplies entering the market in response to increased price incentives.

The history of energy markets and past public policies in the energy field suggest a number of factors that have limited its adjustment capacity. There is, typically, the three-to-five-year lead time for end-use delivery and the common pool problem, rising from ill-defined property rights problems similar to those arising in the fishery problem. Exclusive property rights are created at the instant of capture or drawing oil from a common pool. The incentives, thus, are for several producers sharing a common pool to extract as much oil as possible as quickly as possible. This reduces, however, the total amount of oil recoverable by drilling from the pool, relative to the more paced rate drilling known as the "maximum efficient rate (MER) of production," thus giving rise to physical waste. It is, therefore, preferable to use a slower rate of drilling not to exceed the "maximum efficient rate of production." The idea is to promote joint maximization as in the coordination of production decisions in a cartel of producers.

The long lead time for end-use delivery and the common pool problem are not the only factors causing one of the apparent "malfunctions" in the enrgy market. A historical inquiry, which will be discussed in greater detail in the next section, also reveals that the strong government influence, or perhaps interference, in the past has been to emasculate the capacity of the energy market to respond to the crisis. It is a legacy of the percentage depletion allowance and the demand prorationing system of the 1920s, and the subsequent voluntary and mandatory import quotas on oil products in the 1950s. The problems were further compounded by the U.S. Supreme Court ruling in the Phillips Petroleum Company case in 1954 that the Federal Power Commission must regulate the price of natural gas flowing in interstate commerce.[33] Matters were not helped by price controls on energy imposed in 1971. To some extent, if this is not an oversimplification, it was in reaction to the later U.S. import quotas that the Organization of Petroleum Exporting Countries (OPEC) was formed in 1960.[34]

Consequently, the solutions, according to the "market view," are straightforward if not simple. Public policy must be so designed as to make the energy market more responsive to unexpected shocks and expected changes in market demand and supply conditions. Self-serving domestic power groups acting through the government must be effectively curtailed and brought under control. The "market view" argues that "public policy becomes questionable if it is based exclusively on conserving particular forms of energy, such as oil and natural gas, without explicit regard for the total cost of that policy, including the capital cost, relative to total demonstrable total benefits."[35]

Effects of Past Public Policies

The history of the United States domestic energy industry is a history of output restrictions and limitations on competition. It reveals that the roots of the U.S. energy crisis in the 1970s had been nurtured by past public policy measures. These policies were adopted in response to demands by various segments of the energy industry to avoid the rigors of market competition.

The record of past energy policies has been conflicting and wasteful, indeed. For years policymakers in the United States have focused mainly on various short-run objectives, such as unrealistically low prices, wasteful patterns of consumption, and the too-rapid application of environmental restrictions and controls. Such policy actions have effectually sacrificed the long-run interests of the nation.[36]

This is especially true of policies toward fossil fuels. Past policies and regulations of wellhead prices, for example, had substantially reduced exploration and production of natural gas, and thus inadvertently led to the substitution of normally consumed natural gas with the nearest substitute fuel, oil, by consumers.

Similar effects can also be found in U.S. policies toward coal and nuclear powers. While the Coal Mine Health and Safety Act of 1969 and strip-mining legislation had discouraged the production of coal, failure to build nuclear power plants in a timely fashion had resulted in an extraordinary and unanticipated demand for oil for the generation of electricity. Such failure was due partly to delays in licensing these plants at the federal level, partly to objections to nuclear power plant sites by state and local communities, and partly to legitimate concerns for the safety of nuclear reactors and the disposal of nuclear waste.[37]

Other public policies toward oil had also inadvertently prevented its domestic production from keeping pace with the extraordinary demands being placed upon it. Such policies included reduction of depletion allowance, cancellation of leases for environmental reasons, unnecessary delay in leasing of the outer continental shelf, obstruction of construction of the Alaskan pipeline, and imposition of especially stringent price controls on the industry.

Indeed, at some risk of exaggeration, public policies had the unintended effect of pushing the United States to depend increasingly on foreign oil and, in particular, oil from the Middle East. As the events of the 1973–74 oil embargo revealed, this dependence has posed a major foreign policy and economic problem for the United States.

Limitations on time and space preclude a lengthy discussion of each of these policies. Rather, only those of historical methods of restricting competition as percentage depletion allowance, prorationing, import quota program, and price controls are reviewed relative to the nature and roots of the U.S. energy crisis of the 1970s.

It is noteworthy that, among both academic and nonacademic energy economists, there has been a widespread consensus that government interference in the energy sector was the primary cause of the U.S. energy crisis during the 1970s. Erickson and Spann, for example, wrote that "the energy crisis has been policy induced and is not a result of market power."[38] Yang was more explicit in stating that "the crisis was rooted in the supplanting of the market mode of competition by the political mode. From this perspective, it is difficult to avoid the conclusion that past public policies have been, in large measure, responsible for the energy crisis in the United States."[39] Mancke concluded that "current energy policies have failed to alleviate any of our four energy problems . . . In fact, they have actually worsened each of the these problems."[40]

A brief review of major public policies in the past supports these conclusions.

Percentage Depletion Allowance

Percentage depletion allowances, established by Congress in 1926, provide a tax subsidy designed to attract additional resources to oil and gas exploration. The depreciation allowance rules allow oil and gas producers and royalty owners to receive tax free 27.5 percent of the wellhead value of oil and gas production, subject to a limit that tax-free revenues of oil corporations could not exceed 50 percent of their net profit from oil production. The rationale for this procedure was that there had not been clear relationship between the costs of discovery and the value of deposits discovered. These rules remained in effect until 1969 when tax-free income was reduced to 22 percent. In 1975, legislation removed the benefits of percentage depletion allowances for integrated oil companies, but retained most of them for small gas and oil producers.[41]

A companion tax provision was made, in the late 1920s, for expensing of intangible drilling costs. It allows oil and gas operators to write off as current expenses intangible drilling and development costs of wells, including all costs other than tangible costs with a second-hand value, such as pipes, pumps, and tanks.

These exclusive privileges have been justified on the grounds that oil is, in effect, a capital asset and the net revenue of the oil industry should not be treated solely as taxable income. In particular, a uniform corporate income tax is nonneutral if it is shifted forward as higher prices, and the tax provisions for the oil industry help to reneutralize the effects of the corporate income tax. More importantly, there is the need to stimulate exploration, to protect national defense interests, and to compensate for the extreme riskiness of crude oil production.[42]

The effect of these two policies, at the time of initial implementation, was to allow resource owners to recover several times their original capital costs over the lifetime of the resource. The idea was to make investment in crude oil exploration relatively more attractive and profitable in comparison to investment in other industries without such provisions. However, the high level of investment in oil exploration is coincidental with, rather than induced by, lower taxes, due to the fact that exploration rates are high prior to the implementation of preferential tax treatment provision. As a result, higher after-tax profitability led to increased capital flows into oil and gas exploration and production, thus resulting in lower prices for crude oil and contributing to the historic U.S. low price policy for energy. This in turn led to extravagant consumption habits, treating oil and gas as cheap commodites and consuming these nonrenewable resources excessively.

In any event, the percentage depletion provision was an inefficent form of subsidy to exploration, since it, in effect, subsidized extraction. Whether the provision altered the time path of extraction, shifting production in favor of the present, is dubious at best. The fact is that it hastens resource depletion, and runs counter to national strategies of resource conservation.

To say the least, these two tax policies probably have been the most important evidences of government interference in the petroleum industry. They are examples of preferential government treatment. To such extent, it is difficult to avoid the conclusion that these policies contributed directly to the energy crisis of the 1970s and in general are counterproductive of a conservation goal.

Prorationing

The potential price-depressing effects of depletion allowance were further exacerbated in 1930 by the discovery of the East Texas oil field. This discovery resulted in a large increase in crude oil supplies at a time when demand was declining. As oil prices were falling dramatically and creating a large amount of instability in crude oil markets, producers pleaded for government intervention to reduce instability. The result was the federal authorization, and subsequent implementation by states, of prorationing system.[43]

Prorationing is the term used in the oil industry to describe the old-fashioned cartel practice or restrictive production quotas. It involves two aspects: (a) production controls designed to ensure the maximum, efficient (MER) recovery of oil resources and (b) controls that aim to restrict production levels to market demand. The later is the so-called market demand prorationing, authorized by two laws passed by Congress—an act authorizing the Interstate Oil Compact and the "Connally Hot Oil Act," which provided the enforcement mechanism.

MER-type prorationing allocates production according to the MER of each well. Its rules, with their depth-acreage allowable schedules and well spacing regulations, are purely arbitrary and economically inefficient as a solution to the common property resource externality,[44] because the optimum geological rate is not necessarily the economic optimum. Where the "rule of capture"[45] operated, for example, all production at the MER could lead in some circumstances to overproduction and too fast a rate of depletion.

Market demand prorationing, on the other hand, estimated demand among existing fields so as to "preserve equity." Its primary effect is to shift output from low-cost to high-cost producers. To the extent, it adds additional restrictions on supply and is a substitute for market forces. As a result, the price mechanism is prevented from clearing markets. Price, denied its allocation function, becomes simply a device for determining the incomes of buyers and sellers of crude oil resources.

The high-price policy of the market demand prorationing system, however, was in conflict with the low-price policy of the tax subsidies. At artificially high prices, the U.S. oil market became a lucrative market for imports; and, in effect, U.S. consumers were being required by government action on behalf of the oil industry to support the world price of crude oil. This was an untenable position, requiring severe curtailments in U.S. production.

MER-type prorationing is justified on the grounds of engineering efficiency in order to conserve oil, but market demand prorationing can not be justified on the basis of conservation goals because of its inefficiency. This form of government intervention illustrates the extent to which industry price policies have been due to government regulation rather than to market forces. Historically, competition has not played a major role in domestic crude oil markets.

Mandatory Oil Import Quota Program

The oil import quota program represents another form of government intervention in reducing competition in domestic crude oil markets.[46] As a means of circumventing the dilemma created by the prorationing system, domestic oil producers succeeded in persuading the government to institute a voluntary oil import program in 1957 only to fail as nonmajor producers attempted to import from their recently developed facilities in the Persian Gulf. Unlike the major international producers, the U.S. nonmajor producers did not have the extensive markets and facilities overseas. Instead, they turned to the voluntary import scheme to increase their market shares in the U.S. domestic oil market. As a result, total U.S. imports rose, as a percent of domestic production, from 19.7 percent in 1957 to 22.4 percent in 1959.

Rising imports, however, were opposed by oil industry officials who saw this as a threat to their domestic market shares and by government officials who saw this as a threat to national security. While domestic nonmajor oil producers pressured for protection from cheap foreign oil, government officials rationalized, on security grounds, that such restrictions would create an incentive to maintain a "strong" domestic oil industry and prevent the United States from becoming dependent on foreign sources of crude oil.

As a response to these arguments, the Eisenhower administration instituted a mandatory quota system in 1959 to keep out Middle Eastern crude that could be produced for literally pennies a barrel. In arguing for such a quota program, the oil industry suggested that the rising demand for oil could be met through the expansion of their industrial capabilities which would occur because of the security provided by the import quota program.

The Mandatory Oil Import Program froze the share of imports achieved in 1959, setting a limit of 9 percent on U.S. oil demand that could be met through imported oil. The distribution of import licenses favored small high-cost refiners who, in effect, were subsidized. These licenses had a market value per barrel equal to the difference between the higher-priced, regulated domestic oil and the cheaper, market-priced foreign oil.[47] The effect was to insulate and further emasculate the ability of the domestic oil program successfully to operative competitively.

To such extent, the import quota program had restricted the supply of imported oil, increased domestic prices, and artificially stimulated additional domestic production of this nonrenewable resource. It had also distorted the pattern of oil production worldwide and led to excessive production from rapidly declining U.S. resources, thus inadvertently sowing the seeds of the U.S. energy crisis in the 1970s. An efficient solution to the problem of foreign oil dependence was not introduced until 1975 when the Strategic Petroleum Reserve was authorized by Congress.[48] A Senate study into the causes of the energy crisis suggested that the three-year delay in the lifting of the Oil Quota Program was due, again, to governmental concern for the welfare of the oil industry.

In retrospect, the events set in motion by the Mandatory Oil Import Program of 1959 had a direct causal effect on the formation of OPEC in September 1960. Import quotas based on a fixed share of the U.S. oil market restricted import growth to the rate of growth of U.S. oil production. The nonmajor U.S. oil producers with increasing output from their foreign wells sold their product to other markets with the result that world oil prices declined.

At first glance such a quota-induced decline in prices benefited oil consumers. However, profit-sharing arrangements that major oil producers had with the oil-producing countries were based on "posted prices" and not on "market prices." The major producers unilaterally cut posted prices in 1959 and again in 1960 so as to protect themselves from a profit squeeze.[49] These cuts were vigorously resisted by the oil-producing countries. The et effect was to provide incentive for the oil-producing countries to join in defending their common interests against price cuts by major oil-producing corporations to safeguard their common interests.

By 1970, the disparity between oil production and consumption had become so great that regional petroleum product shortages were developing in the United

States. In response, the White House created a Task Force and charged it with the development of a plan of action that would prevent the spread and increasing severity of these shortages.

The White House Task Force recommended that the quota program be lifted and replaced by a tariff program.[50] In support of its recommendation, the Task Force argued that, because the demand for oil products was so much greater in 1970 than in the 1950s, those arguments against significant oil imports put forth by government and oil industry officials during the 1950s were no longer relevant. As further support of its recommended lifting of the quota program, the Task Force noted that the oil industry expansion, which was anticipated at the time of the institution of the quota program, had not materialized.

The explanation as to why increased domestic oil production had not occurred varies between those who emphasize the effects of the environmental opposition to the operation of refineries and those who emphasize the existence of more attractive return on oil industry capital investment overseas. The Task Force also noted that, by 1970, 40 percent of the U.S. military oil demand was met through foreign suppliers. As an example of the invalidity of the national security arguments against imported oil, the Task Force pointed out that the Vietnam War was run almost completely on foreign oil. The implication is that import quotas isolated, to a large degree, the domestic industry from the influence of foreign competition.

Matters were not put to rest and the oil market received another shock in 1971 with the imposition of a series of price freeze and control programs aimed at fighting inflation. A side effect of such controls by keeping domestic oil prices below the foreign price of oil eliminated the value of import licenses issued under the mandatory quota system.

Price Controls

The price control mechanism was not new. In 1938, Congress passed the Natural Gas Act to govern the charges for transporting natural gas in interstate commerce. The Act, however, made no attempt to regulate the production at one end or the distribution at the other. Its sole purpose was to fill the gap in between, to occupy the area in which the Supreme Court said the states could not act. The responsibility for regulation went to the Federal Power Commission (FPC) as a logical extension of its responsibility for regulating electrical public utilities. The Commission was to regulate the pipelines in two ways commonly found in public utility legislation: controlling rates and controlling facilities.[51]

In 1954, however, the Supreme Court in the *Phillips* v. *Wisconsin* case mandated the Federal Power Commission (FPC) the task of regulating the wellhead price of natural gas on a case by case basis, including all wholesale of natural gas. It also determined that Congress intended controls to cover the wellhead price of natural gas flowing in interstate commerce as well as the act of transporting such gas, but without setting the price itself. Not to be unnoticed, the

Commission must sift through thousands of pages of testimony in trying to establish a fair rate for the Wisconsin public to pay and to regulate the wellhead price of interstate gas on a case-by-case approach.

This was further compounded by the fact that the price set by the Commission was lower than prices that would have been determined by the interaction of supply and demand. As a consequence, domestic producers cut back production and a shortage developed.

Therefore, in 1961, the Commission, overburdened with an enormous backlog of cases and the continuing flood of rate and certificate cases, introduced the Permian Basin method of area-wide rate making. Under this new area system, the Commission would set a ''just and reasonable'' ceiling price for all gas produced within a broadly defined area, such as the Permian Basin in Texas. Just as in the temporary ''freeze'' prices, the Commission established two levels. The lower was for old gas wells and for all wells pumping both oil and gas. The higher price was for new wells producing only gas. The rationale was to encourage drilling for new gas wells without unnecessarily rewarding the old wells for the discovery of gas incidental to the search for oil. The drillers with the capacity to find gas by itself therefore would be encouraged to do so by the new price structure. Three years after the Permian Basin decision, the Commission issued a similar plan for the southern Louisiana area.

The newly established pricing procedure permitted the price to be based on historical cost of low-cost producers in a given area, in favor of artificially low prices. At ''artificially'' low prices of natural gas, the quantity demanded outstripped the quantity supplied, thus creating the usual shortage. At ''artificially'' low prices, natural gas was consumed lavishly and the conservation effort was thwarted, thus leading to increased imports of crude oil and its consequent dependence.

In effect, the new pricing system introduced a downward revision of expected future prices of natural gas, which accelerated downward revision in the desired reserve-to-production ratios in the post-Permian period. Not surprisingly, the accelerated downward adjustment in the reserve-to-production ratio in the 1960s took the form, first, of decelerating growth of reserves and then an outright reduction in reserves between 1968 and 1974. The slowing in reserve accumulation and the eventual reduction in reserves were attributed directly to the delay in the search for reserves as a direct consequence of policy-induced pessimism regarding the prospects for returns on exploration and development activities.

This drawing down of reserves by producers suggests the reason for the peculiar result whereby an ''artificially'' low, controlled price brought forth an increase in the supply of natural gas, owing to the technological peculiarities in the natural gas and oil industry. These peculiarities of the market for natural gas were apparently not sufficiently taken into account by the Commission in its price setting. The result was to create a price incentive for many new industrial and electric utilities to switch from coal to natural gas. As demand for natural gas increased substantially, the "shortage" at the controlled price (created by the Commission) appeared. Consumers began to seek out crude oil as substitutes of energy. This in turn led to increasing demands for crude oil and eventually increased oil imports as a result of oil price controls.[52]

Controls on oil prices began with the 90-day freeze introduced in a series of price freeze and control programs by President Nixon on August 15, 1971, to fight inflation. The effects were, with domestic oil prices being held below the level of import prices, artificially stimulated demand for and artificially restrained supply of crude oil.

The situation was further complicated by distinctions made betwen "old" and "new" domestic crude oil and the resulting two-tier price system, tie-in sales, charges, and countercharges of discrimination and evasions. The two-tier price system, while stimulating new production, created serious problems for the industry and the country, due to the fact hat not every refiner had equal access to "old" and "new" domestic crude oil, nor to domestic and imported crude oil.

Also, significant price differentials appeared between the products of competing refiners, reflecting different access to lower- and higher-priced crude oil. Not only had the new price system undermined the competitiveness of particular segments of the oil industry and increased demands for the breakup of the major oil companies, it had also forced the major oil companies to behave like monopolists, undercutting the prices of some of their smaller, independent competitors. The net result was to create a situation of artificial advantages and disadvantages, when none in reality existed.

Indeed, the U.S. domestic oil market was poorly prepared to cope with such external shock as administered to it by the Arab oil embargo of October 1973. At the time of the "crisis," domestic oil and gas markets were in such chaos that they were tied up in knots due to the effects of the past government policies. Government policy had effectively complicated the necessary adjustment process by consistently allocating the amount of oil for consumption below the sum of domestic production and imports. The result was that the embargo left the U.S. market with a higher stock of petroleum products than in October of 1973.

Following the oil embargo and quadrupling of the crude oil price, those refiners without access to cheaper domestic "old" oil prevailed on the newly created Federal Energy Administration to adopt the Crude Oil Equalization Program in December 1974. The Program was designed to allocate low-cost "old" domestic crude oil proportionately to all domestic refiners through the issuance of tickets or entitlements in much the same way as cheaper foreign oil was allocated by the import licenses during the mandatory oil import quota period. Once again, resort was had to the political arena as a way of "correcting unsatisfactory" economic issues. Once again, as in the import licensing and the demand prorationing programs, most entitlements and tickets went to the smaller refiners.[53]

Such an entitlement system encouraged imports by taxing domestic production and subsidizing imports; and, together with a two-tier pricing system, it had the unintended effect of increasing U.S. dependence on external oil supplies. To some extent, domestic production was reduced below that which would have prevailed in a "free" market by the "uncontrolled" price of "new" domestic oil which was below the world price. In effect, an interventionist policy aimed at dealing with one set of problems created another set of problems as a by-product.

The uncertainty generated by government energy policies shifted producer and consumer attention from market-oriented activities to attempting to influence policies through the political arena. The irony was that it was the oil and gas industry itself which first sought most of the existing regulation. These are the same interests as now call for deregulation of the energy market.

Consequently, in spring 1981, President Reagan removed the price controls on domestically produced crude oil. Partly as a result of the increased quantities of oil supplied and partly because of a decline in consumption—both factors the effects of higher prices for energy products—an oil glut developed in 1980s.

To summarize, there is evidence indicating that public policies instituted by government and supported by industry, have led to monopoly-like control over the output and prices of domestic energy resources. The actions of OPEC in the 1970s had affected events in the domestic market.

There is also evidence indicating that government intervention has reduced the influence of free market forces on the pattern of resource allocation and has been counterproductive with respect to energy resource conservation. Past attempts by various segments of the energy industry to avoid the rigors of free market competition have resulted in public polices that have weakened the ability of the energy market to adjust to man-made and nature-induced shocks.

NOTES

1. Mason Willrich, *Energy and World Politics* (New York: The Free Press, 1975).

2. See Willrich, op. cit. and Exxon Corporation, *Middle East Oil and Gas,* December 1984.

3. Willrich, op. cit., pp. 15–16.

4. The Ford Foundation, *Energy: The Next Twenty Years* (Cambridge, MA: Ballinger Publishing Company, 1979), pp. 169–70.

5. William E. Cline and Sidney Weintraub, eds., *Economic Stabilization in Developing Countries* (Washington, DC: The Brookings Institution, 1981), p. 115.

6. The Ford Foundation, op. cit., p. 169.

7. Willrich, op. cit., pp. 14–16.

8. Ibid., pp. 14–15.

9. Ibid., p. 23.

10. The seven international majors are often referred to as the seven sisters. Five of these, namely, Exxon, Mobil, Gulf, Texaco, and Standard Oil of California, are based in the United States; the other two are British Petroleum, of the United Kingdom, and

Royal Dutch Petroleum Company and Shell Transport and Trading, based in the Netherlands. The history of the seven sisters has been described in dramatic but revealing detail in A. Sampson, *The Seven Sisters: The Great Oil Companies and the World They Made* (New York: Viking, 1975).

11. Rajendra K. Pachauri, *The Political Economy of Global Energy* (Baltimore, MD: The Johns Hopkins University Press, 1985).

12. Exxon Corporation, *Middle East Oil*, 2d ed., Exxon Background Series, September 1980; and, Exxon Corporation, *Middle East Oil and Gas* (New York: Exxon Corporation, 1984).

13. Yoon S. Park, *Oil Money and the World Economy* (Boulder, CO: Westview Press, 1976), p. 12.

14. Pachauri, pp. 56–57; see also, Willrich, op. cit.

15. Ibid.; see also, Fereidun Fesharaki, *Development of Iranian Oil Industry* (New York: Praeger, 1976).

16. "Posted" prices were set by the oil companies as the "list" prices at which they would sell crude oil.

17. Pachauri, op. cit., pp. 57–58.

18. Qatar joined in 1961, Indonesia and Libya in 1962, Abu Dhabi—later the UAE—in 1967, Algeria in 1969, Nigeria in 1971, and Ecuador in 1973. Gabon became an associate member in 1973 and a full member in 1975.

19. Willrich, op. cit.

20. Charles F. Doran, *Myth, Oil, and Politics* (New York: The Free Press, 1977), p. 135.

21. Exxon Corporation, op. cit.; also, Exxon Corporation, *Middle East Oil and Gas* (New York: Exxon Corporation, 1984).

22. Ali Ezzati, *World Energy Markets and OPEC Stability* (Lexington, MA: Lexington Books, 1978), p. 1.

23. Willrich, op. cit.; see also, Doran, op. cit., p. 134.

24. The Council of State Governments, *State Responses to the Energy Crisis*, 1974, p. 4.

25. Federal Trade Commission Staff Report, Investigation of the Petroleum Industry (July 1973).

26. The Council of State Governments, *State Responses to the Energy Crisis*, pp. 4–5.

27. David Howard Davis, *Energy Politics*, 3d ed. (New York: St. Martin's Press, 1982), p. 4.

28. Jai-Hoon Yang, "The Nature and Origins of the U.S. Energy Crisis," *Review*, Federal Reserve Bank of St. Louis (July 1977), p. 2.

29. The Council of State Governments, op. cit., pp. 5–10.

30. See, for instance, The Ford Foundation, *A Time to Choose*, Final Report of the Energy Policy Project of the Ford Foundation (Cambridge, MA: Ballinger Publishing Co., 1974).

31. Walter J. Mead, "The Performance of Government in Energy Regulations," *American Economic Review* 69, no. 2 (May 1979), p. 352.

32. This discussion draws on Yang, op. cit.

33. Edmund W. Kitch, "Regulation of the Field Market for Natural Gas by the Federal Power Commission," *The Journal of Law and Economics* (October 1968), pp. 243–80.

34. Kenneth W. Dam, "Implementation of Import Quotas: The Case of Oil," *The Journal of Law and Economics* (April 1971), pp. 1–60.

35. Yang, op. cit., pp. 5–6.

36. William A. Johnson, "The Impact of Price Controls on the Oil Industry: How to Worsen an Energy Crisis," in Gary D. Eppen, ed., *Energy: The Policy Issues* (Chicago, IL: The University of Chicago Press, 1975), p. 99.

37. Johnson, op. cit., p. 99.

38. E. W. Erickson and R. M. Spann, "The U.S. Petroleum Industry," in E. W. Erickson and L. Waverman, eds., *The Energy Question: An International Failure of Policy,* vol. 2 (Toronto: University of Toronto Press, 1974), p. 7; see also Walter J. Mead, *Energy and the Environment Conflict in Public Policy* (Washington, DC: American Enterprise Institute for Public Policy Research, 1978), p. 17. A similar conclusion can be found in Harry W. Richardson, *Economic Aspects of the Energy Crisis* (Lexington, MA: Lexington Banks/Saxon House, 1975), p. 57.

39. Yang, op. cit., p. 2.

40. Richard B. Mancke, *The Failure of U.S. Energy Policy* (New York: Columbia University Press, 1974), pp. 4–7.

41. See Mead, "The Performance of Government in Energy Regulations," op. cit., pp. 352–56; idem, *Energy and the Environment Conflict in Public Policy* (Washington, DC: American Enterprise Institute for Public Policy Research, 1978), pp. 17–24; Richardson, op. cit.; Gerald M. Brannon, "U.S. Taxes on Energy Resources," *AEA Papers and Proceedings of the Eighty-Seventh Annual Meeting of the AEA* (May 1975), pp. 397–404; and Thomas D. Duchesneau, *Competition in the U.S. Energy Industry* (Cambridge, MA: Ballinger Publishing Company, 1975).

42. Richardson, op. cit., p. 61.

43. See Mead, "The Performance of Government in Energy Regulations" op. cit. pp. 352–56; Duchesneau, op. cit.; Richardson, op. cit.; and Richard B. Mancke, op. cit., pp. 72–76. An excellent analytical study of prorationing is provided in Stephen L. McDonald, *Petroleum Conservation in the United States* (Baltimore, MD: The Johns Hopkins University Press, 1971).

44. Stephen McDonald has proposed an efficient solution in the form of mandatory utilization. See ibid.

45. "Rule of capture" is a principle established by law, which, in the absence of other legislation and controls to mitigate its effects, militates against conservation of petroleum resources. See Richardson, op. cit., p. 59.

46. Analytical studies of the quota program can be found in James C. Burrows and Thomas A. Domencich, *An Analysis of the United States Oil Import Quota* (Lexington, MA: D. C. Heath and Co., 1970); Dam, "Implementation of Import Quotas: The Case of Oil," op. cit., pp. 5–14, 58–60; Cabinet Task Force on Oil Import Control, *The Oil Import Question* (Washington, DC, 1970); and Morris A. Adelman, *The World Petroleum Market,* Resources for the Future, Inc. (Baltimore, MD: The Johns Hopkins University Press, 1972), pp. 150–55.

47. Yang, op. cit., p. 9.

48. Mead, "The Performance of Government in Energy Regulations," op. cit., p. 353.

49. Yang, op. cit., p. 9; see, also, Park, op. cit., pp. 27–35.

50. Cabinet Task Force on Oil Import Control, op. cit.

51. Ralph S. Spritzer, "Changing Elements in the Natural Gas Picture," in Keith C.

Brown, ed., *Regulation of the Natural Gas Producing Industry* (Baltimore, MD: The Johns Hopkins Press, Resources for the Future, 1972).

52. The effects of oil price controls are not as clear as in natural gas. Different conclusions have been drawn by researchers from their empirical studies. For further discussion, see Charles E. Phelps and Rodney T. Smith, "Petroleum Regulations: The False Dilemma of Decontrol" (Rand Corp. R-1951-RC, January 1977); and Robert T. Deacon and Walter J. Mead, "Price Controls and International Petroleum Product Price," final report to the Federal Energy Administration, June 16, 1978.

53. See "Allocations: F.E.A. Adopts Regulations Designed to Equalize Crude, Fuel Oil Costs," *Energy Users Reports,* no. 69 (Washington, DC: The U.S. Bureau of National Affairs, December 5, 1974), p. A-8; also, Yang, op. cit., p. 11.

2

Energy Shocks and Economic Stability

INTERNATIONAL ECONOMIC CONSEQUENCES OF HIGH-PRICED ENERGY

The energy crisis of 1973 took the whole world by surprise, including OPEC. It underlined the end of the long Western boom and marked the beginning of a decade of uncertainty. But that was only the beginning. The first oil shock was followed by successive new surprises and discredited predictions, and historians and forecasters are still wondering what hit them.

The original lack of awareness remains the most remarkable historical fact. The price of oil had been creeping up and some oilmen warned of an impending shortage. But politicians and the public treated OPEC as a joke. Conservation was ignored. For a number of months in 1973 and 1974, the oil crisis included two additional elements: politically motivated supply cutbacks so severe that markets were prevented from clearing even at the new prices and embargoes on the shipment of oil to particular consuming counties whose Middle East policies were considered hostile to the Arab cause.

Over 40 percent of the substantial increase in exports from oil-importing countries was required to pay for the increased cost of their oil imports. Another substantial portion was financed by borrowing from the oil surplus countries via the capital markets.

For those nations whose industrial economic activities were closely linked to a reliable supply of imported petroleum at reasonable prices, increases in oil prices had serious detrimental effects on their domestic economic stabilization. Aggregate demand was reduced in oil-consuming countries as import bills mounted to reflect the increased price of oil. In 1974 alone, for example, the jump in oil prices had amounted to an annual transfer of about 2 percent of GDP from the industrial countries, or roughly half-a-year's growth.

Not only did the rise in the price of energy lower the real wage that was compatible with full employment, but also it led to an incentive to shift away from energy- and capital-intensive methods. This substitution contributed to the slowdown in labor productive growth in industrial countries. To a large degree, but with a lag, the initial deflationary impact was offset by increased exports to OPEC countries, but the recycling process, even though smoother in the event than many had predicted, could restore neither the previous level nor the structure of aggregate demand in oil-importing countries.

As it turned out, the oil decade rammed home the fact of interdependence with a vengeance—in the painful form of unstable currencies, bad debts, frenzied arms sales and a growing list of countries on the brink of bankruptcy.

Shift in Power

Although the crisis of the 1970s can be traced directly to actions taken by the oil-exporting countries, many forces lay behind the changes that had occurred. Even before the shock of politically motivated supply cutbacks and embargoes, it had become increasingly clear that an energy crisis was inevitable unless appropriate actions to avert it were initiated. The problem arose basically from the rapid growth of world energy consumption, the shift from coal to petroleum, and the growing dependence of industrial countries on imported energy, which increasingly meant Middle East petroleum.[1]

The problem was further compounded by oil-producing countries' control over their domestic oil operations and the involvement of state-owned corporations in managing these operations. These actions had substantially changed the traditional role of the major multinational oil companies as the sole power in international petroleum market activities which included exploration, production, transportation, refining, and marketing. In most cases, private oil companies have lost both the ownership of crude oil reserves and the power to determine world crude oil prices, production levels, or production capacity development. These decisions have now been made primarily by the governments of the exporting nations. The shift in control does not mean, though, that the multinational companies no longer have a role to play in the world petroleum market—indeed, they have a vital and lucrative role. They still control and play an important role in much of the transportation and downstream refining and marketing activities. They also retain overwhelming strength in technical know-how and management expertise. That role remained largely intact in the early 1980s.

But the change in power relationships went far beyond the reshaped role of the oil companies. The governments of the principal oil-producing countries now had the capacity to exert concerted market power and to use that power for political as well as economic purposes. Many oil-importing countries were threatened with economic stagnation and severe disruption because of their inability to pay higher oil import bills. At the same time, a number of OPEC members were earning sums vastly in excess of their ability to spend or invest at home. This posed the complex economic and political problems of dealing with the resulting world imbalance in current payments and of managing an accumulation of OPEC claims on the rest of the world on a scale unprecedented in recent history.

Changes in World Payments

Higher oil prices have changed the pattern of world payments dramatically. Prior to the price increases of late 1973, the industrial countries as a group typically earned a balance-of-payments surplus on current account of about $12.7 billion. The developing countries experienced a deficit of comparable magnitude, and this was accommodated by the flow of aid and capital to them.

That situation has changed drastically. In 1974, the developed countries as a group shifted to a current account deficit of almost $23.2 billion; the deficit of those nonoil developing countries rose from $6.1 billion in 1973 to $28.9 billion. At the same time, the oil-exporting countries had developed massive foreign exchange surpluses, jumping from $6 billion in 1973 to more than $60 billion in 1974.

The oil-exporting countries as a group continued to accumulate substantial current account surpluses through early 1980, which resulted in corresponding current account deficits in many of the industrial and nonoil-developing countries. The cumulative OPEC surplus in 1980 was $107 billion compared to $60 billion in 1974.

OPEC countries used their vastly increased oil revenues either to import additional goods and services or to acquire assets in the rest of the world—to the extent that increases in their imports resulted in a somewhat lower standard of living for the rest of the world than it would otherwise have had because it had given up more real resources to pay for the same amount of oil or less. But, by the same token, the current payments problem of the rest of the world was relieved as exports to OPEC countries grew. However, the oil exporters as a group could not absorb all the goods and services that their extra revenues could buy; therefore, they had to acquire assets in the rest of the world. Although the sacrifice of real income in the oil-importing countries was thereby reduced, the deficits in their balance of payments on current account were increased, and more of their assets were owed by OPEC nations.

The Organization for Economic Cooperation and Development (OECD) countries[2] have been forced to adjust to the change in world income distribution by reducing real domestic demand and increasing the quantity of exports, while sometimes facing very large deficits in their balance of payments and high inflation rates. The politico-economic responses to these hard facts have probably contributed significantly to the reduction in real economic growth during the readjustment period.

Different national policy approaches and different domestic economic structures, not direct trade with OPEC, explain most of the trade balance changes of the United States and other oil-importing countries between 1973 and 1978. The U.S. trade balance fell by $26.5 billion over this period; only about $10.8 billion of that drop occurred in trade with OPEC. The combined trade balance of the other industrialized countries rose by $44.9 billion, while their balance with OPEC fell by $1.1 billion. The trade balance of the rest of the world, excluding OPEC, fell by $45.4 billion; about $29.2 billion of this decline occurred in trade with OPEC.[3]

Indeed, many OECD countries had no option but to accept a substantial deterioration in their current account that had to be offset by increases in capital inflows. Some individual countries had attempted to minimize their deficits by means of domestic deflation, exchange rate depreciation, or trade measures designed to discourage imports or stimulate exports. Such measures, however, resulted in the shifting of the payments problem from one importing country to another and led to destructive and self-defeating trade rivalry and worldwide economic depression.

LDC Debt Problems

The large balance-of-payments surpluses realized by the OPEC members in their trade with the rest of the world had their counterpart in the deficits of oil-importing countries. Financing these deficits has created an international debt "overhang" that has been threatening the integrity of the international financial structure since 1982.

Although developing countries borrowed prudently to maintain growth in the face of higher energy costs after the 1973 oil shock, they were beginning to slide into deep debt by the time the second major oil price hike came in 1978–79. By the early 1980s they found themselves pinned down by a combination of events, each of which, by itself, would be troublesome enough: a lingering world recession; high interest rates; slumping exports and generally flat trade; increasing protectionism in the industrialized countries; and low commodity prices. Sluggish growth rates crippled their ability to repay loans. The troubled nations would be obliged to boost export sales to raise more money but that had grown increasingly difficult, because of the rise of protectionist sentiment in the industrialized world. Interest payments fell due, and national treasures were strained to the limits to pay. Everywhere the cost of servicing debt was swallowing an increasing percentage of export earnings.

As a result, the total debt (including short-term) of the nonoil-developing countries (including Mexico and Egypt) multiplied nearly fivefold from 1973 to 1982, reaching approximately $612 billion. For five OPEC countries that are not in capital surplus—Algeria, Ecuador, Indonesia, Nigeria, and Venezuela—total debt was estimated at $80 billion, and net East European debt (in hard currency) added another $53 billion (excluding the Soviet Union). The total debt of these three groups of countries thus stood at approximately $745 billion at the end of 1982.[4]

By mid-1985 Third World foreign debt totaled more than $900 billion, $350 billion of it owed by Latin American governments. The debt morass persisted partly because the debtors had virtually no money left over for productive investments after they made their loan payments.

The risks are without precedent in the postwar world. The banking system of the Western world is now dangerously overexposed. If lending abruptly contracts, there will be an avalanche of large-scale defaults that will inflict damage on world trade and on the political and economic stability of both borrowing and lending countries.

Indeed, never in history have so many nations owed so much money with so little promise of repayment. Much of it may never be paid off, and a major default somewhere, somehow, could trigger far-reaching political and economic reactions everywhere. The overhanging debt of the developing countries is the problem of the 1980s just as OPEC was the problem of the 1970s. And the debt means that economic prosperity is not as high as it could be. The real trick is to ensure that economic growth continue, for without steady growth the world could be headed for a serious decline.

The OPEC Demand for Imports—Respending

The growing export revenues to OPEC countries during the 1970s were almost exclusively due to price increases, whereas the volume of oil exports had hovered around the same level throughout the 1973–80 period.[5] An empirical measure of OPEC respending was constructed and computed for the two oil price hikes in the 1970s by Fabritius and Petersen. Their results show that the impact of respending is positive for all countries—the range of variation between countries is very wide. Fabritius and Petersen also conducted simulation on the impact of a 10 percent oil price increase from the average oil import price level in 1980. Their findings show that for first-year effects, Europe was stimulated more (0.3%) than the United States (0.1%). Within Europe, the large EEC countries were affected the most.

The data for the 1973–78 period indicate that it took at least five years for respending to peak at 73 percent for OPEC (91% for ''high'' and 55% for ''low absorbers''). Average respending over the five-year period was slightly less than 55 percent. In the second round of oil price increases in late 1979 and early 1980, the first-year respending ratio was 5 percent, as compared to 30 percent in 1974. Similarly, the respending ratio for 1980 seemed to be considerably lower than in 1975—24 and 49 percent, respectively.

Again, according to the calculation by Fabritius and Petersen, the impacts of an oil price increase on OECD GDP turned positive, when the respending ratio increased above the 40–45 percent range. The respending ratio passed the 50 percent mark in 1975–76 and average respending during the 1973–78 period was about 55 percent. Hence, real GDP in the OECD countries had not been reduced significantly, or had perhaps even been stimulated due to oil price development and respending since 1973.

The shock itself, that is, the loss of real income in the industrial countries due to terms-of-trade losses, was about 2 percent of OECD GDP in 1979/80, as was the case in 1973/74. But the overall GDP was more depressed in 1979/80 than in 1974/75 due to lower respending. The downturn in Europe in particular was deeper this time, because Europe was influenced more by the reduction in OPEC respending. As the large countries in Europe were hit the worst, this might be an additional explanation for the more evenly distributed balance-of-payments deficits in 1979/80 than in 1973/74.

DOMESTIC ECONOMIC IMPLICATIONS

The importing countries require stable oil supplies at reasonable prices; the exporting countries aspire to economic development, a goal that can only be realized with the technical help of the industrial countries. Both the oil-exporting countries and the industrial countries need a healthy, growing world economy, which in turn requires their assistance to the developing countries that are not oil producers.

Changes that occurred in world energy markets during the 1970s were dramatic, compared to the relatively stable environment of prior decades. Although there were substantial international responses to energy shocks among the oil-importing countries and also broad scope for constructive cooperation between oil-exporting and oil-importing countries, the capacity of importing countries to absorb the burden of higher oil prices depends, first of all, on the health and vitality of their own economies. When the huge oil price increases occurred, many OECD countries were already plagued by the twin economic problems of high inflation and weakness in production. The increases further exacerbated both problems and greatly complicated the task of domestic economic management in many oil-importing developed countries.[6]

The impact of an increase in the price of oil on the developed economies can be roughly illustrated as the outcome of three elements which may vary in strength between countries. These elements are (a) worldwide inflationary pressures, (b) depressing world output and employment, and (c) adjustment problems.

Inflation

The oil shock of the early 1970s, coinciding with a food price shock as a result of bad crops in both the United States and Soviet Russia, came at a time of unsustainable worldwide demand pressures, an acute inflation problem, widespread speculation on commodities, and a build-up of inventories. The effect of the jump in oil prices—from $3.50 per barrel in 1972 to $13.50 in 1974—on this fragile situation was devastating. All 24 OECD economies suffered a slowdown in aggregate economic growth. All but one (Switzerland) experienced an intensification of consumer price inflation. Inflation rates rose from an already higher average 8 percent in these industrial countries in 1973 to a double-digit range in 1974, as compared with an average 3.9 percent range in 1960–73 (see Table 2.1). Overall economic growth of the OECD countries as measured by the annual GNP growth slowed from 4.9 percent during 1965–73 to 2.7 percent during 1973–79.

In the late 1970s and early 1980s, supply shocks again led to an increase in inflation and a sluggishness in worldwide economic activity. Overall inflation as measured by the CPI reached a higher point in this episode than in the earlier one, as a result of the rising OPEC oil prices from $13.50 to $34.50. Just as in the early 1970s, supply shock inflation was followed by a slowing in economic activity, a decline in real output, rising unemployment, and a major disequilibria in balance of payments worldwide.

The OPEC action had provided strong impetus to inflation in two ways: first, by directly increasing the price of a product as basic as petroleum (and indirectly increasing prices for all other forms of energy) and, second, by stimulating higher wage demands from workers seeking to protect their incomes from erosion by rising prices. The increase in oil prices implied a deterioration in the terms of trade and a consequent overall loss of real income for each importing country. To the extent that particular groups within an importing country sought to avoid sharing in this loss, the burden was passed on to other groups, who in turn reacted in ways that might have prolonged the inflationary spiral. The tendency to resist such sharing was further accentuated by the income shifts associated with earlier and continuing inflation and had greatly complicated the task of domestic economic management in oil-importing countries in the 1970s.[7]

Output and Employment

While high oil prices gave a new boost to worldwide inflationary pressures and disrupted progress toward regional equilibrium in the world's balance of payments, they also dealt a severely depressing blow to world output and employment, which were already weakened. During the 1973–74 period, the annual growth of developing countries as a group fell sharply, from 5.8 to 4.6 percent, but there was a more drastic deceleration in industrial countries, from 5.1 to 2.4 percent. The total loss in output from the 1974–75 recovery in industrial countries, though part of it may have followed from factors unrelated to oil, was about $350 billion. In the United States alone, higher prices of energy resources, relative to the prices of labor and capital resources, had permanently resulted in a loss of economic capacity, or the potential output of its

Table 2.1
Inflation Rates in Selected Industrial Countries, 1973–84 (annual percentage change)

Country	1960–73	1973–79	1973	1974	1975	1976	1977	1978	1979	1980	1981	1982	1983	1984
Canada	3.3	9.2	7.5	10.9	10.8	7.5	8.0	9.0	9.1	10.2	12.4	10.8	5.8	4.3
France	4.6	10.7	7.2	13.9	11.8	9.6	9.4	9.1	10.7	13.8	13.4	11.8	9.6	7.4
Germany	3.3	4.6	7.0	7.0	5.9	4.3	3.7	2.7	4.1	5.4	6.3	5.3	3.3	2.4
Italy	4.7	16.1	10.8	19.1	17.0	16.8	17.0	12.1	14.8	21.2	17.8	16.5	14.7	10.8
Japan	6.1	10.2	11.7	24.4	11.8	9.3	8.0	3.8	3.6	8.0	4.9	2.6	1.8	2.3
United Kingdom	5.1	15.7	9.2	15.9	24.3	16.6	15.8	8.3	13.4	18.0	11.9	8.6	4.6	5.0
United States	3.2	8.6	6.2	11.0	9.1	5.8	6.5	7.6	11.3	13.5	10.4	6.2	3.2	4.3
Industrial Countries	3.9	9.6	7.6	13.3	11.1	8.3	8.4	7.2	9.1	11.9	9.9	7.5	5.0	4.8

Source: IMF, *International Financial Statistics,* 1984.

economy, by 4 to 5 percent. The productivity of existing capital and labor resources was sharply reduced.[8]

Indeed, the sluggish economic growth in the 1970s is in good part the consequence of past misdirected energy policies in the industrial nations in general and in the United States in particular. The problem was further compounded by the price-setting activities of the OPEC cartel so that world economies are now struggling with various conservation measures that are costly in terms of utilization of existing capital resources. However, efforts to restrain the emerging inflationary pressures by applying restrictive monetary and fiscal policies tended to impede the industrial countries' economic growth, and, given the high degree of interdependence in the world economy, stymied economic progress worldwide. In the second half of 1979, for example, the combined GNP of the 24 industrial countries comprising the OECD was growing at an annual rate of around 3 percent, compared with 4.3 percent in the second half of 1978. A further significant slowdown to less than 1 percent growth was observed in the industrial countries in early 1980 (see Table 2.2).

During this period, unemployment in the industrial countries increased sharply and remained at high levels in most of them during the recovery. In Europe unemployment was between 9 and 11 percent of the labor force, while in the United States the unemployment was between 6 and 7 percent. The unemployment rate in the United States, however, has declined substantially since the recent recession to an annual rate of 5.3 percent by the end of 1988, which was a 14-year low.

Indeed, rising oil prices increase unemployment and inflation in ways that are difficult for policymakers in oil-importing countries to manage; on the other hand, they depress domestic demand and employment. Policymakers attempt to control part of the inflation, at the cost of increasing unemployment. Policymakers typically do not fully offset the effect on employment because they simultaneously try to hold down the rate of inflation.

To judge from available U.S. evidence, the sharp increases in energy prices in 1974–75 and in 1975–80 reduced both potential output and productivity, and temporarily increased the inflation rate. The pattern suggests that the reduction in output owing to an increase in energy price initially is smaller than the decline in potential output, then overshoots it, before returning to the size of the permanent decline. A similar pattern is also found in unemployment rate developments: The unemployment rate declines initially, then rises to higher levels before falling sufficiently so that, after six quarters, an energy price increase has no effect on the unemployment rate.[9]

According to some estimates for the U.S. economy, the 40 percent change in the relative price of energy which occurred in 1973–74 and 1978–80 permanently reduced potential output and productivity in the private business sector. The rise in the relative price of energy also reduced the desired capital-labor ratio as a result of energy price increases that occurred from 1978 to 1980.[10]

Table 2.2
Growth of Real GDP in Selected Industrial Countries, 1973–84 (annual percentage change)

Country	1960–73	1973–79	1973	1974	1975	1976	1977	1978	1979	1980	1981	1982	1983	1984
Canada	5.6	3.2	7.5	3.6	1.2	5.8	2.0	3.6	3.2	1.1	3.3	-4.4	3.3	4.7
France	5.6	3.1	5.4	3.2	0.2	5.2	3.0	3.8	3.3	1.0	0.5	1.8	0.7	1.6
Germany	4.4	2.5	4.6	0.5	-1.7	5.5	3.1	3.1	4.2	1.8	–	0.9	1.0	2.6
Italy	5.3	2.7	7.0	4.1	-3.6	5.9	1.9	2.9	4.9	3.9	0.2	-0.5	-0.4	2.6
Japan	10.4	3.7	8.8	-1.2	2.4	5.3	5.3	5.1	5.2	4.8	4.0	3.3	3.4	5.8
United Kingdom	3.2	1.5	7.9	-1.1	-0.7	3.9	0.9	3.8	2.1	-2.2	-1.3	1.8	3.2	1.6
United States	4.1	2.7	5.5	-0.8	-0.9	5.3	5.5	4.9	2.4	-0.3	2.6	-2.0	3.8	7.1
Industrial Countries	4.9	2.8	6.0	0.6	-0.4	5.0	3.9	4.0	3.3	1.3	1.6	-0.2	2.5	4.4

Source: IMF, *International Financial Statistics*, 1984.

It is now recognized that policy formulations must take into account the permanent reduction in U.S. economic capacity and reduced productivity of existing capital and labor. Failure to consider the permanent nature of these changes, especially in the face of persistent unemployment, contributed to an overstatement of the benefits of an expansionary monetary and/or fiscal policies, as manifested in the recessionary U.S. economy in the early 1980.[11]

Indeed, the large increase in the cost of energy resources in the 1970s had profound effects on productivity, investment, and the long-term growth path of the U.S. economy. To some extent, the rise in the relative price of energy and its adverse effects on productivity created incentives to reduce the desired capital labor ratio in production through a reduction in the growth rate of capital formation. This was shared by a heterogenous group of countries, worldwide. Although there are a number of alternative explanations as suggested by economic theory, they do not appear to be able to account for the entire problem. The changing composition of the labor force, for example, is advanced by some observers as having adversely affected productivity. So too the relatively slow pace of capital formation, decline in research and development, and government-mandated environmental programs which may have been responsible for diverting capital formation from the market economy to environmental goals of clean air, health, and safety programs.

Uncertainty generated by inflation, along with the diversion and transfer of resources caused by it, provided significant disincentives for expanding productive capacity. This suggests that monetary policy plays a substantial role in promoting productivity growth. A stable rate of growth in the money supply will enhance productivity growth by reducing inflation.

Adjustment Problems

Sudden and sharp increases in oil prices had serious detrimental effects on inflation in the world economy, especially in industrial nations. They created extraordinary difficult adjustment problems for the world economy. Economic policymakers found that traditional demand management policies were seriously constrained by the continued coexistence of strong inflationary pressures and substantial excess capacity. The inflationary recessions of the 1970s, if not exclusively attributable to the OPEC price increases, were certainly worsened by them.

Paradoxically, the recessions these events induced were unexpectedly prolonged. In the industrial countries, economic policies that had successfully coped with earlier cyclical downturns, and even to some extent with the recession of 1974–75, are proving inadequate, and growth has faltered. The developing countries, despite the rise in their current account deficits from $40 billion in 1979 to $115 billion in 1981, have been much more successful than the industrialized countries in adjusting to the new situation. Many have been helped by policies they instituted in response to events of the early 1970s, by their high investment rates, and by the helpful developments of the later 1970s in international trade and capital flows. Nonetheless, even for thriving middle-income countries, the economic environment in the 1970s was fraught with difficulties. For many people in the poorest developing countries—particularly in sub-Saharan Africa, where income per person has not grown for more than a decade—the ability to maintain even basic production activities might have been compromised.[12]

Different countries adjusted in different ways, depending on the relative availability of indigenous energy resources and degree of dependency on imported oil. Some countries adjusted to more expensive energy by boosting their exports and borrowing. For the world as a whole, however, a large part of the adjustment was made more directly, through changes in the supply and demand for energy itself. These took place through substituting other fuels for scarce petroleum, reducing the energy required per unit of GDP, and changing rates of growth of GDP.

It is noteworthy that, among developing countries, the low-income sub-Saharan countries were least able to make structural adjustments; but in India and China, with large, relatively self-sufficient economies, the effect of adverse external events was more than offset by high domestic investment and good agricultural performance. The industrialized countries, however, were unable to restrain consumption, and the least developed countries had little hope of doing so.

Immediate Concerns

Reactions to the oil shocks in the 1970s reflected several immediate concerns—whether the response to higher oil prices should come through government action or through the market price mechanism, and whether it should come on the supply side or on the demand side. There was a great deal of talk on the government side, including international action, but with very modest, if any, results. On the energy front, the temporary embargo of oil shipments by Arab states spawned instant analysis, grand plans, but little in the way of effective actions in the industrial world. A program for energy independence in the United States, for example, floundered and remained mostly rhetoric.

On the multinational basis, the International Energy Agency (IEA) was organized, largely with the aim of building some protection against interruptions of petroleum supplies by stockpiling and developing plans for sharing supplies in an emergency. But the difficulties of organizing the IEA seemed to exhaust the energies of the participants. Other efforts to coordinate an international approach to OPEC to attempt to stabilize oil prices and production levels also failed to produce significant results.[13]

On the financial front, massive OPEC deposits overloaded the international banking system creating an unmanageable flood of liquidity, while, on the other hand, many developing countries facing enlarged deficits were unable to obtain

the massive new credits they needed to finance them. This was further exacerbated by the continuing inflationary pressure, which severely disrupted progress
toward regional equilibrium in the world's balance of payments.

Indeed, for decades, oil had a special mystique because experts said it was
"price inelastic": Regardless of price, consumption would grow in lockstep
with economic growth. That theory was a casualty of the last decade. Petroleum has become the fuel of last resort.[14]

Regardless of the way the world economy reacted to the difficulties, the
global adjustment over the period until 1983 entailed huge transfers of income
and wealth to the OPEC countries, the piling up of tremendous debts by many
oil-consuming countries, and the threatening shadow of financial collapse for
the weaker importing countries.

ECONOMIC CONSEQUENCES OF THE 1986 OIL PRICE COLLAPSE

The energy crisis is over, at least for the short term. Almost all oil output
around the Persian Gulf has been cut by half since 1980. The Iraq-Iran War
has slashed the production of those two countries—from a combined output of
9.3 million barrels per day in the mid-1970s—to less than 3 million barrels per
day in November 1985. Saudi Arabia, which was daily pumping 10.3 million
barrels in 1981, had tumbled to an unprecedented 2 million barrels per day in
mid–1985, and has remained at the level of less than 5 million barrels until late
1988.

Yet the world would be awash in an oil glut unparalleled in the 14 years
since the first OPEC price shock of 1973, and it has been estimated that the
glut would last at least through 1990. Energy conservation, alternate energy
use, and the rise in non-OPEC oil production had conspired to drive the price
of oil down. Once as high as $40 a barrel and seemingly headed inexorably for
$60, $80, $100, or more, the prices of crude oil fell to $12 a barrel in the first
half of 1986, back to the level of 1974 and, when adjusted for changes in the
general price level, close to the real oil price that prevailed in 1973 just before
the first OPEC price increase.

The problem has been further exacerbated by a cease-fire that ended the
eight-year Iraq-Iran war on August 20, 1988. During the Iraq-Iran conflict, Iraq
exceeded its OPEC production quota of 1.54 million barrels a day because of
a desperate need for oil revenues to fuel its war machine. Now that the fighting
has ended, Iraq, with 100 billion barrels of reserves, ranks second only to
Saudi Arabia among the world's producers, and will have enough pumping
capacity to increase its production even more, from a current level of 2.7 million barrels a day to about 3.5 million barrels a day within a year or so.

Moreover, fearing a loss of market share to other OPEC producers, the three
leading gulf producers—Saudi Arabia, Kuwait, and the United Arab Emirates—have now opened their spigots, increasing OPEC's total oil production

by nearly 10 percent. This has led to the overflow which has inadvertently created a price-dampening glut. There are expectations among oil traders that the glut may soon inspire OPEC to cut its production. If it does not, prices could drop below $10 per barrel and remain at that level for early 1989. That would mean a repeat by next spring of the oil-market collapse of early 1986, when OPEC overproduction sent prices crashing to less than $10 per barrel.

The question again is: Is the Middle East still important to the stability of the world economy? The answer, obviously, is yes. Because even as the supply of oil from the Middle East is in decline, the amount of turmoil it can create worldwide seems to be on the increase.

The Elusive Price of Oil

In the mid-1970s, economists were trying desperately to predict the impact of sharply rising oil prices. Many of the forecasts, which ranged all the way to international financial disaster, proved to be far too pessimistic. In the mid-1980s, economists were trying to predict the impact of collapsing oil prices. Their forecasts once again varied widely, but on average they tend to be quite optimistic.

In the early 1980s, with demand softening for oil in general—and for OPEC oil in particular—surplus capacity built up. It exerted downward pressure on market prices and caused financial strains in several OPEC states, notably those with large populations and a high need for imported products (sometimes referred to as the *high absorber countries*). In March, 1982, OPEC members, in an effort to sustain prices, established a total OPEC production ceiling of 17.5 million barrels a day, compared with 1981 output of 22.7 million barrels a day, as well as production quotas for individual member countries.

As 1982 progressed, demand for OPEC oil remained depressed, and world crude market prices continued to soften. In an effort to raise more revenues, some members produced above their quotas and sold at discounts off official government selling prices. This resulted in total OPEC production of more than 1 million barrels a day in excess of the official ceiling. In December of the year, OPEC sought to formalize the new production level by increasing the quota to 18.5 million barrel a day for 1983. This accomplished little, however, in the face of stagnant world demand and the inability of OPEC members to agree on lower prices.

Oil prices, however, continued to tumble on the spot market, the market-savvy Soviet Union had cut the price of its crude exports by $1.50 a barrel, and U.S. refiners where reducing the amount they would pay for new oil liftings. Worst of all for the producers, Saudi Arabia had at least temporarily abandoned its role as OPEC's stabilizing force and had actually abetted the free fall in prices. Indeed, the oil cartel has been fighting a losing battle.

A fundamental oversupply situation has caused world prices to drop 25 percent since early 1981. OPEC can sell only about 60 percent of the oil it can produce, and the cartel has agreed to limit its production to prevent a ruinous glut. Saudi Arabia, OPEC's biggest producer, is supposed to adjust its production up and down if demand rises or falls from the agreed-to level. The trouble was that many of the other 12 countries in OPEC cheated on their quotas and the oversupply persists.

The glut worsened in early 1984 as colder-than-normal weather forced refiners to produce more heating oil. Because each barrel of crude they "cracked" to get heating oil also produced gasoline, inventories of that fuel swelled. Oil users and speculators also stocked up when they thought—incorrectly, it turned out—that the tanker bombings in the Persian Gulf would reduce oil shipments. It was a time for Saudi Arabia to cut its production. But the Saudis wanted to buy 10 Boeing 747s without depleting their cash reserves, and they decided to pay in oil—playing exactly the opposite market role from the one they were supposed to.

To further underline how peculiar the economics of energy has become, increased natural gas shipments from Russia to Europe obviously benefit the Soviet Union. But they also help depress oil prices, since they are inducing many Europeans to switch to the substitute fuel. Europe likes the idea partly because Soviet gas is not priced in U.S. dollars and thus is relatively cheap in their own currencies. In effect, Soviet sales had been going so well that there were plans for a second pipeline in 1985, so the flow of Russian gas could be increased considerably.

Market pressures were too much for Saudi Arabia and the rest of the cartel to cope with in any case. Fierce competition in the sales of gasoline and other oil products, especially in the United States, was reducing prices and pulling down the price of crude oil. Weakness in oil prices continued into early 1986 and throughout the years of 1987 and 1988. If the glut continues, weakness in oil prices will undoubtedly persist to the end of this decade.

Effects of Low-Priced Oil

For the world at large, the continuing plunge of oil prices is a plus: lower energy prices help check inflation and fuel economic recovery around the globe. But a sharp drop in world oil has also negative repercussions, and they extend well beyond the tight little world of OPEC producers. The profits of major oil companies have suffered, and both the drop in current cash flow and prospective future prices have caused the oil industry to impose severe cutbacks in its exploration and production spending. The impact will be that long in coming, because it usually takes about five years to move from initial exploration efforts to bring a new field into production.

Falling prices have also cut sharply into the revenues of the oil-producing countries, pushing many of them to the edge of financial ruin, and thus limiting their ability to purchase goods and services from the rest of the world.

While falling oil prices are picking up the world economy, they are shaking it at the same time. The repercussions could go well beyond economics as those countries express their resentment toward consuming countries, many of which are rich industrial lands. The crisis could inflame tensions in the Middle East, in particular, where oil revenues dropped from $237 billion in 1980 to an estimated $110 billion in 1985. Many politicians called the oil plunge a threat to peace in the Middle East and urged Western countries to begin a modern-day Marshall Plan to aid the region, using some of the money saved by lower oil prices.

Developing countries from Mexico to Indonesia that had built their economies and dreams on oil revenues now watched in anguish as those hopes of prosperity evaporated. Each $1-a-barrel drop in the price of crude oil reduced Venezuela's export earnings by $470 in 1985, for instance. Heavily indebted Mexico, a non-OPEC producer, was even more hard pressed to pay off its huge foreign debt. And the British pound had fallen further in relation to the dollar as Great Britain's North Sea oil treasure declined in market value.

The United States has a sore spot as well. Low prices discourage new exploration and make some existing wells uneconomical to operate. The oil-patch states of Texas, Oklahoma, and Louisiana have been so severely affected that their troubles could affect the nation's economy, at least in the short run. At the same time, the oil bust has spoiled the economics of alternative energy sources as well. Many of the ballyhooed 1970s-era programs to extract petroleum from oil shale and tar sands have been mothballed because they cost too much to operate.

Inevitably, the drop in oil prices raises the question of economic vulnerability once more. A strategic petroleum reserve (SPR), for example, can help deal with a relatively short-term disruption in world supplies, such as the Arab embargo of 1973, imposed for political reasons. However, it can do little to shield the United States or other importing nations from the economic effects of long-term cartel-like behavior by the Organization of Petroleum Exporting Countries.

Another strategic question is how the Soviet Union will respond to the loss of revenue from its oil exports to Europe and Japan. Sales of about 1.3 million barrels a day in mid-1985 provided the Kremlin with about 60 percent of the currency it spent on Western grain and technology. The Soviets could retaliate by trying to increase their influence over troubled oil producers like Libya. They have routinely characterized the oil-price decline as a conspiracy by "Western monopolists."

The most immediate threat to the United States, however, is financial. Bankers fear a default by hard-pressed oil producers, notably Mexico, which owes $97 billion, or Nigeria, a $17 billion debtor. Mexico alone owes about $70 billion to U.S. institutions. The banks, and probably the whole financial system, would be staggered if Mexico were to walk away from its debts.

Indeed, like the energy crisis of the past decade, which threatened the industrial might of the West, the oil slide is changing the balance of economic power.

The price drop has greatly reduced the flow of billions upon billions of dollars from oil-consuming countries to the producers. The so-called petrodollar drain of 1979–83 had contributed to the worst global economic slump since the Great Depression. But cheap oil will act as a giant tax cut, or perhaps a lottery jackpot, for the consumers and businesses of such large industrial countries as the United States, West Germany, and Japan.

On the other hand, however, if OPEC succeeds in raising the prices again under the impetus of a fresh agreement to limit production, it may restore the economic viability of oil-producing countries, at the cost of negative effects on consuming countries, especially in Europe. It would be one factor in helping to push inflation rates higher in all oil-importing countries.

What Is the Correct Price of Oil?

In the political debate over collapsing oil prices, one idea frequently advanced is that prices have come down too fast, "destabilizing" the economies of the producing countries. This notion usually is coupled with a search for the "correct" price for oil, one that would reflect some mystical level fair to both producers and consumers.[15]

Those who worry about the precipitate drop in oil prices (from $32 a barrel late in 1985 to below $10 at one point in 1986 and edged upward to about $13 per barrel in 1988) rarely mention the precipitate rise. Thus, against the 50 to 55 percent drop from the peak, oil rose 40 percent from 1978 to 1979; another 73 percent from 1979 to 1980; and yet another 47 percent from 1980 to 1981. Not surprisingly, the "correct" price advocated by those who worry about the decline turns out to be substantially higher than the current price of oil.[16]

The Amex Bank Review, published in London, argues that $15 a barrel "is emerging as a desirable level for a new floor for oil prices." A collapse to single digits would benefit the world economy only if a later oil price hike could be ruled out, the review says. Other economists and analysts, however, argued that oil at $15 a barrel is too cheap.

By compiling a historical record of oil prices going back to 1901, in dollar and inflation-adjusted terms, Paul Mlotok and Michael C. Young contend that "current 'low' oil prices are not really an anomaly; rather, they are in line with historical real prices." Thus, over the period 1901–85, the real price of oil averaged just under $5 a barrel. To match that price in current dollars, oil today should cost no more than $12 a barrel.

The only rationale for higher prices, they conclude, would be rooted in political, rather than economic, considerations. Yet, efforts to achieve an artificially high "correct" price for oil may be doomed to failure in view of the enormous oil surplus.

NOTES

1. Committee for Economic Development, *International Consequences of High-Priced Energy* (New York: Georgian Press, Inc., September 1975), p. 18.

2. The 24 OECD member countries are Australia, Austria, Belgium, Canada, Denmark, Finland, France, Federal Republic of Germany, Greece, Iceland, Ireland, Italy, Japan, Luxembourg, the Netherlands, New Zealand, Norway, Portugal, Spain, Sweden, Switzerland, Turkey, the United Kingdom, and the United States.

3. U.S. Congressional Budget Office, "The Effect of OPEC Oil Pricing on Output, Prices, and Exchange Rates in the United States and Other Industrialized Countries," CBO Study (February 1981), p. 64.

4. William Cline, *International Debt and The Stability of The World Economy* (Washington, DC: Institute for International Economics, 1983), p. 9.

5. This discussion draws on Jan F. R. Fabritius and Christian Ettrup Peterson, "OPEC Respending and the Economic Impact of an Increase in the Price of Oil," in Lars Matthiessen, ed., *The Impact of Rising Oil Prices on the World Economy* (London: Macmillan, 1982), pp. 80–96.

6. Committee for Economic Development, *International Consequences of High-Priced Energy* (New York: Georgian Press, Inc., September 1975), p. 17.

7. Committee for Economic Development, ibid.

8. See Robert H. Rasche and John A. Tatom, "The Effects of the New Energy Regime on Economic Capacity, Production, and Prices," *Review*, Federal Reserve Bank of St. Louis (May 1977), pp. 2–12.

9. See, for instance, J. A. Tatom, "Energy Price, and Short-Run Economic Performance," *Review*, Federal Reserve Bank of St. Louis (January, 1981), pp. 3–17.

10. Tatom, ibid., p. 5; See also, Tatom, "Energy Prices and Capital Formation, 1972–1977," *Review*, Federal Reserve Bank of St. Louis (May, 1979), pp. 2–9.

11. Rasche and Tatom, "The Effects of the New Energy Regime on Economic Capacity, Production, and Prices," op. cit., pp. 2–12; see also, D. S. Karnosky, "The Link Between Money and Prices—1971–76," *Review*, Federal Reserve Bank of St. Louis (June, 1976), pp. 17–23; A. N. Filipello, "A Question of Capacity," *Business and Government Outlook* (Fall 1976), pp. 1–3; B. Bosworth, "Capacity Creation in the Basic-Materials Industries," *Brookings Papers on Economic Activity* 2 (1976), pp. 297–341.

12. *World Development Report 1982*, The World Bank, p. 7.

13. Paul A. Volcker, Congressional Testimony, September 1979 and February 2, 1983.

14. Henry C. Wallich, "The Limits to Growth: Revisited," Remarks in the Manville Public Policy Lecture Series, Rockford College, Rockford, Illinois, April 7, 1982.

15. This discussion draws on Hobart Rowen, "Globally Slow Pace Continues," *The Washington Post* (January 11, 1987), p. G1.

16. Rowen, ibid.

3

Economic Theory and Cartel

The ability of the Organization of Petroleum Exporting Countries (OPEC) to raise oil prices and the effectiveness of its control over the supply of crude oil in the 1970s has given rise to numerous discussions on the nature of the OPEC cartel[1] and the requisites for successful cartelization of world commodity markets. Although the cartelization of world commodity markets is not a new phenomenon, there has been the growing concern about the future prospects for long-term successes of cartelization and the strong likelihood of an increasing domination of world commodity markets by cartels in the future.

For some, cartelization is merely a political maneuver of developing nations to achieve their political goals in international arena. For others, cartelization is an implicit transfer of monopoly and monopsony power from developed to developing countries. It, therefore, is "an essential and justifiable component of the New International Economic Order (NIEO)," for which the LDCs have spearheaded to seek a greater share of the action in the markets for their raw materials and primary product exports. And the eruption of "new oligopolists" into world markets dominated by "old oligopolists" has, in effect, led directly and indirectly to greater competition and a close approximation of textbook ideals of oligopolistic market situation.[2]

Historically, however, the experience of "old oligopolists" in cartelization of international commodity markets has not been completely successful. The majority of the attempts to cartelize the markets for most of the major internationally traded commodities were failures. The cartel either dissolved after a limited period of time, or in some cases the cartel remained in force officially, but had little or no real impact on price and member revenues. In effect, of the

51 formal cartel organizations documented by Paul Lee Eckbo,[3] only 19 could be considered successful in the sense of being able to maintain a price significantly higher than what it would have been in the absence of agreements.

Paul L. Eckbo arrived at the conclusion that "OPEC has also many of the characteristics of the earlier international commodity cartels that were successful for limited time periods."[4] This limited time period was four to six years for the earlier cartels. On this basis, OPEC was expected to collapse by the end of the 1970s, but OPEC has survived to surprise even some of its own members.[5] Even after the OPEC cartel demonstrated its unity, many economists insisted that OPEC would disintegrated, but the cartel held together. The prophets of doom were also discredited.

Indeed, the oil crisis underlined the end of the long Western boom and marked the beginning of a decade of uncertainty. There is perhaps no other myth in the great petroleum polemic which is as compelling as that of OPEC cohesion. More than a decade has passed since a small group of developing countries precipitated the most profound economic crisis of the postwar period and began what was to become the greatest transfer of wealth in history. The industrialized nations, which had based their economies on the assumption of limitless supplies of oil, were caught by surprise when the then little-known OPEC exercised its newly acquired authority as the world's main supplier of crude oil to raise the price for its "black gold."

The temptation to attribute the rise of the world oil price in the 1970s to the effective monopolization of the world oil market by OPEC has been reinforced by the empirical results of many studies.[6] Some studies have made a motivational hypothesis that OPEC was interested in maximizing profits (the "wealth maximizing monopolists") and have confirmed that the price rise after 1972 could be traced basically to the virtual monopolization of the international oil market. Other studies have considered the optimal behavior of an oligopolistic corporation with a significant position in several markets.[7] The implication of these results is rather significant in the stabilization of oligopolistic markets situation.

The question is whether the pricing strategy and policy of OPEC cartel are in its own long-term interest or whether it has set the price of crude oil at too high a level, in the sense that it has provided strong incentives to others to substitute for crude oil with other energy sources, the existence of which undoubtedly will undercut monopoly power of OPEC cartel. Such questions can not be answered in the absence of an explicit reference to some construct that builds on OPEC's intertemporal oligopolistic behavior.[8]

THE OLIGOPOLY PROBLEM AND CARTEL

Oligopoly is essentially a market situation intermediate between the cases of pure monopoly and pure competition. In pure monopoly only one seller is in the market; competition does not exist. The monopolist faces the market demand curve for his product. Pure competition and monopolistic competition represents the opposite. There are so many firms in the markets that the actions of each are expected to be imperceptible to the others. There is competition in the technical sense, but little or none in the popular sense. The demand curve faced by the purely competitive firm is horizontal at the equilibrium market price, the monopolistic competitor faces a downward sloping highly elastic demand curve. This is due to the fact that the monopolistic competitor is so small relative to the entire market that by itself it cannot affect other firms in the industry.

In oligopoly, technically, competition is lacking but sometimes there is intense rivalry or competition in the popular sense. With regard to the number of firms in the industry, oligopoly lies between the extremes of pure competition and monopolistic competition on the one hand and pure monopoly on the other. Its primary characteristic is that there are few enough firms in the industry for the activities of one firm to have repercussions on the price and sales of the other firms. Hence, rivalries develop under oligopoly. The demand curve faced by a single seller depends upon what reactions of rivals cannot be predicted; the demand curve faced by the firm is indeterminate. The rivals may try to second guess each other; they may tacitly agree to compete by advertising but not by price changes; or, recognizing their monopoly potential, they may form a coalition and cooperate rather than compete.

Typically, the firms in an oligopolistic industry produce and sell "differentiated products." The products of all firms in the industry are very good substitutes for each other, as they have high cross elasticities of demand, but that of each firm has its own distinguishing characteristics.

Some industries, however, approach a situation called pure oligopoly. Here the firms of the industry produce virtually identical products. Purchasers have little cause for preferring the product of one firm to that of another on any basis except price. Examples of industries approaching the pure oligopoly category are the cement industry, the aluminum industry, the steel industry, and the petroleum industry. Even here there are elements of differentiation among the products sold in a particular industry. Locational factors, service, political factors, and even personal friendships may differentiate the products of the various sellers in an industry.

Indeed, there is no satisfactory theory of oligopoly behavior. The classical treatments of oligopoly have been based upon the assumption that firms act independently of one another even though they are interdependent in the market. Most other studies, however, focus on explicit or implicit collusion among firms. This is due to the fact that the oligopolistic market situation tends to invite collusion among the firms in an industry. There are at least three major incentives leading oligopolistic firms toward collusion. First, by limiting the scope of competition among the firms it can enable them to act monopolistically and increase their profits by so doing. Second, by acting in concert the firms can reduce the likelihood of any one firm taking actions detrimental to the interactions of the others, thus decreasing oligopolistic uncertainty. And, third, collusion among the firms already in an industry will facilitate blocking newcomers from entering the industry. At the same time, once a collusive arrangement is in existence, any single firm is provided with a strong profit incentive to break away from the group and to act independently,[9] as illustrated by OPEC members in the early 1980s.

According to the degree of collusion occurring in the industry, oligopolistic situations can be classified as perfect and imperfect collusion. Imperfect collusive cases consist primarily of tacit informal arrangements under which the firms of an industry seek to establish prices and outputs and yet escape prosecution under the antitrust laws. Cases of perfect collusion, however, are made up for the most part of cartel arrangements. When a collusive arrangement is made openly and formally, it is called a cartel. Specifically, while collusion is a covert, informal agreement among firms in an industry setting prices for their output, a cartel is a formal organization of the firms or producers within a given industry, whose objective is to limit the scope of competition forces within a market. In a cartel, the member firms enter into an enforceable arrangement pertaining to price and possibly other market variables. This is perhaps best illustrated by the German Kartelle and the Organization of Petroleum Exporting Countries. It may also be formed by secret collusion among sellers for collusive price fixing. Many examples of this exist in U.S. economic history.

There are also numerous international cartels existing today, primarily in natural resources. International cartels control markets for such basic resources as copper, tin, bauxite, diamonds, chrome, phosphate, coffee, bananas, and most important of all, petroleum. These cartels are all either controlled by or in cahoots with the governments of the major producing countries.

In terms of the conditions for profit maximization, there is absolutely no difference between the optimal managerial strategy of a cartel and that of a monopolistic or oligopolistic firm that has several different plants. Still, the cartel's management does face the additional problem of distribution of profits among its members once the profit-maximizing price has been established, and there is no particular rule that must be followed in that distribution. The main difference between the cartel and an oligopolistic firm with several plants is that the latter must estimate a demand curve that is something other than the market demand curve.

Therefore, of the variety of services a cartel performs for its members, price fixing[10] and market sharing are of central importance. They are the two major problems confronting cartel members. Because a tight-knit cartel is effectively a shared monopoly, the logical approach is to price like a monopolist and sell the monopoly output. In other words, maximization of the cartel's profits is essentially a monopoly problem since in reality a single agency is making decisions for the industry as a whole. Profits will be maximized at the industry output and price at which industry marginal revenue equals industry marginal cost.

Cartel and Price Fixing

The cartel marginal cost curve is simply the horizontal sum of the component marginal cost curves of the cartel members. Since the primary function of the management group is to determine cartel marginal cost, the problem is the simple one of determining the price that maximizes cartel profit—the monopoly price. In the short run, cartel's profit will be maximized if members collectively produce at the cartel-established monopoly price.

This will have two effects, which can easily be illustrated by petroleum resources, but it could equally well apply to other natural resources. First, the higher uniform price will provide a powerful incentive to increase the capacity of world production. As oil becomes more profitable, for example, there will be strong incentives for nonoil-producing countries to locate new deposits and go into production and for other oil-importing countries such as the United States and the United Kingdom to increase their own production and to become self-sufficient. Second, the higher oil price will result in reduction in quantities demanded as conservation efforts are intensified and cheaper substitute energy sources are utilized. These efforts shift the supply schedule to the right, thus resulting in an "oil surplus" (as they were, in fact, by the end of 1974).

In order to maintain the fixed price, however, output must be reduced to the original output capacity of the cartel and production must be limited. With consequential cutbacks and restriction in production, the cartel-established common price must either represent a compromise between the optimal prices for individual member countries or imply a strategy that yields widely divergent benefits among member countries. If the resource is exhaustible and absorptive capacity for oil receipts is limited, the economic case for some output restriction and market sharing is very strong.[11]

Undoubtedly, under such circumstances, the cartel members will urge new producers to join the cartel and bear their share of the cutbacks. But the newcomers, happy in their sudden affluence, will probably reason that they are better off to stay out and produce without restraint. So all, or nearly all, of the cutbacks may fall on the original cartel members.

With reduction in the original output capacity and smaller profits, there is likely to be dissension among members of the cartel over "fair sharing" of the output cuts. There is also a strong temptation for a country to produce beyond its quota and to sell the extra oil quietly at a cut-rate price. But if everyone starts doing this, the cartel will break down. Therefore, as long as the abnormally high price is maintained, there will be a strong incentive for every country to keep looking for oil and increasing potential output capacity. The supply schedule will keep moving to the right, so the production cutbacks necessary to protect the price will become larger, and the problem of policing these cutbacks will become steadily more severe. The problem confronting the cartel management now is how to distribute the total sales among the member nations.

Cartel and Market Sharing

Market sharing of one type or another is characteristic of cartel arrangements. Under certain conditions, it can result in "ideal" monopoly price and output for a particular industry—the industry profit-maximizing level of price and output; but it is also likely to deviate from the monopoly position.

Fundamentally, there are two methods of sharing markets: nonprice competition and quotas. Under the nonprice competition, a uniform price is fixed and each cartel member is allowed to sell the product it can at that price. The only requirement is that members not reduce price below the cartel-established common price. The sellers compete with one another but not by price variations.

The second method of market sharing is the quota system, of which there are several variants. Under this system, there is no uniform principle by which quotas can be determined. In practice, however, the bargaining ability of the representative of a cartel member and the importance of the member to the cartel have been the most important elements in determining a quota. In effect, the cartel negotiations, as Bjarke Fog observed correctly, have been characterized by "reciprocal suspicion and distrust, not only as to what would be the optimum level for the others, but also regarding their motives and sincerity." [12] It is a political process in which various cartel members have different amounts of influence. Those with the most influence and the shrewdest negotiations are likely to receive the largest sales quotas, even though this increases total costs of the cartel.

Moreover, high-cost member producers are likely to receive larger sales quotas than cost minimization would dictate, since they would be unwilling to accept the small quotas dictated by cost minimization. In the late 1960s, for example, efforts were made through OPEC to establish export quotas. They failed. Saudi Arabia, Iran, and other Middle East countries resisted proposals that would have reduced the market advantage they derived from their lower production costs. Prior to the Middle East War, only Kuwait and Libya had restricted output. In effect, OPEC's membership as a whole has never grappled successfully with the question of quota allocation. To some extent, market restrictions have been carried out not by an OPEC cartel, but by a wealthy Arab cartel.

Beyond this there are two popular methods for determining the quotas. The first method relies on either the relative sales of the member in some precartel base period or the "productivity capacity" of the cartel member. As a practical matter, the choice of base period or of the measure of capacity is a matter of bargaining among the members of the cartel. Thus, the most skillful bargainer is likely to come out best. The second method for the quota system is based on geographical division of the market. While quota agreement is quite difficult in practice, in theory some guidelines can be laid down. A reasonable criterion for the cartel management group would be "minimization of total cartel costs."

This is identical to the short-run problem of allocating monopoly output among plants in a multi-plant monopoly.[13]

If the aim of the cartel is to maximize cartel profits, it will allocate sales to member producers in such a way that the marginal cost of all producers is equal. However, this allocation of output—or the so-called "ideal" allocation—is unlikely to occur, since allocation decisions are the result of negotiation between producers with varying interests and varying capabilities.

There are several factors that may stand in the way of achieving an "ideal" monopolistic price and output. Costs of production for the individual producers, for example, are likely to differ rather than be identical. Market sharing largely precludes the transfer of output quotas from producers with higher marginal costs to those with lower marginal costs at the output level produced by each. Differing political views (e.g., Iran vs. Iraq) and differing economic interests of the cartel members may result in compromises that stand in the way of profit maximization for the cartel as a whole. Individual members, assigned market shares and given a common price, may deliberately or in good faith overestimate the quantities of output that constitute their respective proportions of the total market and thus may encroach on the markets of other cartel members. In addition, the degree of independent action left to individual cartel members may provide further incentives to break away from the cartel and may in effect increase the possibilities for their doing so. All of these factors make pricing and output problems much more uncertain than they appear to be.[14]

Undoubtedly, subversion of the cartel by an individual member producer can be extremely profitable to that producer. With the industry operating at the level of monopoly price and output, the demand curve facing an individual producer is likely to be highly elastic, provided that other cartel members do not know or, if they do know, do not retaliate against, its action of lowering the price. To wit, the availability of significant profits to a member producer who cheats on the cartel, coupled with the ease with which secret price concessions can be made, makes policing cartel agreements extremely difficult.

Failure to establish a market share arrangement is likely to open possibilities for fragmentation. OPEC, for example, has attempted to set a monopoly price for oil. This would require member countries to curtail production to keep prices high. On several occasions, however, smaller countries (Nigeria, Iran, Ecuador) have refused to cut production. In 1982, as a result, OPEC was forced to reduce its price to balance supply and demand.

The OPEC cartel's loss of market control in late 1985 and early 1986 provides another example of a cartel that failed primarily because members could not agree on a market sharing scheme. Pressure from new entrants attracted by the relatively high oil prices and profits added to the cartel's problems.

But perhaps the most dangerous of all threats from the viewpoint of cartel members is that high prices and profits will induce potential competitors to develop substitute products. Since the OPEC cartel became effective and increased the price of oil by over 1000 percent over the period 1973–80, there has been increasing emphasis on developing alternatives to petroleum as an energy source. These problems combine to make cartel survival difficult.

Therefore, with the presence of the potential monopoly gains, a cartel is most likely to succeed if it can find solutions to the problems of organization and stability. The question, then, is whether a group of producers with sufficient potential monopoly power to dominate the market can agree on an optimal level of aggregate production, an equitable division of output, and a selection of an effective means of detecting and deterring cheating.

CARTEL ORGANIZATION AND STABILITY

Historically, cartels have been fragile, lasting only a short period of time. Accordingly, many economists maintain that cartels are inherently unstable because of external and internal problems they face. The external problem is to predict and, if possible, to discourage production by noncartel producers that affects the demands for members' output (the location problem). The internal problems include those of determining the contract surface, which requires information about demand and costs, selecting a point on the cartel contract surface (a division of output and profits—the sharing problem), detecting cheating by members, and deterring cheating.[15] These organizational problems have generated a great deal of empirical interest and have been the focus of most attempts to evaluate the future prospects for successful cartelization. The likelihood of existing and potential cartels to solve these problems has often been debated and used as the major argument to support forecasts of a potential proliferation of cartels.[16]

Hindrances to Cohesion

Locating the cartel's contract surface and detecting and deterring cheating are evidently serious problems. Determination of the contract surface, as Bjarke Fog pointed out, is most likely to be complicated by differences in opinion over the characteristics of demand and competitive supply, the existence of substitutes, and so on.[17] More importantly, cartel members may operate under different constraints with different time preferences. These constraints are further complicated by the unpredictable behavior of the noncartel producers. Variations in the total output of these producers change the members' profit functions of cartel members, thus shifting the contract surface about.

Except for the rare conditions of identical profit functions, there will always be disagreement among the cartel members about the appropriate share of the market. Some members will feel victimized and be tempted to cheat. There will always be powerful incentives for those who are not victimized to cheat, because of the positive marginal profits, ceteris paribus, at the output quotas.[18] If cheating takes place, loyal oligopolists, confronting a residual market, may be worse off than if they had followed competitive policies. They may be left holding large stocks in a declining market—a situation that can lead to political upheaval as well as economic collapse. Recognizing that other members of the cartel are cheating, the formerly obedient members must themselves reduce price in order to remain viable. Would-be cartelists are likely to abandon co-operation if they distrust their partners. The suspicion of cheating becomes a self-fulfilling prophecy. The cartel will accordingly collapse.

Demonstrating the incentives to cheat, or for a cartel member to leave the cartel, is rather an easy matter; demonstrating its capacity to cheat successfully is much more problematic. Consider the graphical representation of oligopolis-tic behavior depicted in Figure 3.1. Market demand for the homogeneous com-modity (such as oil) is given by DD, so the marginal revenue curve is given by the dash line MR. The demand curve dd and corresponding marginal reve-nue curve mr represent the market situation facing an individual member of the cartel that attempts to cheat or to leave the cartel.

As shown, the curves for the individual members are much less steep, that is, more elastic, than those for the cartel as a whole (DD and MR). While the demand curve DD is based on the supposition that all producers raise or lower their prices by the same amount as the individual producer, demand for the individual members is assumed to be much more subject to price than is true for the cartel as a whole. The individual cartel member can increase or decrease

Figure 3.1
Incentive to Cheating by a Cartel Member When Other Members Adhere to the Pricing Agreement

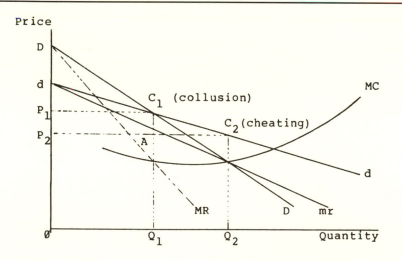

price and obtain a much greater change in the quantity of oil sold than the cartel acting as a whole in the market.

Therefore, if the individual member/producer increases its price and if other cartel producers maintain their prices, the producer in question can expect a considerable decrease in sales, since it will lose business to other producers in the cartel (because buyers will switch allegiance). Assuming that each member/producer expects its actions to go unheeded by its rivals, each producer believes its demand curve to be quite elastic (as shown by dd).

If a cartel elects to set a collusive price P_1 at the intersection point of marginal revenue MR and marginal cost MC for the cartel as a whole, the cartel sells OQ_1 quantity of oil at the collusive price, P_1. Under these circumstances, the maximum profit of an individual member producer, should it leave the cartel or secretly lower price to P_2, will be attained if it sells an output of OQ_2, at a price of P_2, where its marginal cost curve MC intersects its marginal revenue curve mr. This price would result in a revenue bonus of $AC_2Q_2Q_1$, which is higher than if the producer in question were to conform to the price and sales quota dictated by the cartel, thus inducing great incentives to cheat or to leave the cartel.

Without effective legal sanactions, the life of a cartel is likely to be brief. There will be a constant threat to the existence of a cartel; and there will always be an incentive to cheat or to leave the cartel as long as there are potential gains with price concessions. Once a few do so, other members of the cartel will follow. Price concessions made secretly by a few "chiselers" or openly by a few malcontents cut into the sales and profits of cooperative cartel members who are likely induced to match them, so long as the cartel does not punish it in some way. As the ranks of the unfaithful are expanded, the cartel is very likely to become disarrayed and incoherent and ultimately disintegrate completely.

Insensitivity of Oligopolistic Prices

Recognized interdependence and uncertainty of rivals' reactions, however, have often combined to make oligopoly prices insensitive to market forces. This "stickiness" or relative stability of price in an oligopoly market lies in the phenomenon of administered price, or the so-called "kinked" demand.

The kinked demand curve, d_1CD_2 as shown in Figure 3.2, arises from the assumption that an individual producer in the cartel, acting independently under normal economic conditions and uncertain about rivals' reactions, might expect rivals not to match its decision to raise its price above the collusion price P, but will expect rivals to at least match a decision to lower price. The individual producer in question would view its demand curve d_1d_2 as highly elastic for prices above the prevailing price, but for prices below the kink at the prevailing price P, the producer would expect the more inelastic demand segment CD_2 to

Figure 3.2
Administrated Prices Achieved by Cartel Leadership

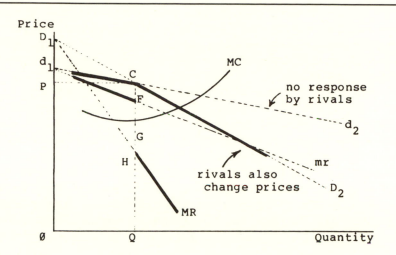

apply. Specifically, d_2CD_1 is the demand curve that applies if other producers in the cartel did not follow an individual producer when it changed price. On the other hand, demand curve CD_2 applies when all other member/producers will follow a price change made by one individual producer. With the assumption specified above, the demand curve for the producer has a kink in it at P and Q, which is critical to the cartel price fixing. It occurs at the kink in the demand curve, where other cartel members reduce price as well.

If the individual producer raises price above the point C and moves along the upper portion dC of dd, it will do so at its own risk because the remaining members of the cartel undoubtedly will refuse to go along and simply expand their market share at its expense. Consequently, the producer that raises its price beyond the point C will experience a large drop in the quantity of its product. On the other hand, if the individual producer attempts to cheat by lowering its price below the established market price (at the point below C), the other members of the cartel will counter with similar price cuts and demand moves along the lower portion of the demand curve DD for the cartel member under conditions of joint price movement. They will refuse to allow any single member by itself to lower price and thus earn a revenue bonus. Consequently, price tends to rest at the point C—the "posted," or agreed, sale price for oil.[19]

In this situation, because of the kinked demand curve at the point C, the effect on the marginal revenue curve is to introduce a vertical gap, FH, between the marginal revenue curve mr for the individual producer and the marginal revenue curve MR for the cartel as a whole. Again, if the individual producer should attempt to raise price alone, marginal revenue increases slowly along the segment dF of the mr curve. If the individual producer in question tries to cheat by lowering price, marginal revenue drops from F to H and from there along MR for the cartel. Thus, by attempting to cheat, the individual cartel member suffers an immediate and precipitous decline in marginal revenue. This, in effect, is by itself a sufficient deterrent to delinquency, perhaps, for most cartel members.

In most cases, the producer's marginal cost curve will pass through the "gap," FH, at Q. It can be shown that OQ is the most profitable output—and P the most profitable price—of the producer and will remain so even if there are considerable changes in marginal cost curve or some changes in demand, as long as the kink remains at the same price level.

Put differently, as long as the marginal cost curve of the individual producer in question passes through the gap in the marginal revenue curve at Q, the producer will maximize profit by producing OQ units of output and charging a price equal to P. However, if the producer's marginal cost curve were to intersect mr at a level of output less than OQ, the producer would maximize its profit by raising its price and producing a lower level of output. If the marginal cost curve were to intersect MR at a level of output greater than OQ, the firm would maximize its profit by lowering its price and producing a level of output greater than OQ. Under these circumstances, one might expect price to be quite rigid or sticky.

The Problem of Detecting Cheating

The problem of detecting cheating is not inherently insoluble, particularly if the cartel produces a good that is fairly homogeneous (for example, as oil), or if sales can to some extent be centralized. Unfortunately, rather than adopting measures to exacerbate the cartel's organization and stability problems, noncartel members of the industry might take actions to encourage cheating by making its detection more difficult. Governments of consumer nations have often abetted collusion by supporting the oligopolistic practices of multinational corporations, or by protecting high cost domestic producers. In the petroleum market, for example, corporate behavior has facilitated collusion among exporting countries. Not only have the oil companies willingly participated in a tax structure that discourages competitive behavior, they also have regulated output themselves. More perniciously, they have created an artificial pricing system and have capitulated to demands for price increases. In dealing with the oil companies, as Krasner commented, "OPEC's members hit mush and, following Lenin's dictum, pushed on." As a consequence, the benefits petroleum-exporting nations derived from their association with multinational corporations surpass those bestowed on any other group of Third World exporters.[20]

A cartel may indeed solve its organizational problems, but this does not guarantee its success. The ability to solve the organizational problems may depend very much on the potential for monopoly profits, the existence of which, in turn, depends not only on market concentration, but also on the elasticity of demand. If monopoly and competitive prices differ only slightly, no organizational strategy can result in cartel success. There are still other costs involved in the organization and maintenance of a cartel. These include political costs, costs of price-output coordination, and, for each cartel member, costs associated with the risk of being undercut and losing significant short-term profits. Hence, it would not be worthwhile to bear these costs if the expected resulting gains were not at least as large.[21] One reason for the formation of OPEC and later success in maintaining itself as a cohesive cartel in the 1970s lies in the large gains to its member producers from cartelization in the world petroleum market. The history of commodity cartelization has shown that those cartels were most successful for which potential monopoly profits were the greatest.

Unless the cartel can exert some form of coercion against the noncartel members, the cartel may also face the problem of the outsider. Some producers may find it more profitable to remain outside the cartel. The outsider may sell at the cartel's monopoly (or near monopoly) price without being restricted to any market share.

Under such circumstance, it would be in the interest of cartel members to bring the outsider into the cartel. Where the cartel's control is partial, or perhaps limited pricing, there is often considerable rivalry among cartel members. If the cartel controls market share as well as price, with output quotas assigned on the basis of capacity, members may attempt to increase their capacity. Without a strong monopolistic cartel, as well as the legal and economic power to punish the recalcitrant producers, the market share and profit of each cartel member are most likely to decrease.[22]

To say the least, the future stability of OPEC cartel depends in part on how closely OPEC can be made to approximate a monopoly by eliminating certain differences between member countries and by unifying their goals. This can be achieved, as Ezzati suggested, through either an effective and widely accepted production prorationing program, or by establishing a joint OPEC fund to provide low-interest-rate loans to member countries in order to discourage them from producing more than their ration and in order to prevent OPEC as a whole from producing more than what is demanded from it. Greater political unity and/or the establishment of regional economic pacts would also minimize the conflict among member countries and bring the OPEC "cartel" closer to an OPEC monopoly.[23]

PROSPECTS FOR SUCCESSFUL CARTELIZATION: THEORETICAL ISSUES

Theoretically, it is not possible to state definitely when collusion will take place. There are, however, two basic market conditions, in addition to oligopolistic-monopolistic market structure and political constraints previously discussed, that make durable cartel behavior more likely.

Supply Unresponsive to Price

Successful collusion is more likely in an industry where there are effective economic and/or technical barriers to the entry of new producers. Where barriers to entry into the industry are substantial, price competition is often "out-of-bounds." Where informal (or formal) arrangements on operating rules are satisfactory to all, price is quite insensitive to market forces under oligopoly. On the other hand, if higher prices prompt large increases in production, collusion is less attractive in the long run, because of rapid erosion of the cartel members' market share and consequent reduction of their profits as a result of additional supplies.

An analysis of the supply of and demand for petroleum in the non-OPEC nations shows that unresponsiveness of supply to price plays a substantial role in the success of OPEC cohesion in the 1970s. First, there has been only a small increase in petroleum output by non-OPEC nations following the sharply higher prices in 1973, indicating that supply of petroleum in non-OPEC nations is relatively price inelastic. Although the price of petroleum increased about twelvefold during this period, petroleum output in non-OPEC nations increased only 24 percent.[24] It is estimated that the long-run price elasticity of the non-OPEC oil supply is between 0.33 and 0.67. In other words, a 1 percent increase in price of oil will cause output to increase about 0.5 percent.[25]

Part of the reason for short-run inelastic supply of petroleum by non-OPEC nations is the dominant position of OPEC in the petroleum industry. From 1945 to 1979, about three-fourths of world oil discoveries were in the Middle East (largely the OPEC area). In 1973, when OPEC began restricting production, it was producing about 31 million barrels of oil per day, more than four-fifths of which was exported. OPEC supplied 83.4 percent of all petroleum exports in 1978. Specifically, worldwide petroleum production contracted in growth in the 1970s at a time when distortions in distribution were already forcing supply in some areas to lag behind the demand that otherwise would have occurred at prevailing prices.[26] Not only was U.S. petroleum production actually falling, but extraction of new, North Slope oil in Alaska had been delayed.

Without being oversimplified, it is safe to conclude that successful cartelization depends in part on the supply elasticity of the output of the industry. The less elastic the supply curve, the longer the cartel is likely to survive. If a large increase in price elicits only a small increase in output by noncartel producers, there will be less pressure on the cartel.[27]

Demand Unresponsive to Price

Likewise, the more inelastic the demand curve for the cartel's product, the higher the price can be raised without drastically reducing the quantity demanded and the greater the potential profit for the cartel as a whole. Put differently, the less responsive demand is to price, the greater the benefits of collusion. Even if the demand for an industry's product is relatively inelastic, the demand for the product of a single producer representing a fraction of the industry's output, is highly elastic. Collective action in such a situation could be used to exploit the global inelasticity of demand.[28] If good substitutes are available for the cartel's product, however, this will not occur. Instead, sizable increases in the price of the cartel's product will result in larger purchases of these substitute goods. In this case, the cartel is not very likely to increase its profits for too long by restricting output and raising prices. Even if both the demand and supply relationships may appear to be quite inelastic in the short run, demand and supply conditions will change over time in response to higher prices.[29]

The maintenance of high prices over a long period, however, could induce some unintended effects: lower demand for energy consumption; a more favorable social environment for energy conservation; the extensive search for new discoveries of oil and other fuels by oil importing nations; the substitution of other cheaper fuels; increasing research into energy-saving technologies; more research and development in alternate fuel technologies such as nuclear, oil shale, and coal and gas liquefaction; and an import-restriction strategy.[30] These changes will undoubtedly induce the instability of the cartel.

Succinctly, the success of the OPEC strategy in 1973 was, to some degree, due to the low elasticities, at least in the short run, of petroleum demand by non-OPEC nations and the absolute scarcities consequent upon the embargo. A relatively small decrease in quantity demanded, as a result of the large increase in price, was confirmed by petroleum consumption in the major industrialized countries from 1973 until mid-1980. Although petroleum prices had risen about twelvefold, consumption in the these nations declined only about 10 percent, or equivalently a reduction of approximately 4.1 million from 35.2 to 31.1 million barrels per day.[31] In particular, in the United States, on the demand side, the long-run price elasticity of demand for gasoline has been estimated at about -0.8, which indicates that an increase in price of 1 percent causes a reduction of about 0.8 percent in quantity demanded. As the output of the cartel members is being reduced, intense rivalry for greater market shares will develop among cartel members, thus making it more difficult for cartels to exist for extended periods.

In short, the OPEC cartel has been successful because of special supply and demand conditions for petroleum, which assured an increase in profits to cartel members when production was restricted.

WHETHER OPEC IS A CARTEL

The world has witnessed a remarkable assertion of economic and political power by the oil-producing nations grouped into the cartelized organization.

Perhaps, for the first time several primarily less developed countries have combined to flex their muscles with the developed, industrialized world. The prospect that certain developing countries will be able to combine to exercise similar control over other vital natural resources, particularly mineral resources, has caused a great deal of concern among industrialized nations. Officials and scholars of several developed industrial economies have chided developing countries' attempts at concerted action—often branding them as cartelists or exploiters. Such an accusation is, nonetheless, unfounded, even for the successful grouping of oil-exporting countries.[32] Professor Zuhayr Mikdashi pointed out that

Such criticism overlooks the fact that the developed industrial economies are not faithful to the model of competitive markets, and that oligopolistic-monopolistic market structures predominate in leading sectors with active or passive support for the home governments concerned.[33]

It has often been argued in the oil-importing countries that the OPEC price in the 1970s was purely the result of the exercise of monopoly power, and that this price was in no way fair or efficient. Despite OPEC's obvious market power, it is not clear that prices during the period since 1974 have been unreasonable. Although OPEC takes the form of an open collusion, it does not meet the strict definition of a cartel in all respects. There are dominant "firm" and "property rights" theses which provide arguments for this observation.

Dominant "Firm" Thesis

Many economists have treated OPEC as the dominant *firm* that sets and lets the small producers sell all they want at the official price. The dominant firm in the alleged cartel is clearly Saudi Arabia. In the years from the strong crude oil market in 1973 to the relatively weak markets in 1975–77, Saudi Arabia expanded its market share from 24.2 to 30.4 percent of OPEC production. Although Saudi Arabia and its close neighbors (Kuwait and smaller Gulf countries) control approximately 60 percent of the productive capacity of OPEC, Saudi Arabia has not been able to persuade some smaller and fractious members of OPEC to limit production as a way of maintaining OPEC's control on world oil markets. In 1982, Saudi Arabia was formally designated by OPEC to be the "swing" country. By so designating, Saudi Arabia would allow the other countries to produce a given amount, while setting its own production in order to maintain the cartel's official price. This evidence is not consistent with either a fixed market share or a dominant firm price-leadership model of oligopoly behavior. On the other hand, OPEC output, in the aggregate, is consistent with cartel behavior. The OPEC share of world crude production declined from 55.5 to 52.5 percent during the increasingly weak markets from 1973 to 1977.[34]

"Property Rights" Thesis

Using a *property rights* explanation of the rise in crude oil prices, Ali D. Johany argues that OPEC is not a cartel.[35] He has shown that movements of crude oil prices from approximately $3 per barrel in the early 1970s to approximately $12.5 per barrel in 1974 are rational in terms of maximizing the present value of the resources of oil-producing countries. Johany pointed out that during the 1970s and 1960s there was a progressive awareness on the part of international oil companies holding oil concessions in the Middle East that their property rights were in jeopardy as a result of OPEC nations' nationalization of international oil company interests, seizing control of the international flow of oil and extending the decolonization process that began after World War II. Fear of loss of property rights caused international oil companies to accelerate their foreign production. From 1950 through 1970 the compound annual growth rate in oil production from the Middle East was 10.9 percent, compared to the growth rate of 15.0 percent from 1970 through 1973.[36] These output increases were matched by worldwide demand with only modest increase in nominal prices. In effect, the prices of world crude oil were relatively stable during this period of time.

By the end of 1973, however, OPEC nations, who had firmly established their property rights, were in complete control of output within their borders. From 1973 to 1977, Middle Eastern oil output increased at a compound annual rate of only 0.7 percent. As a consequence, crude oil prices in world markets rose sharply from 1970 to early 1982, a fact which can be explained without the aid of a cartel theory. In fact, the oil shortages in the early 1970s were the result not of an OPEC cartel, nor even an Arab cartel, but of actions taken by four countries—Libya, Kuwait, Abu Dhabi, and most importantly, Saudi Arabia.

OPEC Cohesion: The Myth of Perpetual Unity?

Whether OPEC cohesion is the myth of perpetual unity or just ephemeral temperament has been subject to extensive debates. The fact is that, as the fifteenth anniversary of the Arab oil embargo approaches, OPEC's power over the world oil market has clearly waned. The first two years of the 1980s saw increased bickering among OPEC nations over production quotas and pricing policy as each sought to maintain its sale in a shrinking market. At an emergency meeting in London in March 1983, OPEC established new production ceilings and voted to lower its benchmark price by $5 to $29. It was the first time in its 23-year history that OPEC had announced a price reduction. In effect, the OPEC cartel has already lost much of its international market to non-OPEC suppliers. Subsequently, the oil price plunged to below $10 a barrel at one point in 1986 as a result of the world oil glut.

Although OPEC's power has waned, its action has clearly succeeded in achieving its main objectives. The Arab oil embargo in political, economic, and symbolic terms was one of the most important events to occur since World War II and caught everyone by surprise. The consequences are still unfolding.

While many observers eagerly anticipated the breakup of OPEC as due punishment for its own greed, members' resolve to stick out the oil glut appears greater than expected. The producing countries have gotten their act together and prices stick. The oil prices, which plunged from $32 a barrel late in 1985 to below $10 a barrel at one point in 1986, have now recovered to about $13 and are most likely to climb to more than $15 per barrel in 1989 under the impetus of a fresh agreement among the Organization of Petroleum Exporting Countries to limit production. If OPEC succeeds, it may restore the economic viability of oil-producing countries, at the cost of negative effects on importing countries, especially in Europe. It would be one factor in helping to push inflation indexes higher in all importing countries.[37]

Hence, far from being a sign of imminent collapse of the cartel, this is more likely an adjustment to the greater long-run demand elasticity, and might be a sign of successful adjustment to change. But the cartel must muster enough internal discipline to hold the line for several more years since demand shows no signs of reviving significantly. In effect, there is no other group of Third World producers who now possesses, or is likely to possess in the foreseeable future, similar advantages to those enjoyed by those OPEC nations. These advantages include tacit assistance from multinational corporations, surfeit revenues, and highly salient shared values.[38]

Certainly there had been a triumph of OPEC restraint. But the real reason was much more fundamental: The non-OPEC oil producers had no desire to break the cartel and were doing everything possible to help keep the price up.

But it was not the new oil producers who were now siding with OPEC. It was a vast network of oil companies, arms companies, construction companies, and above all bankers. The banks had loaned billions to such countries as Mexico, Venezuela, and Nigeria, who were suddenly impoverished by a new drop in revenues. And so the banks used their lobbying power to support the high oil prices.

The 15-year sequence of shocks and revelations has brought about the ultimate irony. The cartel is now supported by many industrial nations. And many bankers and investors who had fought to beat the oil price down were now still more determined to keep it up.

NOTES

1. The OPEC cartel may not meet the strict definition of a cartel in all respects, but this term is used to facilitate discussion.

2. Diaz-Alejandro has termed the LDC's spearheading the drive for the NIEO the "new oligopolists." See Carlos F. Diaz-Alejandro, "International Markets for LDCs—

The Old and New," *American Economic Review Papers and Proceedings* (May 1979), pp. 264–69; see also, Robert S. Pindyck, "The Cartelization of World Commodity Markets," *American Economic Review* 69, no. 2 (May 1979), pp. 154–58.

3. See Paul L. Eckbo, "OPEC and the Experience of Some Non-Petroleum International Cartels," M.I.T. Energy Lab, Working Paper (June 1975); and Robert S. Pindyck, op. cit., p. 154.

4. Paul Lee Eckbo, *The Future of World Oil* (Cambridge, MA: Ballinger, 1976), p. 108.

5. R. K. Pauchari, *The Political Economy of Global Energy* (Baltimore, MD: The Johns Hopkins University Press, 1985), p. 61.

6. William D. Nordhaus, *The Efficient Use of Energy Resources* (New Haven, CT: Yale University Press, 1979), Chapter 5. Nordhaus has shown that the market price in the late 1960s and early 1970s was virtually equal to the calculated efficiency price.

7. Ibid.

8. See Robert Pindyck, "Gains to Producers from the Cartelization of Exhaustible Resources," *Review of Economics and Statistics* 60 (1978), pp. 238–51; also J. Cremer and M. Weitzman, "OPEC and the Monopoly Price of World Oil," *European Economic Review* 8 (1976), pp. 155–64.

9. Richard H. Leftwich, *The Price System and Resource Allocation*, 3d ed. (New York: Holt, Rinehart and Winston, 1966), p. 214.

10. A nontechnical survey of some theoretical analyses of the pricing of exhaustible natural resources and the incentives for developing resource substitutes under oligopoly is conducted by Partha Dasgupta. See Partha Dasgupta, "Resource Pricing and Technological Innovations under Oligopoly: A Theoretical Exploration," in Lar Matthiessen, ed., *The Impact of Rising Oil Prices on the World Economy* (London: The Macmillan Press, Ltd., 1982), pp. 149–77.

11. Harry W. Richardson, *Economic Aspects of the Energy Crisis* (Lexington, MA: Lexington Books/Saxon House, 1975), p. 127.

12. Bjarke Fog, "How Are Cartel Prices Determined?," *Journal of Industrial Economics* 5 (November 1976), pp. 16–23.

13. C. E. Ferguson, *Microeconomic Theory*, 3d ed. (Homewood, IL: Richard D. Irwin, Inc.), 1972.

14. Leftwich, op. cit., p. 221.

15. D. K. Osborne, "Cartel Problems," *American Economic Review* 66, no. 5 (December 1976), pp. 835–44; see also, Robert S. Pindyck, "The Cartelization of World Commodity Markets," *American Economic Review* 69, no. 2 (May 1979), pp. 154–58.

16. C. F. Bergsten, "The Threat Is Real," *Foreign Policy* 14, (Spring 1974), pp. 84–90; and Zuhayr Mikdashi, "Collusion Could Work," *Foreign Policy* 14 (Spring 1974), pp. 57–68.

17. Fog, op. cit., pp. 16–23; see also, Pindyck, "The Cartelization of World Commodity Markets," p. 157.

18. Osborne, op. cit., p. 835.

19. Charles F. Doran, *Myth, Oil, and Politics* (New York: The Free Press, 1977), p. 139.

20. Stephen D. Krasner, "Oil Is the Exception," *Foreign Policy* 14 (Spring 1974), pp. 77–78; see also, Pindyck, "The Cartelization of World Commodity Markets," pp. 156–57.

21. Ibid., p. 157.

22. Allan J. Braff, *Microeconomic Analysis* (New York: John Wiley & Sons, Inc., 1969); pp. 205–06.

23. Ali Ezzati, *World Energy Markets and OPEC Stability* (Lexington, MA: Lexington Books, 1978), p. 132.

24. U.S. Department of Energy, *Monthly Energy Review* (December 1980), pp. 88–89; see also, Exxon Corporation, *Middle East Oil Gas,* 2d ed. (December 1984), p. 26. Part of the apparent inelasticity, however, reflects the impact of the price controls in the United States and Canada.

25. Michael Kennedy, "A World Oil Model," in Dale W. Jorgenson, ed., *Econometric Studies of U.S. Energy Policy* (Amsterdam: North-Holland Publishing Company, 1976), p. 139.

26. Doran, op. cit., p. 134.

27. Clifton B. Luttrell, "A Bushel of Wheat for a Barrel of Oil: Can We Offset OPEC's Gains with a Grain Cartel?," *Review,* Federal Reserve Bank of St. Louis (April 1981), p. 14.

28. Zuhayr Mikdashi, "Collusion Could Work," *Foreign Policy* 14 (Spring 1974), p. 61.

29. Luttrell, op. cit., p. 14.

30. Richardson, op. cit., pp. 127–28.

31. U.S. Department of Energy, *Monthly Energy Review* (December 1980), p. 90.

32. See C. Fred Bergsten, "The Threat from the Third World," *Foreign Policy* 11, pp. 102–24; also, M. A. Adelman, "Is the Oil Shortage Real?" *Foreign Policy* 9, pp. 69–107.

33. Mikdashi, op. cit., p. 58.

34. Walter J. Mead, "The Performance of Government in Energy Regulations," *American Economic Review* (May 1979), p. 354.

35. See Ali D. Johany, "OPEC Is Not a Cartel: A Property Rights Explanation of the Rise in Crude Oil Prices," unpublished doctoral dissertation, University of California–Santa Barbara (June 1978); also, Walter J. Mead, "The Performance of Government in Energy Regulations," *American Economic Review* (May 1979), p. 354.

36. Mead, ibid., p. 354.

37. Hobart Rowen, "Globally Slow Pace Countries," *The Washington Post* (January 11, 1987), p. G-1.

38. Krasner, op. cit., p. 79.

4

Demand for Energy

A growing dependence on oil caused both by the rapid growth of world output and by a shift to oil from coal and other sources has been characteristic of global energy developments since World War II. Until 1970, rates of discovery of oil in the Middle East and elsewhere were far in excess of demand. As a result, the real price of petroleum fell steadily. Oil and natural gas supplied over 80 percent of the increase in world use of primary energy between 1950 and 1970. Cheap energy made an important contribution to the unprecedentedly rapid growth of world output.

The record of energy transition is very significant in industrial nations, particularly in the United States. Even those nations that did not possess the advantages of indigenous oil production were overwhelmed by the sheer economic benefits of using oil and did so, even in some cases to the disadvantage of indigenous coal production. The displacement of coal was very rapid, considering the vast amount of coal-using capital stock built up during the second half of the nineteenth century. There was little changeover of coal-using equipment to oil use, but oil captured a larger share merely through the design of new industries for fuel oil use. Much the same developments took place in Europe and Japan during their rapid industrialization after World War II. The centrally planned economies have been no exception to this trend even though their dependence on oil is somewhat lower.[1]

At the other end of the spectrum, most of the developing nations have followed a transition path that goes directly from the use of traditional fuels like firewood and animal and vegetable waste to the use of oil and natural gas. Their choice of oil was influenced by (a) the availability of oil-using technologies and industrial plants, (b) the effectiveness of the multinational oil companies in marketing oil products at the constantly declining prices during the 1950s and 1960s and (c) the eagerness of Western equipment suppliers to design for oil use. And, at the same time, the developing countries began to develop programs to improve transportation routes and to expand construction of electric utilities in order to satisfy economic and social needs for their countries.

Indeed, the post–World War II period has brought major structural changes in the economies of most countries. In some nations, particularly in the industrialized West, these changes occurred in response to actual and anticipated changes in factor price ratios. In the developing countries, on the other hand, the economic structure has moved from a great reliance on agriculture to rapid growth in industry and other sectors, notably transport and services. The rapidity of change in economic structures and activities has made the post–World War II period particularly revealing of transitional trends in the use of energy.

The energy crisis of the early 1970s, however, had ushered in a new era of energy awareness. The pattern of energy consumption in the industrial nations has changed substantially during the past decade as a result of a rise in the relative price of energy, the emergence of new technologies, the imposition of environmental constraints, and other factors. Whereas the developed countries have achieved significant reductions in energy use per unit of output, the developing countries, as a group, have shown only a slight decline and are likely to continue with higher intensities of energy use for many years to come. This is due to the fact that the developing countries are at the beginning of a period of intensive industrialization, modernization of transport systems, and a shift from traditional fuels to commercial sources of energy.[2]

WORLD ENERGY CONSUMPTION

The rising price of oil in the 1970s has had a profound impact on the world economy. It contributed importantly to the slowdown in economic growth, to surging inflation worldwide, and to the disintegration of the international financial structure. The OPEC cartel had acted on the widely held assumption that energy—particularly oil—was so essential to economic growth in the industrial West and that price had little influence on demand. However, the market forces unleashed by the surging oil prices brought forth positive responses in the world economy.

The high price of oil spurred oil conservation measures on the part of oil consumers and industries worldwide. The greatest scope for conservation lies with the industrialized countries; they account for more than half of world energy consumption (and more than a third of production). On average the industrialized countries use about eight times as much commercial energy per person as the middle-income developing countries and more than 40 times as much as the low-income countries. This is partly because they are more industrialized;

but their agriculture and households are also more energy intensive. They have been reducing the ratio of energy use to GNP.

Industrial Countries

Prior to 1973, annual consumption of oil in industrial countries grew some 2 percent faster than production. Between 1973 and 1980 oil consumption per unit of output actually declined at a rate of 2 percent annually. The rate of decline has accelerated to over 6 percent since 1980. This has meant a saving of about 15 percent, or 10 million barrels a day of oil equivalent in 1980, compared to the demand that would have been expected if there had been no increase in real energy prices. The conservation measures in different industrial countries had resulted in different energy use ratios. Between 1973 and 1977 this ratio fell 16 percent in Japan, 13 percent in France, 12 percent in the Federal Republic of Germany, 10 percent in both the United States and Italy, 9 percent in Canada, and 7 percent in the United Kingdom. Moreover, Japan and Western Europe have held their absolute volume of petroleum use constant since 1973, and the United States has done so since 1978.

The quantity demanded in the major industrial nations is relatively small, compared with the large increase in prices of crude oil. Prices of crude oil rose about twelvefold from 1973 to 1982, but consumption in these nations declined only 10 percent, from 34.2 to 31.1 million barrels per day during the same period. The implication is that the demand for crude oil by non-OPEC nations is price inelastic, at least in the short run.

Even so, the 1973–74 oil price increases have had a marked effect on energy consumption of oil-importing countries, especially the industrial countries. The conservation measures, combined with the marked slowdown in world economic growth, have led to a gradual reduction in the worldwide demand for oil. By the end of 1982, the total world demand was some 6 percent below the level that prevailed at the end of 1973.

The increase in prices of imported oil has gradually been passed through to consumers, cushioned by the slower rise in taxes and in the prices of other types of energy. In the major industrial countries, real price to final users rose by 62 percent between 1973 and 1979. The available data show a similar rise in oil-importing developing countries but much less in oil-exporting countries.[3] It is not clear, however, how much of the reduction in energy demanded is attributable to price changes and how much is the effect of reduced economic activity and decline in income.

Nonmarket Industrial Economies

While the share of petroleum in energy consumption in the nonmarket industrial economies of the U.S.S.R. and the countries of Eastern Europe continued to grow over the decade after the 1973 energy crisis, the share of solid fuels continued to decline during this period. However, these countries retained a higher dependence on coal than did the industrial countries of the non-Communist world. In 1980, for instance, the nonmarket industrial economies consumed only 13.1 mbd of oil, but 20.9 mbd of solid fuels, which constituted 30.5 percent and 48.6 percent, respectively, of their total energy consumption. The share of petroleum in energy consumption, however, is expected to level off through 1990, while natural gas will continue to play a major role in the nonmarket industrial economies.

Oil-Exporting Developing Countries

Trends in energy consumption in the oil-exporting developing countries show a very high relative dependence on petroleum (e.g., 64.5 percent in 1980) and an almost negligible level of coal consumption. Larger quantities of natural gas, approximately 25.5 percent of energy consumption, have also been used in their industrial plants and are expected to continue to increase in its share in energy consumption through 1990. The most significant feature about past energy trends in the oil-exporting developing countries is the rapid increase in consumption that took place between 1973 and 1978, amounting to a total of 54.5 percent.

Oil-Importing Developing Countries

The oil-importing developing countries, on the other hand, have shown a lower dependence on oil, accounting for 12.2 percent only. The available data show that this group of countries registered an actual decline in oil consumption between 1978 and 1980, largely as a result of higher prices, and that real prices to final users rose by 62 percent between 1973 and 1979. In effect, since the late 1970s, there has also been an increase in the use of primary electricity in these nations, and large-scale investments have been made, which indicate that use of electricity may grow more rapidly than that of other energy sources, taking up the slack from the decline in the use of oil.[4]

In general, about half of all the energy production of low-income oil-importing countries is noncommercial—from wood and dung, for example. As their economies develop, much of this will have to be replaced by commercial energy. The study by the World Bank shows that even with appropriate pricing and other conservation measures, the consumption of commercial energy in these developing countries is expected to rise more than 80 percent in the 1980s, compared with a GNP growth of about 70 percent. By 1990 the oil-importing developing countries' commercial energy requirements are likely to rise to around 17 percent of world use.[5]

In sum, the aggregate consumption of energy continues to grow despite a downward trend in the industrial nations, which, significantly, are the world's largest consumers. However, the most encouraging trend since 1980 has been the decrease in oil consumption, which eased the pressure on the world's oil market.

THEORETICAL ISSUES

Over the decades since World War II, trends in the demand for oil for different groups of countries have been diverse, bringing about varying rates of growth. The demand for energy is a function of many variables. Generally, the structure of demand for energy in the long run would be given by the function:

$$D = f(K, L, M, Y, P_E, P_K, P_L, P_M) \tag{1}$$

where D is the demand for energy for any set of activities, K is the stock of capital employed, L is the labor employed, M is the quantity of raw materials used, Y is the level of output, P_E is the price of energy, P_K is the price of capital, P_L is the wage rate for labor, and P_M is the price of raw materials used.

The main factors affecting demand for energy can be divided into an income effect and a price effect (with conservation measures being part of the latter). Many studies have attempted to estimate the long-run elasticity of demand for energy. Michael Kennedy, for example, has shown that the long-run price elasticity of demand for gasoline in the United States has been at about −0.8, indicating that an increase in price of 1 percent causes a reduction of about 0.8 percent in quantity demanded.[6] Paul MacAvoy, however, has found no statistically significant or believable elasticities or lags in his fitted demand equation for energy.[7]

Even though some later work using the translog form has provided very useful results from a number of research efforts,[8] most global studies use much simpler aggregation. Typically, for predicting energy demand some estimates of long-run price and income elasticities are combined with assumptions of future increase in energy prices and incomes in the region being considered. The World Bank (1981) used this approach to develop forecasts of demand for energy by groupings of countries for the years 1985 and 1990.

The World Bank study shows that income elasticity tends to be higher in developing countries than in industrial ones, reflecting the rapid increases in industrialization and urbanization that accompany the early stages of growth. As shown in Table 4.1, for every percentage point increase in income, energy consumption rises by about 1.3 percent in developing countries, compared to 1.0 percent in industrial countries.

Although the flexibility in the energy system provides many means to accommodate the higher costs, minimizing the economic effects for those developing countries that are not energy exporters, this flexibility is not available, as in those industrialized nations. This is due to the fact that the structures of the economies in the developing countries are different from those of the industrialized nations.

Table 4.1
Typical Income and Long-Term Price Elasticity for Energy

Country Group	Income Elasticity	Price[1] Elasticity
Industrial Market Economies	1.0	0.4 (0.2-0.6)
Developing Countries	1.3	0.3 (0.1-0.5)

[1] At user prices. The range of estimates is indicated in parentheses.

Source: The World Development Report 1981.

The limited investigation conducted by Pindyck and others indicates that price elasticities tend to be somewhat lower.[9] Over the 1973–81 period, each 10 percent increase in price has led to a reduction in energy demand of about 4 percent in the industrial countries but only 3 percent in the developing countries. The full effects of higher energy prices will take place over 15 to 20 years as energy-using equipment is replaced. The observed effects of price rises over the past decade are therefore perhaps half of the estimated long-term effects.[10]

Many economists have argued that energy is unique and that the behavior of the energy demand can not be explained with "conventional econometric models." Some, however, contend that the demand for energy is a fundamental building block of the energy market. Hence, the uncertainties in energy demand are, in effect, related to four fundamental issues of the demand theory: the long-run income elasticity of the demand for energy, the long-run price elasticity of the demand for energy, the time distribution of the response to the recent price increases, and the response of energy to relative prices, income, population, and other determinants.[11]

To explain the behavior of the demand for energy with the conventional econometric model, Nordhaus assumes that society's preferences can be represented as a well-behaved preference function of the final goods and services consumed and that the preference function is spearable over time. By maximizing an index of consumption, C_t, taking nonenergy goods as numeraire, that is,

$$\text{Max } C_t = X_t + \sum_{i=1}^{n} A_i E_{it}^{-\alpha_i} (X_t + \sum_{i=1}^{n} w_i E_{it})^{\beta_i} \qquad (2)$$

subject to the budget constraint

$$Y_t = \sum_{i=1}^{n} p_{it} E_{it} + X_t \tag{3}$$

where X_t is an index of nonenergy goods, E_{it} different energy services, p_{it} current year energy prices of energy services relative to nonenergy prices, A_i, α_i, β_i are parameters of the utility functions, and w_i the base period weights for energy in terms of other goods, Nordhaus was able to derive a quantifiable energy demand function

$$E_{it} = k_i p_{it}^{-\gamma_i} Y_t^{\delta_i} \qquad\qquad i = 1, 2, \ldots, N \tag{4}$$

where $k_i = (\alpha_i A_i)^{1/(1-\alpha_i)}$, $r_i = (1-\alpha^i)^{-1}$, and $\delta_i = \beta_i (1-\alpha_i)^{-1}$ $\tag{5}$

This equation was used to estimate net energy consumption for the period 1955–72.

Nordhaus' estimates of energy demand rely on a combination of techniques for estimating the price responsiveness of energy demand in the United States and Europe. The basic result is that energy demand is shown to be moderately elastic with respect to price, with elasticities in the range of -0.5 and -1.0, depending on the sector, country, and specification.

MacAvoy, on the other hand, fitted a demand equation for energy. His solution is to take elasticity estimates presented elsewhere in the literature, insert these into the model, and solve for equilibrium prices and quantities. This procedure is repeated with alternative coefficients to generate a number of different solutions, and the solution set of simulated prices and quantities that most closely approximates actual prices and quantities in certain years is then used as the source for the estimated values of the elasticities. The ad hoc nature of the methodology, however, deprives the model's predictions of reliable confidence intervals and other statistical properties.

Although the reliability of elasticity estimates is of prime importance in assessing future scenarios, uniform estimates of energy price elasticities do not exist as yet. There is even scantier evidence on the relationship between energy and other factors of production. Earlier estimates of energy price elasticities fall short of reality when one examines the downturn in energy demanded during 1981–82. The energy-capital complementarity question has not been answered despite some rigorous work in the field.[12]

Even so, it has been recognized that world demand for energy is highly correlated to economic growth, the level of energy conservation, and OPEC's pricing strategy. A great effort has been made to reduce petroleum consumption through conservation, but there is still substantial potential for further reduction in transportation, residential, and industrial consumption. Price strategies on the part of OPEC and tax strategies by governments of oil-importing countries have also dampened the demand for petroleum products. The impact of other

Table 4.2
Commercial Primary Energy Consumption, by Country Group, 1970, 1980, and 1990 (millions of barrels a day)

Country Group	1970			1980			1990		
	Consumption	Share of World Total (%)	Share of Total Energy for Country Group (%)	Consumption	Share of World Total (%)	Share of Total Energy for Country Group (%)	Consumption	Share of World Total (%)	Share of Total Energy for Country Group (%)
Industrial countries	60.6	61.2	100.0	72.4	53.4	100.0	87.0	47.0	100.0
Petroleum	29.9	69.1	49.3	35.0	58.6	48.3	37.4	51.6	43.1
Natural gas	12.8	72.3	21.1	15.0	61.7	20.7	16.2	47.4	18.6
Solid fuels	13.3	42.2	21.9	14.0	36.2	19.3	19.1	34.6	22.0
Primary electricity	4.6	69.7	7.6	8.4	65.6	11.6	14.3	61.6	16.4
Centrally planned eco.	27.6	27.9	100.0	43.0	31.7	100.0	62.1	33.5	100.0
Petroleum	7.2	16.6	26.1	13.1	21.9	30.5	17.3	23.9	27.9
Natural gas	3.8	21.5	13.8	7.0	28.8	16.3	12.3	36.0	19.8
Solid fuels	15.7	49.8	56.9	20.9	54.4	48.6	29.4	53.3	47.3
Primary electricity	0.9	13.6	3.3	2.0	15.6	4.7	3.1	13.4	5.1
Capital-surplus oil-exporting co.	0.3	0.3	100.0	0.9	0.7	100.0	1.7	0.9	100.0
Petroleum	0.2	0.5	66.7	0.7	1.2	77.8	1.1	1.5	64.7
Natural gas	0.1	0.6	33.3	0.2	0.8	22.2	0.6	1.8	35.3
Solid fuels	-	-	-	-	-	-	-	-	-
Primary electricity	-	-	-	-	-	-	-	-	-

Oil-exporting developing count.	2.8	2.8	100.0	5.5	4.1	100.0	10.0	5.4	100.0
Petroleum	1.8	4.2	64.3	3.6	6.0	64.5	5.5	7.6	55.0
Natural gas	0.7	4.0	25.0	1.4	5.8	25.5	3.5	10.2	35.0
Solid fuels	0.1	0.3	3.6	0.1	0.3	1.8	0.3	0.5	3.0
Primary electricity	0.2	3.0	7.1	0.4	3.1	7.3	0.7	3.0	7.0
Oil-importing developing count.	7.8	7.9	100.0	13.7	10.1	100.0	24.3	13.1	100.0
Petroleum	4.2	9.7	53.8	7.3	12.2	53.3	11.2	15.4	46.1
Natural gas	0.3	1.7	3.8	0.7	2.9	5.1	1.6	4.7	6.6
Solid fuels	2.4	7.6	30.8	3.7	9.6	27.0	6.4	11.6	26.3
Primary electricity	0.9	13.6	11.5	2.0	15.6	14.6	5.1	22.0	21.1
Bunkers	2.9	-	-	3.1	-	-	4.6	-	-
Total	99.1	100.0	-	135.5	100.0	-	185.1	100.0	-
Petroleum	43.3	-	43.7	59.7	-	44.1	72.5	-	39.2
Natural gas	17.7	-	17.9	24.3	-	17.9	34.2	-	18.5
Solid fuels	31.5	-	31.8	38.7	-	28.6	55.2	-	29.8
Primary electricity	6.6	-	6.7	12.8	-	9.4	23.2	-	12.5

Source: World Development Report 1981, The World Bank.

factors on demand have also been substantial as shown by development in 1980 and 1981. The combination of higher prices, slower economic growth, energy conservation, and fuel switching (primarily coal and gas) not only reduced the demand for oil but caused it to fall far more than was expected. With demand softening for oil in general, surplus capacity has built up and the world has been awash in an oil glut unparalleled in the 14 years since the oil crisis in 1973. It has been estimated that the glut will last at least through 1990.

Even so, and even with the North Sea oil field, Europe will still be dependent on oil imports for the majority of its oil requirements. Until recently, for example, more than 90 percent of Europe's oil requirements were satisfied by oil imported from OPEC countries. Japan is most dependent of all, and almost all its current demand for petroleum must be satisfied with imported oil.[13]

The main problems the oil-importing countries face now are how to maintain their economic growth, how to maintain and increase the security of foreign sources of supply, and how to develop more indigenous energy resources. Even with the current worldwide oil glut, increased conservation and improved efficiency in fuel use prove necessarily the right steps to take to alleviate some of the problems.

FUTURE ENERGY DEMAND

Projecting the future energy requirements is a highly speculative exercise, in particular for the period after 1990. Most studies dealing with the future of global energy are based principally on trends, relationships, and—to some extent—plans that emerged in the years between the two oil crises. They do not draw much on events since 1981, but rather assume stable energy prices and specified economic growth rates in their projections of possible future energy development.

A study of global energy prospects through 1990 by the World Bank (1981)[14] indicates that the change in shares expected for the various groups of countries and for the various fuels in each country group is of greater significance than the aggregate growth in energy demand. With an exception of the centrally planned economies, oil will remain the dominant source of energy. As shown in Table 4.2, in 1980 about 58.6 percent of the world's consumption of petroleum took place in the industrial nations, but by 1990 this share will drop to about 51.6 percent. To such extent, demand for oil in the future is expected to be heavily affected by developments in the industrialized countries. A decline in the share of oil in all regions is accompanied by an increase in the share of solid fuels, except in the case of the capital surplus oil-exporting nations.[15]

As for developing countries, their share will grow to almost 20 percent by 1990, even though they consumed only 14 percent of the world's total in 1980. This observation is based on (1) higher growth rates of gross national product than in the industrial nations, (2) growth rates of energy consumption higher than growth rates of gross national products, and (3) higher rates of urbanization, industrialization, and growth of transportation than in the past. In effect, in view of historical rates, the growth rate of energy demand is more likely to be higher in regions where energy prices were not completely adjusted to world market levels than in regions where energy prices were completely adjusted to world market levels.[16]

The study by the U.S. Department of Energy, on the other hand, predicts that oil consumption in the non-Communist world will remain almost constant at around 50 million barrels a day through the year 2000, although total primary energy consumption will continue to grow at 2 percent a year for the 1980–2000 period. At the same time, while OECD consumption is projected to decline to under 30 million barrels a day by the year 2000, OPEC consumption of oil is projected to grow rapidly as a result of high growth rates of economic output and subsidized energy prices.

The projections of possible future development in Northeast Asia are found in the study by Joseph A. Yager (1984) of the Brookings Institution. Assuming stable energy prices and specified economic growth rates, the study projects an increase of 50 percent in the primary energy requirements of the Northeast Asian countries from 1980 to 1990. According to the study, the energy requirements of individual Northeast Asian countries are expected to expand more rapidly than the requirements of comparable countries in other parts of the world. To such extent, then, the share of Northeast Asia in international energy markets is also likely to expand.[17]

In sum, possible world energy developments have several important implications. Future world energy requirements will depend, to some extent, on the rates of economic growth and the energy intensities of each individual economy. The shift to technology intensive activities that is already under way could continue and could help to sustain both respectable rates of growth and a gradual decline in energy intensities. Consequently, in adjusting to possible future large increases in energy prices (though much unlikely to occur soon given the current worldwide glut), governments of both developed and less-developed nations must choose between the partly competing goals of economic growth and price stability. Although governments cannot control all of the factors that determine the overall energy intensity of an economy, they do influence energy intensity by a conscious decision to give priority to goals other than energy conservation.

NOTES

1. Rajendra K. Pachauri, *The Political Economy of Global Energy* (Baltimore, MD: The Johns Hopkins University Press, 1985), p. 13.

2. Ibid., pp. 13–15.

3. The World Bank, *World Development Report 1981* (1981); p. 36.

4. Pachauri, op. cit.

5. The World Bank, op. cit., p. 15.

6. Michael Kennedy, "A World Oil Model," in Dale W. Jorgenson, ed., *Econometric Studies of U.S. Energy Policy* (Amsterdam: North-Holland Publishing Company, 1976), pp. 139–45.

7. Paul W. MacAvoy, *Crude Oil Prices: As Determined by OPEC and Market Fundamentals* (Cambridge, MA: Harper & Row, Balinger, 1982).

8. See, for instance, E. R. Berndt and D. O. Wood, "Technology, Prices, and the Derived Demand for Energy," *Review of Economics and Statistics* 58 (1976); and J. M. Griffin, "Interfuel Substitution Possibilities: A Translog Application to Intercountry Data," *International Economic Review* (October 1977), pp. 149–64.

9. Robert S. Pindyck, *Structure of World Energy Demand* (Cambridge, MA: MIT Press, 1979).

10. The World Bank, op. cit., p. 37.

11. William D. Nordhaus, *The Efficient Use of Energy Resources* (New Haven, CT: Yale University Press, 1979); ibid., "Oil and Economic Performance in Industrial Countries," *Brookings Papers on Economic Activity* 2:1980, pp. 341–50.

12. See for example, E. R. Berndt and D. O. Wood, op. cit., pp. 256–68.

13. Ali Ezzati, *World Energy Markets and OPEC Stability* (Lexington, KY: Lexington Books, 1978).

14. The World Bank, op. cit.

15. Pachauri, op. cit., p. 37.

16. Ibid., p. 37.

17. Joseph A. Yager, *The Energy Balance in Northeast Asia* (Washington, DC: The Brookings Institution, 1984), p. 4.

5

Supply of Energy

Energy resources are scarce and limited in supply. Those resources that are most economical are those that have the most severe ultimate limitations on availability. Over the long run, however, it is the amount of recoverable resources left in the ground, including those volumes as yet undiscovered, that will have the definitive effect. It is this, along with the cost of finding recoverable reserves, that will be a determining factor in the availability and supply of energy resources and the relative production shares of various energy forms.[1]

PROBLEMS, OBSTACLES, AND LIMITATIONS

The primary forms of energy resources include coal, oil shale, petroleum, and uranium (nuclear). There exists a high degree of interresource substitution among these sources of energy, effectuated by available and prospective technology in the areas of desulfurization, coal gasification and liquefaction, synthetic fuel from shale, nuclear reactors, offshore exploration, secondary recovery, among others. To some extent, the supply of alternative primary energy forms is a function of costs and availabilities of energy resources and the level of technology used in exploration, production, transportation, refining, and other energy conversion processes. The supply of and demand for each of these energy forms, along with related technologies, jointly and simultaneously determine equilibrium prices and quantities of energy resources.

Petroleum Resources

The superior qualities and the ease with which it can be transported have made petroleum the most important energy source and the preferred fuel in the world since 1920. The result is the heavy dependence of developed economies upon the availability of petroleum resources, to the extent that the world economy is rapidly approaching the same dependence that industrialized nations now experience.

Classification Problems

Petroleum resources are defined as all the oil and gas believed to be eventually recoverable by means of known or expected technologies. Some of these resources have already been found and are referred to as discovered resources. Those expected to be found in the future are undiscovered potential resources. The sum of the two constitutes the total resource base.

A more limited but also elusive concept is that of economically (or commercially) producible reserves—the segment of discovered resources that is thought to be recoverable at current or forecast prices with the existing technology. Economically producible reserves consist of proven and unproven (or probable) reserves. Proven reserves are those the existence and quantity of which are well known and verifiable with a high degree of confidence and which are commercially producible. They are those reserves that can flow now from existing wells in already developed reservoirs. As more wells are drilled into a reservoir, the estimate of proven reserves may be revised up or down. The ultimate potential of a field may be up to twice that of initial estimates.

In contrast, the existence of unproven reserves is less known, but they are expected to be economically feasible in the future. There are indicated and inferred unproven reserves. Indicated reserves are those that are determined by limited drilling with some certainty as to the extent of additional oil and gas in geologically related reservoirs of the same oil field. On the other hand, inferred reserves are those the existence of which is inferred on the basis of information from exploratory drilling and geological extrapolation and producible at current prices and costs.

In addition to economically producible energy resources, exploratory drilling may confirm the presence of other deposits. If these are not exploitable at current prices or with existing technology, they are designated subeconomic reserves. In a sense, they are the noncommercial portion of the discovered resources and are sometimes called the static reserves. A subeconomic reserve may become economically feasible and commercially producible and will move into the category of proven or unproven reserves, if costs are justifiable by price rises, or if a remote area is developed because of new discoveries of other oil fields nearby and construction of a pipeline, or if the volume of a reserve is found to be higher than originally estimated. The rest are the unrecoverable reserves left behind in reservoirs.

As yet undiscovered resources may exist where exploratory drilling has not yet taken place but where geological and other data provide suggestive evidence. Estimates of undiscovered resources are inevitably highly uncertain.

There are still many other ways in which petroleum resources can be conceptually categorized, but they are themselves poor guides to the availability of energy for consumption. Despite many efforts to develop uniform sets of terms and classifications, there is no universally accepted classification system for petroleum resource concepts. Confusion and misuse of terms continue to appear in the energy literature. No matter what classification system is used, however, the geologic and economic distributions are not precise. What is geologically known and/or economically and commercially feasible is not fixed but subjected to changes with time and circumstances. The challenge is finding reserves that are recoverable at a reasonable cost, not finding substantial volumes of petroleum reserves.

Resource Estimation

It has been widely assumed that oil and gas will together supply more than half the world's energy for the rest of this century, with a substantial portion for many years thereafter, but no one knows for sure the amounts of energy resource that remain in the earth. Major uncertainties inhere both in resource estimation techniques and in the economic factors governing reserves.

Depending on the amount and quality of information available, there are three general approaches used in estimating the amount of oil and gas recoverable from an existing field. These include geological extrapolations based on a field's past production, theoretical calculations based on an existing field's geological and geophysical characteristics, and comparisons with other similar fields for which more data are available. Often, economic considerations determine how much of the discovered resources should be classified as economically (or commercially) producible reserves. Usually, the published estimates of remaining reserves for already discovered fields are in reasonably close agreement. Differences are due mainly to variations in the estimates of how much is likely to be obtained from application of improved recovery methods and/or technologies.

On the other hand, the bases for estimating undiscovered potential—and for identifying locations for exploration—are geologic studies of the world's sedimentary basins. Although drilling exploratory wells could provide valuable knowledge and information, they are extremely costly, and if undertaken indiscriminately, would make the discovery of hydrocarbons prohibitively expensive. Even with more sophisticated analytical techniques, such as computer technologies, the assessment of undiscovered potential requires a great deal of informed judgment. When little information is available, the experts must rely principally on their interpretations of comparisons with better known basins that appear to have similar geologic characteristics. As exploration proceeds and the availability of geologic information increases, the quality of reserve calculations improves.

Because of the uncertainties in the assessment process, experts typically assign probabilities to each of the various geologic factors that affect the existence and recovery of hydrocarbons. Such probabilities reflect the chance that the data used might be imperfect and the necessary geologic elements might be nonexistent. As a consequence, an overall estimate of future undiscovered potential obtained by such various assessments is most likely to be inaccurate at best.

Government Intervention

The availability of petroleum as a world energy resource and its annual production depend upon several factors, some of which relate to geology of the earth and levels of technologies for oil exploration and development, but many of which are dependent upon economics, governmental policies and regulations, equipment, and operating supplies.

The historical decline in exploration and development of oil and gas in the United States, for example, are largely attributable to government policies and regulations, rather than by market forces of supply and demand. Government intervention has been systematic and comprehensive, ranging from policies designed to stimulate production to policies that attempt to control output in order to support prices of crude oil and natural gas. These policies resulted in long-term decline in the real price of domestic crude oil, low incentives for investment in exploration and development, high tax burdens on oil and gas producers, uncertainties about oil import programs, and increasing costs and difficulties experienced by the industry in finding new oil and gas reservoirs.

The problem is further compounded by environmental concerns that have further delayed discoveries of crude oil reserves and impeded the expansion of producing capacity. Alaskan North Slope production and offshore leasing, for example, have been delayed for this reason. As a result, resource allocation decisions are mainly the result of government decision making and the role of free market competition has been substantially reduced.[2]

The Common-Pool Problem

The common-pool problem rises from ill-defined exclusive property rights that are created at the instant of drawing oil from a common pool. The incentives are for co-owners of the oil pool to extract as much of the oil as each can. This, however, reduces the ultimate amount of oil recoverable by drilling, relative to the slower rate of drilling. Although geologists can estimate the so-called "maximum efficient rate (MER)" of production, it may be difficult for the individual owners to agree on how much each can take, since each would like a larger share and might drill more wells to obtain it.

Thus, this "rule of capture" effectively distorts the optimal path of resource extraction by discriminating heavily against the future in favor of present production. It also gives rise to physical waste, since too fast a rate of extraction frequently reduces the total amount of oil recoverable from the pool.[3]

The Long Production Cycle

Usually, it will take three to five years, from the time the research for promising areas begins, to complete the refinery process and deliver the product to the market. Development and delivery can be accelerated slightly, but higher product prices will have only a minimal effect on output in the short run.

In the long run, however, the response to supply will be greater than in the short run. Higher prices will induce producers to increase their search and development activities and stimulate efforts to achieve more complete extraction from a petroleum pool. Currently, oil is produced from a reservoir primarily by utilizing the natural pressure which causes the oil in the reservoir to flow toward the well. However, such pressure decreases with production, and only about 25 percent of the oil in the place is typically recovered by these primary methods. Extracting the rest can be done by artificial methods, but such methods are simply too costly. Higher prices can make it more attractive to develop new and more elaborate means of recovery such as pumping water or natural gas into the reservoir, heating the oil by injecting steam or diluting the oil by injecting solvents. Again, it takes time for producers to adjust to price changes, to install the necessary equipment, and to extract the extra oil and transport it to the refinery.

While higher real prices and improved cost-reducing technologies will provide incentives to accelerate development and delivery, they will also create supply-demand adjustment problems, leading to disequilibrium market conditions. Not only would sufficient price increases depress growth in demand below the level anticipated, but increases would also stimulate efforts to develop low-cost substitutes for crude oil and natural gas. In particular, higher prices would induce additional importation or encourage the development of other domestic resources of energy such as solar energy and nuclear power by oil-importing countries. These unintended by-products of higher prices certainly would negate the efforts to provide increased supplies of oil and gas at reasonable prices. To say the least, technological advances and development would offer the best alternative in reducing exploration and development costs, improving oil and gas recoveries, and increasing supplies at a reasonable cost.[4]

Inventories and Energy Supplies

The Arab oil embargo in 1973–74, the interruption in Iranian exports in 1978–79, and the outbreak of war between Iraq and Iran were all periods in which the level of inventories was cited to explain why supply shortages were either more or less serious than might have been expected under the circumstances. Still more recently, inventories, well above historic levels, have been widely cited as a factor contributing to a glut of oil supplies in the mid-1980s.

Indeed, inventories are one of the factors that influence the energy supplies. Inventories provide the industry with the means to offset reasonably foreseeable fluctuations in the supply and demand of oil by making allowance for day-to-day fluctuations and normal seasonal variations in product demand. But in times of more than normal uncertainty, protection against the unforeseeable looms large. Sudden disruptions of established supplies can create serious logistical problems in the industry and thus lead to supply-demand disequilibrium situations in the market. To the extent possible, inventory management attempts to anticipate such developments and mitigate their impact. But, at best, it does so imperfectly.[5]

But, the size of inventories is as much a consequence of unforecast developments in the market as the result of deliberate planning. It affects supply, demand, or both. It would be uneconomical for petroleum producers to incur the cost of holding substantial larger amounts of inventories.

Explicably, in the oil and gas industry, proven reserves are essentially the same as inventories in other areas of business. They allow producers to adapt to uncertain future market conditions, but it is costly to identify, purchase, and hold petroleum resources, just as it is costly to hold inventories in other businesses. Thus, at any given time, energy producers will choose to verify and hold a limited amount of the earth's energy-producing reserves.

The OPEC Cartel

Pricing and production levels of crude oil established by OPEC members have for a number of years been the dominant factors which influence the supply of energy. With about half of the world's production controlled by these countries, their political and economic policies have an obvious effect.

The formation of OPEC and its emergence as the dominant force in the global oil market were the consequence of pricing decisions in earlier periods. After the emergence of OPEC as an effective organization, and even more recently, prices have been closely linked with output decisions by OPEC and, more significantly, have been responsible for the expansion of oil production outside OPEC.

Not surprisingly, the prices and the production levels of crude oil and petroleum products in the oil-importing countries are highly correlated with the prices of imported crude oil from OPEC member countries. Future prices of imported crude oil, natural gas, and liquefied natural gas from OPEC member countries will probably depend upon OPEC's oil revenue requirements, the degree of participation, production policies, and price escalation clauses built into concession agreements.[6]

Shale Oil Resources

The global shale oil resource base is huge. It, along with coal, represents potential unlimited supplies of feedstock for refined liquids, by some estimates, up to the year 2050. It is, however, very capital intensive.

Oil shales are shale deposits that contain the solid hydrocarbon wax organic materials (kerogen) which, when heated (retorted), can be converted to oil and gas. The United States is currently estimated to have over 1000 billion barrels of shale oil, and the world resource is estimated at over 5000 billion barrels. The primary obstacle to use of this oil shale is in finding an economically, commercially, and environmentally acceptable process for extracting the oil from the shale.

Despite the extensive efforts in research and development by the oil industry during the past four decades, it remains marginally economical to produce shale oil on a commercial basis. There are severe environmental problems associated with oil shale exploitation. The existing technology of surface processes requires large amounts of water to capture the dust created by crushing the shale which may give rise to air pollution. It has been estimated that about three barrels of water are normally required in order to yield one barrel of oil. There are also large quantities of spent shale that must be disposed of. As a consequence, there is considerable doubt whether shale operations could meet environmental standards of air quality in the foreseeable future.

In effect, the potential environmental impacts of oil shale development have often been used as an argument suggesting that shale oil development will be limited in the United States. Water availability has also been cited as a potentially major constraint on shale development in the western United States.

Problems of waste disposal and water usage, however, can be considerably reduced by using *in situ* retorting, which shatters the deposit by explosives and then retorts the shale underground. In effect, *in situ* technologies for extracting oil from shale provide the most promising prospect for cost reduction. Not only will it eliminate the necessity for disposing of large quantities of spent shale, it may also require substantially less water per barrel of oil produced, if it proves feasible on a larger scale. However, this process is not fully developed; it is still only in the research stage and has not been proved economically feasible.[7]

The cost and abundance of shale oil suggest that it may form a liquid fuel backstop which will relegate other unconventional liquids to a relatively small role. But, whether oil shale will be a significant source of oil over the next decade remains relatively doubtful.

Coal Resources

Coal presents not only the greatest number but also the most complex problems among the primary energy resources. Over two-thirds of the recoverable coal reserves are concentrated in only four nations—the United States, the U.S.S.R., China, and Australia. A number of factors have been responsible for the decline in coal production in these countries during the past decades. Environmental concerns have constrained growth in most industrial nations. In the United States, for example, about one-half of the estimated 3210 billion tons of coal resources may be recoverable, but many of these resources have such a high sulfur content that they cannot be sold under existing emission regulations. Further, there exist large reserves of high-quality coal suitable for strip mining, but this technique has been a prime target of objection on the part of ecologists and legislators.[8]

In China, however, lack of adequate transportation has prevented the distribution of the coal produced in the northern provinces from reaching other parts of the country, while in Australia initial growth in coal production was constrained by the small size of the country's population and the consequently small domestic demand.

Historically, the tonnage of coals used for electric power generation, has increased over time, but its share has decreased. Continued improvements in technologies of mining, transportation, and utilization have kept coal prices competitive with other fossil fuels. These technological advances have partially offset increased production costs, including higher cost of health, safety, and environmental regulations.

Despite certain advantages of coal over other synthetic fuel sources, there are three major obstacles in converting coal to synthetic hydrocarbons: the need for the massive inputs of hydrogen and water, the large investment risks involved in the construction of necessarily large plant units, and the need for tremendous amounts of coal at a single plant. There are also other constraints such as a severe shortage of miners, strict coal mine health and safety laws, stringent environmental regulations and requirements, severe restrictions on strip mining, and increased costs of coal mining. These constraints are apparent not only in the United States but also, to some degree, in other countries. These are further compounded by the fact that the responsiveness of coal supply to changes in price is quite sensitive to the time span within which the incremental tonnage is to be produced.

The lead time needed to develop large underground mines is about four to five years. Surface mines, the predominant mining practice in the western United States, can be developed more quickly, but the process is still time consuming. For this reason, coal supply is not particularly elastic in the short run. That is, within the short-term time frame, coal supply seems to be quite insensitive to changes in price.

In the long run, however, coal supply seems quite sensitive to changes in price, since the entry of new firms is not impeded by institutional constraints, economies of scale, or high capital costs. Long-term equilibrium coal prices are expected to approximate the costs of production, defined to include an economy-wide average rate of profit.

Nonetheless, there are a number of factors that could affect the long-term supply of coal. These include (a) adequate supply of miners, (b) availability of an adequate transportation system, (c) the production costs, (d) the level of technology, (e) government policies, (f) adequate coal reserves, especially low-sulfur coal, and (g) the ability of industry to generate the capital required for growth. Not only could these factors limit the capacity of the industry to grow, they could also affect the cost of producing coal at various growth rates or with time.[9]

For the next decade at least, the speed with which coal replaces oil will largely determine whether energy supplies grow sufficiently to sustain economic growth. Other sources such as shale oil, hydroelectricity, and nuclear power are also expected to play a substantial role in the increase in primary energy in the next decade, but their lead times are so long that they are less responsive to current market conditions. While oil readily replaced coal in the 1950s and 1960s, it is now much harder to reverse this process.

Nuclear Power

Nuclear power has the potential to replace petroleum resources as the world's primary energy source, but growing environmental concerns in several industrial countries (such as the United States, Germany, and Great Britain, in particular) have inhibited the growth of nuclear power. The major risks concern not only the chance of a reactor accident (possible meltdown, for example) and potential for thermal and radioactive pollution, but also the hazards associated with the disposing of nuclear waste and the transportation, storage, and possible illegal diversion of high-level nuclear fuels and wastes. Although the production costs of nuclear power appear to make it competitive at current prices of fossil fuels, such possible hazards may make these cost comparisons fuzzy or even irrelevant.

Nuclear power has some of the disadvantages of coal without sharing in coal's major advantage of plentiful reserves available at tolerable mining costs. Power from nuclear fission is dependent upon the use of relatively high-cost enriched uranium that has to be extracted from uranium ores, which prove to be in relatively short supply.[10]

To the extent possible, nuclear power is an option open only to very large countries. Its capital cost is high, and smaller countries do not have grids with the minimum capacity to handle the minimum reactor output efficiently. If countries also lack the skilled labor and management needed for a nuclear program, the peculiar hazards of nuclear energy production may make it an unwise choice. The justification for nuclear power for the electric utility industry is economics, although there are other factors such as the limited supply of fossil fuels and environmental risks and impacts.

The promise nuclear power held out in earlier decades has not been realized, and current development is moderate. Major increases in nuclear power have been planned only in the U.S.S.R., France, and Japan. The French and the Japanese policies favoring rapid nuclear growth are based on their country's vulnerability as major importers of oil from the Middle East. This vulnerability will largely be offset by aggressive nuclear power development, which will enable France, as well as Japan, to generate over half of their power supply from nuclear sources. Although there have been indications that the world's nuclear capacity may at best double by the year 2000 from its 1980 level, this growth is likely to be concentrated in the very few countries that have the industrial capacity for design, manufacture, and installation of nuclear plants.[11]

With nuclear fission reactors slowly growing in number, and being scrutinized regarding their environmental safety, attention is turning to the potential for nuclear fusion. Whereas nuclear fission gets its energy from large nuclei as they break up, thermonuclear fusion reactions yield energy when two light nuclei fuse together to form a heavier one which produces quantum fusion powers. The challenge is to establish a workable fusion reactor in practice.[12]

The fusion reactor, if achieved, will have many advantages. It will provide the ready and inexpensive availability of fuel with fewer environmental hazards than do the fission reactors. Neither will there be long-lived heavy-element isotopes and production (or handling) of the biologically dangerous and radioactive plutonium, nor will there be the need for transporting radioactive fuel elements as all processing would be done on site.

Fusion may be the safest source of energy for the future with a minimal environmental impact, but it will probably be another decade or two before a commercially useful fusion reactor is available. The advantages of fusion power are chiefly environmental and social ones, but present developments are not sufficient to enable us to determine whether fusion power is a dream or will become a reality.[13]

Indeed, the future of nuclear power is extremely uncertain. The certainty is that costs have escalated tremendously in the past decade and are likely to continue escalating. How nuclear power fares in the future depends not only on environmental considerations, but also on the relative cost of electric-generating technologies and the demand for electricity in general.

AVAILABILITY OF WORLD ENERGY RESOURCES

No one knows for sure the amounts of energy resources that remain in the earth. Estimates of the availability of the world energy resources vary widely, and experts disagree about the size of reservoirs and about the total world energy resources. Major uncertainties inhere both in resource estimation techniques and in the economic factors governing reserves.

Petroleum Resources

Variations in estimates of prospective supplies have been the greatest for oil and natural gas.[14] Uncertainties about future exploration efforts, the probability of new discoveries, and the geology of reservoirs from which oil is produced make valid predictions difficult. As shown in Table 5.1, the most recent estimates by Exxon Corporation from a variety of industry sources place the world's total resource base between 3000 and 5000 billion barrels oil equivalent,[15] of which nearly a third (1000–1200 billion barrels) is now considered proven reserves—that is, oil and gas producible in today's circumstances.

Proven oil reserves, the most important part of the resource base at least for the short term, are distributed quite unevenly among nations as illustrated in Table 5.2. In 1982, of the top ten countries, five (including Saudi Arabia and Kuwait) are in the Middle East. Saudi Arabia accounts for 25 percent of the total; the top five, 62 percent; and the top 15, 92 percent.

By country groups, the 13 members of the Organization of Petroleum Ex-

Table 5.1
World Oil and Gas Resource Base, 1981

	Billions of Barrels Oil Equivalent
Remaining Proven Reserve	1000-1200
Unproven Reserves	300-600
Total Remaining Commercial Reserves	1300-1800
Cumulative Production to Date	700
Total Resources Discovered to Date	2000-2500
Undiscovered Potential	1000-2500
Total Oil and Gas Resource Base	3000-5000

Source: Exxon Corporation, *How Much Oil and Gas?* (May 1982), p. 10.

porting Countries (OPEC), led by Saudi Arabia, have about 65 percent of the world's total proven oil reserves. The Centrally Planned Economies (CPE)[16] of the U.S.S.R., People's Republic of China, Eastern Europe, and Southeast Asia have 14 percent. Only 10 percent are estimated to be in the 24 principal industrial nations which form the Organization for Economic Cooperation and Development (OECD) and which are the world's major energy consumers. The remaining 12 percent are in the rest of the world. This means that all the non-OPEC developing countries, with the principal exception of Mexico, must import a greater portion of their energy supplies.

Like proven oil reserves, proven gas reserves also distributed quite unevenly at least in the short run as illustrated in Table 5.3, but the list of principal countries shows different rankings and includes four which were not among the top 15 in oil. The U.S.S.R., accounting for 40 percent of the world's total, has the largest estimated proven natural gas reserves. This is followed by Iran, the United States, Algeria, and Saudi Arabia. These first five account for 72 percent; and the top 15, 89 percent.

Aggregate gas reserves by country groups are also shown in Table 5.3. About 35 percent of the world's proven gas reserves belong to the 13 OPEC nations. About 41 percent are in the Centrally Planned Economies, mainly the U.S.S.R. Only about 16 percent are estimated to be in the principal industrial nations of the OECD group, reflecting the significant reserves of the United States and the Netherlands. The remaining 8 percent of proven gas reserves are in the rest of the world, again led by Mexico.

In addition to discovered resources, undiscovered potential resources have been estimated at the range of 1000 to 2500 billion barrels oil equivalent. Some

Table 5.2
Estimated Proven Crude Oil Reserves (billions of barrels)

Country	1/1/82	Percent	Rank	1/1/77	Percent	Rank	1/1/72	Percent	Rank
Leading Countries									
Saudi Arabia*	167.9	25.0	1	113.2	18.9	1	157.5	24.9	1
Kuwait*	67.7	10.1	2	70.6	11.8	3	78.2	12.4	2
U.S.S.R.	63.0	9.4	3	78.1	13.0	2	75.0	11.9	3
Iran	57.0	8.5	4	63.0	10.5	4	55.5	8.8	4
Mexico	57.0	8.5	5	7.0	1.2	14	4.5	0.7	19
Abu Dhabi	30.6	4.6	6	29.0	4.8	7	18.9	3.0	8
United States	29.8	4.4	7	31.3	5.2	6	37.3	5.9	5
Iraq	29.7	4.4	8	34.0	5.7	5	36.0	5.7	6
Libya	22.6	3.4	9	25.5	4.3	8	25.0	4.0	6
Venezuela	20.3	3.0	10	15.3	2.6	12	13.9	2.2	9
P.R.C.	19.9	3.0	11	20.0	3.3	9	20.0	3.2	7
Nigeria	16.5	2.5	12	19.5	3.2	10	11.7	1.9	11
United Kingdom	14.8	2.2	13	16.8	2.8	11	5.0	0.8	18
Indonesia	9.8	1.5	14	10.5	1.8	13	10.4	1.6	12
Algeria	8.1	1.2	15	6.8	1.1	15	12.3	1.9	10
Country Groups									
OPEC	439.0	65.5		404.2	67.5		438.7	69.4	
CPE	85.9	12.8		101.1	16.9		98.5	15.6	
OECD	63.9	9.5		64.0	10.7		63.7	10.1	
All Others	81.9	12.2		29.7	4.9		31.0	4.9	
World Total	670.7	100.0		599.0	100.0		631.9	100.0	

*Including 50 percent of Neutral Zone.

Source: Calculated by the author from tables presented in the *Oil and Gas Journal*, December 1971–July 1982, various issues.

Table 5.3
Estimated Proven Natural Gas Reserves (trillions of cubic feet)

Country	1/1/82	Percent	Rank	1/1/77	Percent	Rank	1/1/72	Percent	Rank
Leading Countries									
U.S.S.R.	1160	39.8	1	918	39.8	1	546	31.7	1
Iran	484	16.6	2	330	14.3	2	200	11.6	3
United States	198	6.8	3	220	9.5	3	270	15.7	2
Algeria	131	4.5	4	126	5.5	4	107	6.2	4
Saudi Arabia*	118	4.1	5	66	2.9	5	56	3.2	7
Canada	90	3.1	6	56	2.4	7	54	3.1	6
Mexico	75	2.6	7	12	0.5	22	12	0.7	17
Qatar	60	2.1	8	28	1.2	13	8	0.5	20
Netherlands	56	1.9	9	62	2.7	6	83	4.8	5
Norway	49	1.7	10	19	0.8	19	10	0.6	18
Venezuela	47	1.6	11	41	1.8	9	25	1.4	12
Nigeria	41	1.4	12	44	1.9	8	40	2.3	8
Kuwait*	35	1.2	13	34	1.5	10	35	2.0	10
Indonesia	27	0.9	14	24	1.0	17	5	0.3	33
Iraq	27	0.9	15	27	1.2	14	22	1.3	14
Country Groups									
OPEC	1022	35.1		783	34.0		554	32.1	
CPE	1195	41.1		953	41.3		558	32.3	
OECD	466	16.0		460	20.0		518	30.0	
All Others	228	7.8		108	4.7		95	5.6	
World Total	2911	100.0		2304	100.0		1725	100.0	

*Including 50 percent of Neutral Zone.

Source: Calculated by the author from tables presented in the *Oil and Gas Journal* (December 1971–July 1982), various issues.

studies have shown that the world's annual oil and gas consumption is expected to average 30–40 billion barrels oil equivalent per year over the next couple of decades. If so, then there are sufficient reserves at present. However, by the year 2000, there won't be enough reserves to permit production at levels now foreseen, unless substantial quantities of new petroleum are discovered in the interim.

Coal Resources

World reserves of coal far exceed those of petroleum. At present prices, some 640 billion tons of proven reserves are economically recoverable, enough to maintain current production levels for over a hundred years. About 90 percent of the production and use of coal is in the industrial economies, market or nonmarket. According to World Bank estimates, an additional production of 25 million tons of coal (equivalent to 125 million barrels of oil) would be possible from these sources by the end of the 1980s. The limits to coal expansion lie in the need for large investments in transport, coal-using equipment, and pollution control.

The total coal resources amount to more than 11 trillion tons of coal equivalent (tce), the distribution of which is quite uneven. Among these, as shown in Table 5.4, the United States, the Soviet Union, and the People's Republic of China account for about 80 percent of the world's total coal resources and over 65 percent of the recoverable proven reserves. And by country groups, OECD countries as a whole possess about 39.7 percent of the total coal resources and 45.8 percent of the recoverable proven reserves, compared to 56.7 percent and 46.7 percent for the Centrally Planned Economies (CPE), respectively. Only 3.5 percent of the total resources and 7.5 percent of the recoverable reserves are found in all other countries in Africa, Latin America, and Asia, and over half of these resources and three-fourths of these reserves are accounted for by South Africa and India. The absence of significant quantities of coal resources throughout most of the less-developed countries is as striking as the large quantities known to exist in the OECD and CPE countries.

Some of these disparities are due to differential exploration effort; however, a large amount may derive from an uneven distribution of the resource. A rough way of judging the adequacy of coal reserves is to suppose continued growth in annual production and determine the number of years known amounts would last.

The projections of the World Bank study for future coal production are shown in Table 5.5, indicating that the share of production in the industrial countries and the oil-importing developing countries would go up slightly between 1980 and 1990, while the share of the centrally planned economies would show a slight decline. Most of the shift from oil to coal is therefore expected to take place in the industrial countries. Although there will be some substitution in developing countries, about half of their consumption will continue to rely on

Table 5.4
Global Coal Resources and Reserves (10^6 tons of coal equivalent)

Country	Proven Reserves In Place		Proven Recoverable Reserves		Additional Resources		Total Resources	
	tce	Percent	tce	Percent	tce	Percent	tce	Percent
Leading Countries								
United States	344,195.4	31.8	190,890.0	27.5	2,529,090.0	25.0	2,873,285.4	25.7
U.S.S.R.	211,390.8	19.5	169,063.7	24.4	4,469,845.0	44.2	4,681,235.8	41.9
P.R.C.	99,000.0	9.2	99,000.0	14.3	1,339,838.0	13.3	1,438,838.0	12.9
Poland	65,598.9	6.1	30,600.0	4.4	92,558.8	0.9	158,157.7	1.4
West Germany	63,574.6	5.9	34,977.0	5.0	186,300.0	1.8	249,874.6	2.2
Australia	59,496.2	5.5	36,302.0	5.2	611,600.0	6.1	671,096.0	6.0
South Africa	58,749.0	5.4	25,290.0	3.6	33,762.0	0.3	92,511.0	0.8
United Kingdom	45,000.0[1]	4.2	45,000.0	6.5	146,892.0	1.5	191,892.0	1.7
India	21,392.0	2.0	13,134.0	2.0	91,231.7	0.9	112,623.7	1.0
Canada	12,579.0	1.2	4,586.8	0.7	403,925.0	4.0	416,504.0	3.7
Country Groups								
Middle East/OPEC	385.4	0.0	193.0	0.0	215.0	0.0	600.4	0.0
CPE	425,564.8	39.4	323,841.7	46.7	5,920,358.1	58.6	6,345,922.9	56.7
OECD	551,950.4	51.0	317,524.2	45.8	3,890,851.0	38.5	4,442,801.4	39.7
All Others	103,455.7	9.6	51,711.1	7.5	290,933.3	2.9	394,389.0	3.5
World Total	1,081,356.3	100.0	693,270.0	100.0	10,102,357.4	100.0	11,183,713.7	100.0

[1] According to the WEC, the proven in-place reserves of the United Kingdom and China in their survey are unknown and should really have been set higher than the estimates of proven recoverable reserves.

Source: Calculated by the author from tables presented in the World Energy Conference (WEC), *Survey of Energy Resources 1980*, Part B, tables 1–4.

Table 5.5
Commercial Primary Energy Production, by Country Group, 1970, 1980, and 1990 (millions of barrels a day)

Country Group	1970			1980			1990		
	Production	Share of World Total (%)	Share of Total Energy for Country Group (%)	Production	Share of World Total (%)	Share of Total Energy for Country Group (%)	Production	Share of World Total (%)	Share of Total Energy for Country Group (%)
Industrial countries	43.2	41.9	100.0	50.6	36.6	100.0	64.3	33.9	100.0
Petroleum	12.7	26.8	29.4	14.5	23.3	28.6	16.4	21.6	25.5
Natural gas	13.0	72.6	30.1	13.8	56.8	27.3	13.2	38.1	20.5
Solid fuels	13.0	41.3	30.1	13.9	35.4	27.5	20.4	36.4	31.8
Primary electricity	4.5	69.3	10.4	8.4	65.6	16.6	14.3	61.6	22.2
Centrally planned eco.	28.8	27.9	100.0	45.2	32.6	100.0	63.4	33.4	100.0
Petroleum	8.0	17.0	27.8	13.7	22.0	30.3	17.9	23.6	28.2
Natural gas	3.8	21.2	13.2	7.7	31.7	17.0	12.6	36.4	19.9
Solid fuels	16.1	51.1	55.9	21.8	55.5	48.3	29.8	53.1	47.0
Primary electricity	0.9	13.8	3.1	2.0	15.6	4.4	3.1	13.4	4.9
Capital-surplus oil-exporting co.	12.8	12.4	100.0	18.6	13.4	100.0	21.7	11.4	100.0
Petroleum	12.7	26.8	99.2	18.3	29.5	98.4	20.4	26.9	94.0
Natural gas	0.1	0.6	0.8	0.3	1.2	1.6	1.3	3.8	6.0
Solid fuels	-	-	-	-	-	-	-	-	-
Primary electricity	-	-	-	-	-	-	-	-	-
Oil-exporting developing count.	13.7	13.3	100.0	16.7	12.0	100.0	25.2	13.3	100.0
Petroleum	12.7	26.8	92.7	14.2	22.8	85.0	18.3	24.1	72.6
Natural gas	0.7	3.9	5.1	2.0	8.2	12.0	5.9	17.1	23.4
Solid fuels	0.1	0.3	0.7	0.1	0.3	0.6	0.3	0.5	1.2
Primary electricity	0.2	3.1	1.5	0.4	3.1	2.4	0.7	3.0	2.8

Oil-importing developing count.	4.7	4.5	100.0	7.5	5.4	100.0	15.1	8.0	100.0
Petroleum	1.2	2.6	25.5	1.5	2.4	20.0	2.8	3.7	18.5
Natural gas	0.3	1.7	6.4	0.5	2.1	6.7	1.6	4.6	10.6
Solid fuels	2.3	7.3	48.9	3.5	8.9	46.6	5.6	10.0	37.1
Primary electricity	0.9	13.8	19.2	2.0	15.6	26.7	5.1	22.0	33.8
Bunkers	–	–	–	–	–	–	–	–	–
Total	103.2	100.0	–	138.6	100.0	–	189.7	100.0	–
Petroleum	47.3	–	45.8	62.2	–	44.9	75.8	–	40.0
Natural gas	17.9	–	17.4	24.3	–	17.5	34.6	–	18.2
Solid fuels	31.5	–	30.5	39.3	–	28.4	56.1	–	29.6
Primary electricity	6.5	–	6.3	12.8	–	9.2	23.2	–	12.2

Source: World Development Report 1981, The World Bank.

93

oil until the end of the 1980s. In the long run, however, the developing countries also have a considerable scope for raising coal production.

For most developing countries, coal is still a minor fuel used mainly in electricity generation and—in larger coal producers (such as India, Turkey, South Korea, and Yugoslavia)—in industrial applications. Coal can substitute for oil in electricity generation, but the potential for increased use is limited largely to new capacity, since converting existing plants is often uneconomical.[17]

Shale Oil Resources

The global shale oil resource base is huge. The best known and most widely quoted estimates of its size are Duncan and Swansen's 1965 estimates given in Table 5.6. Duncan and Swansen referred to the estimates as "orders of magnitude." The higher grade resource base estimates of $4,000,000 \times 10^{15}$ Btu are well over 10,000 times 1979 global energy production. There is little reason to dispute Duncan and Swansen's estimates in terms of the resource base.[18]

THE WORLD'S CRUDE OIL PRODUCTION:
FUTURE PROSPECTS

Although the OPEC cartel has been in existence since September 1960, its capacity to exercise monopoly power over the price of oil was limited in early years by the oil production capacity of the United States.[19] In those years, the United States was not only able to supply its own needs but was also able to act as a marginal supplier of oil to the rest of the world. As oil consumption grew rapidly worldwide under the stimulus of a relatively low price, the capacity of the United States to fulfill these roles dwindled rapidly. And as the reliance on oil was well integrated into the industrial structure of the world, with the demand far exceeding the capacity of the oil-consuming nations to supply it, the stage was set for OPEC countries to produce an increasing portion of the world's crude oil output.[20] In the 1960s, OPEC's crude oil output accounted for only 37.6 percent of the total world production.

By 1970 the 13 members of the Organization of Petroleum Exporting Countries (OPEC) produced half of the world's petroleum and held three-quarters of the world's reserves. The subsequent transfer of ownership of oil-producing facilities to the governments of these countries has had several long-term effects on petroleum supplies. Most fundamentally, supply decisions were now viewed as part of the overall development strategy of each country. The larger, more populous, and more diversified economies such as Algeria, Indonesia, Iran, Venezuela and Nigeria, tended to maximize their oil production. But the countries with substantial production and reserves in relation to their development needs—Saudi Arabia, Iraq, Kuwait, the United Arab Emirates, Libya, and Qatar—were able expand imports rapidly without spending all of their pe-

Table 5.6
Global Oil Shale Resource Base—Orders of Magnitude Estimates (10^{15} Btus)

| Region | Energy Content of Organic Shale | |
	10-65 Percent Organic Matter	5-10 Percent Organic Matter
North America	570,000	2,900,000
United States	310,000	1,600,000
Europe	310,000	1,600,000
Australia & Zealand	230,000	1,200,000
Asia	1,300,000	6,500,000
Africa	960,000	4,900,000
South America	470,000	2,300,000
TOTAL	4,000,000+	20,000,000+

Source: Adapted from O. C. Duncan and V. E. Swansen, "Organic Rich Shale of United States and World Land Areas," (U. S. Geological Survey Circular 523, 1965). Estimates are rounded.

troleum revenues. This group has produced two-thirds of OPEC supplies, playing a pivotal role in the world petroleum market.

Nor surprisingly, 37 of the less-developed, non-OPEC nations produced an average of only 12 percent of their consumption. Among them, only Egypt, Syria, and Mexico have sizable quantities of petroleum exports, and the combined exports of these countries totaled less than 10 percent of U.S. imports in 1982. Among the developed industrial nations, the United States, one of the world's largest petroleum-producing nations, imported more than 50 percent of its petroleum. Western Europe produced only 12 to 14 percent of its domestic consumption. South Africa and Japan imported essentially all of their petroleum.

Since late 1979, following the second major price increase, however, OPEC's output has declined rapidly as importing nations imposed draconian conservations measures and turned increasingly to alternative energy sources and to such non-OPEC oil producers as Mexico, Britain, and the Soviet Union.

Caught between declining demand and rising alternative sources of supply, OPEC, in order to maintain the world price set by it, was under continuous pressure to reduce its own supplies. OPEC's crude oil production was reduced steadily, from 33 million barrels per day in September 1973, to 17 million barrels per day, which accounted for only 35 percent of the global market, in October 1983, and then to less than 16 million barrels per day in the first half of 1986. The production cutbacks placed increasing strains on the cohesiveness of the cartel. Some members who had embarked on ambitious economic and military programs, became increasingly reluctant to implement the cutbacks and thus faced a reduction in their revenues. "Cheating" became prevalent. The resulting increases in supply of oil put an additional downward pressure on world prices.

Given the dominant position of OPEC and the length of time required for the exploration and development or petroleum resources or petroleum substitutes, the slow response of output by the non-OPEC world to the higher price of oil is to be expected. That is, supply of petroleum in non-OPEC nations is relatively price inelastic. It is estimated that the long-run price elasticity of the non-OPEC oil supply is between 0.33 and 0.67. In other words, a 1 percent increase in price of oil will cause output to increase only about 0.5 percent.[21] As a result, two-thirds of the adjustment to the slowdown in oil production has taken place through curbing demand growth and only one-third through accelerating the production of other energy supplies.

In terms of extra supplies, petroleum will no longer make the largest contribution. Having provided more than 60 percent of the increment to energy supplies in the 1960s, its share is expected to continue to shrink. By the end of the century, it may account for only 30 percent of world primary energy, compared with its peak of 50 percent in 1973. This decline will have to be offset largely by a revival of coal and coal-based fuels and a significant increase in nuclear energy and synthetic fuels, as well as other energy sources.

NOTES

1. Further discussion on these two issues can be found in William D. Nordhau, *The Efficient Use of Energy Resources* (New Haven: Yale University Press, 1979), Chapter 5; Ali Ezzati, *World Energy Markets and OPEC Stability* (Lexington: Lexington Books, 1978); Richard C. Dorf, *Energy, Resources, & Policy* (Reading: Addison-Wesley Publishing Company, 1978); and Jae Edmonds and John M. Reilly, *Global Energy: Assessing the Future* (Oxford: Oxford University Press, 1985).

2. Thomas D. Duchesneau, *Competition in the U.S. Energy Industry* (Cambridge: Ballinger Publishing Company, 1975), p. 21.

3. Harry W. Richardson, *Economic Aspects of the Energy Crisis* (Lexington: Lexington Books/Saxon House, 1975), p. 58.

4. Ezzati, op. cit., p. 21.

5. Exxon Corporation, *World Oil Inventories* (August 1981), pp. 2–3.

6. Ezzati, op. cit., p. 26.

7. Dorf, op. cit., p. 132.

8. Ezzati, op. cit., p. 22.

9. Ibid., p. 24.

10. James M. Griffin and Henry B. Steele, *Energy Economics and Policy* (New York: Academic Press, 1980), p. 26.

11. Rajendra K. Pachauri, *The Political Economy of Global Energy* (Baltimore: The Johns Hopkins University Press, 1985), p. 45.

12. Dorf, op. cit., p. 253.

13. Ibid., p. 262.

14. This discussion draws on Exxon Corporation, *How Much Oil and Gas?* Exxon Background Series, Exxon Corporation (May 1982).

15. Oil equivalent means crude oil, plus natural gas expressed as its energy equivalent in oil, plus liquids removed from the gas.

16. U.S.S.R., People's Republic of China, Eastern Europe, Cuba, Mongolia, North Korea, Viet Nam, Yugoslavia, Laos, and Kampuchea.

17. The World Bank, *World Development Report 1980* (1980), p. 17.

18. Edmonds and Reilly, op. cit.

19. See, *International Letter,* Federal Reserve Bank of Chicago, no. 496 (March 25, 1983); also Clifton B. Luttrell, "A Bushel of Wheat for a Barrel of Oil: Can We Offset OPEC's Gains with a Grain Cartel?" *Review,* Federal Reserve Bank of St. Louis (April 1981), pp. 13–21.

20. *International Letter,* op. cit.; also, Luttrell, op. cit., pp. 13–21.

21. Michael Kennedy, "A World Oil Model," in Dale W. Jorgenson, ed., *Econometric Studies of U.S. Energy Policy* (Amsterdam: North Holland Publishing Company, 1976), p. 139.

6

Energy and Economic Growth

In the history of the economic growth and development in the industrial world, energy has been considered a nearly ubiquitous good—essential but abundant and inexpensive. The Arab oil embargo in late 1973, however, dramatically signalled the end of the era of abundance. Not only has an unanticipated four-fold increase in the price of crude oil had significant impacts on the levels of economic activity in the oil-importing and industrial economies, it has also changed the structures of relative prices, induced structural changes in production and consumption, and altered paths of economic growth.

Although the ability of improvements in technical efficiency to offset the tendency to stagnation implied by the diminishing returns resulting from a rising capital-labor ratio has been quite fascinating in the history of the economic growth, the energy sector has been viewed in isolation from the remainder of the economy. The analysis of energy policy has always been performed without consideration of the broader impacts. Typically, the GNP and other macroeconomic indexes are taken as given—as though they were unaffected by the energy sector. The energy crises of the 1970s, however, manifest that a sudden large increase in energy prices can have deleterious macroeconomic effects. The energy sector affects the rest of the economy through shortages and/or income transfers from rising energy prices. The future macroeconomic environment of the industrial nations will depend in part on developments in the energy sector; others will result from the implementation of specific government policies and decisions of foreign oil-producing countries.

Specific energy sector developments impact on the economy and are, in turn, affected themselves. Although such feedback effects between the general economy and the energy sector may be significant, with the notable exception of the Hudson-Jorgenson model, little work has been done to construct models that recognize both sources of interactions. Most macroeconometric models are final demand oriented. Models with an explicit supply sector typically aggregate energy and nonenergy variables, do not allow for input substitution possibilities between energy and nonenergy inputs, or both.

Much of this chapter, though, has direct relevance to the theme of economic growth, and places greater emphasis on the energy-economy interactions and the impacts of higher oil prices on the paths of economic growth in the Western industrial economies.

ENERGY-ECONOMY INTERACTIONS

The problem of economic growth has engaged the attention of many economists throughout the history of the discipline. Adam Smith, David Ricardo, John Stuart Mill, Thomas Malthus, Karl Marx, Alfred Marshall, Joseph Schumpeter, J. M. Keynes, and the other great figures either made growth the central problem of their work or felt compelled to relate their work to it. The classical economists found the essence of growth in a growing labor force. The role of capital was purely subsidiary. It was seen as necessary to provide the "wage fund" to employ a growth population. Keynes,[1] Harrod,[2] and Duesenberry,[3] on the other hand, were all concerned with the question whether, or under what conditions, a modern economy might generate sufficient aggregate demand to permit continued growth. All were concerned with the role of capital accumulation as a possible inhibitor of growth, but they came up with quite different answers regarding whether this threat was serious. Despite their differences, all three approached the growth problem from the demand side. Output and its ability to grow were seen to be limited by aggregate demand. The problem of growth is the problem of demand.[4]

As supply shortages of energy resources in the early 1970s resulted in escalating prices which have inhibited growth at rates comparable to those that prevailed during the previous decades in the United States, as well as other industrial nations, works on economic growth have focused on energy-economy interactions and the strength of the energy-growth link. The problem of growth has become the problem of energy supply.

Indeed, energy pervades a modern industrial society in ways that make it difficult to decide what is an energy problem and what is a problem of economic growth, income distribution, environment, or international politics. Energy touches every aspect of life, playing a major role in some and a minor role in others.

The consumption of inanimate energy played the critical role in advancing the material well-being of mankind—both by providing an essential input into economic growth and by satisfying a diverse range of wants made possible by the resultant increases in real income. The large-scale application of inanimate energy forms through new technologies began with the Industrial Revolution in the late eighteenth century. Of these inanimate energy forms, coal was initially the strategic element in the emergence of industrial civilization. It made a significant contribution to the development of the iron and steel industry, to railways, and to factory mechanization. In the twentieth century, electrification and motorized transport, nonetheless, served to sustain this historic process and to step up tangible economic progress.[5]

Hypothesis of Inseparability

Historically, in the developed world in general and in the United States in particular, there has been a close relationship between economic growth, rising living standards, and increasing energy consumption. In a sense, the economic history of the industrialized world might be written in terms of the increasing use of energy and the substitution of more for less productive energy-using technologies.

The mechanization of industry, the succession of revolutions in transport, the improvement in material living standards and the social history of changing life-styles—all these phenomena can be understood only within a context that stresses the increase in supply and transformation of energy resources. The implication is that economic growth and increasing energy consumption per capita are inseparable and that energy consumption is in part a necessary condition for economic growth and part a consequence of growth. Generally, this inseparability is based upon three types of evidence: the economic history of industrialized countries; the similarity over decades of experience in the United States between annual growth rates in GNP and in energy consumption; and cross-sectional international evidence suggesting a strong relationship between level of economic development energy consumption per capita.[6]

Depending upon the observer's assessment of the energy supply situation, there are two distinctive opposing inferences on the hypothesis of inseparability. The first inference contends that to cut back on energy consumption is not only unnecessary, it is dangerous. It reasons that even though the resource base of fossil fuels is finite, only a fraction is economically recoverable. Through higher prices and improved technology, the economically recoverable resource base can be expanded despite the fixity of the total resource base. It, therefore, believes that if we attempt to conserve energy, growth will abandon us. In particular, new energy supply technologies such as nuclear reactors and coal-based synthetic fuels are essential if the future rate of economic growth is not to be slowed down. Thus, according to this view, the potential for expanding energy supplies is considerable,[7] and conservation only results in unnecessary sacrifices. Measures to promote energy conservation can be implemented only at the expense of economic growth, and to risk disturbing the growth of the economy may wipe out the sources from which technological advance is possible.

The second inference argues that the supply of energy resources, in danger of running out, has become a severe constraint on growth. It holds that the rate of economic growth ought to be slowed down or abandoned—precisely in order to conserve energy resources and to avoid the safety and environmental consequences associated with nuclear energy and with coal. The only way to bring energy consumption and growth into correspondence and to prevent total economic and social collapse is to cut back on the pursuit of growth and hence on consumption. It contends that energy conservation will be relatively easy to achieve, while supply stimulation, particularly for domestic oil, gas, and nuclear fuel, is quite limited.[8] Therefore, conservation must be used as the primary policy vehicle. Neither position, however, is very optimistic about the prospects for breaking the nexus between energy consumption and growth.[9]

Still another viewpoint is logically possible—one that rejects the hypothesis of a strong linkage between energy consumption and economic growth. According to this third viewpoint, there are many ways to reduce energy consumption without having a major impact on the GNP. In some cases, this would have no direct costs, but would require a change in life-styles. In other cases, it would be necessary to substitute other economic goods in place of energy. Each of these conservation measures would eventually become cost-effective if there were a sufficient rise in the price of energy. Opinions, however, differ on the magnitude of the price increase that would be needed in order to induce significant amounts of conservation.

Even if energy conservation were desirable, others point out that energy conservation is not simply a matter of reducing ''wasteful'' energy consumption. The most extreme version of this position is that energy conservation is not achievable unless per capita GNP is reduced proportionately with per capital energy consumption.[10]

Indeed, the debate has brought us to more realistic interpretation and understanding of the relationship between energy consumption and economic growth. However, there remains considerable room for improvement if policy decisions are to be based on these hypotheses. A reading of economic history of the industrial world suggests that the energy consumption required to provide society with a given set of amenities may display considerable flexibility. But thinking, which assumes the presence of an energy-conservation ethic and abhorrence of waste ''over there,'' in contrast to the disregard for such things in the United States, reflects notions at odds with fact and is simplistic in its view of the world.

Although evidence is abundant in support of a strong positive correlation between per capita energy consumption and per capita real gross domestic product in industrial countries, correlations do not prove causality. The possibility exists that energy consumption and economic growth are inextricably intertwined. Even assuming causation, it is not clear if the direction of causation runs from energy to economic growth or vice versa.[11]

Measuring Energy-Economic Growth Relationship

The relationship between energy consumption and economic growth can be expressed as a ratio which measures the amount of energy consumed per dollar of GNP (E/GNP ratio). This ratio is the simplest expression that measures a very complex and constantly changing relationship. This relationship can also be found in the concepts of energy coefficients—the E/GNP elasticity. The E/GNP elasticity is the percentage growth rate in energy consumption compared with the percentage rate of growth of GNP. It is a unitless statistic that can be compared across countries.

Care, however, must be exercised in drawing conclusions from comparing E/GNP ratios among countries. Various studies have pointed to low E/GNP ratios in European countries as evidence that the United States, for example, should or could consume radically less energy. The merit of these contentions depends on the interpretation of meaning and significance of E/GNP ratios. The explanations for differences in E/GNP ratios among different countries include pricing policies, import dependence, product mix, energy embodied in imports and exports, GNP accounting differences, real product (exchange rate) conversion problems, climate, and geography, to name a few.

Despite the similarities of industrial societies, each is composed of a unique mixture of factors, resources, and prices that dictate, within a relatively narrow range, the level of energy consumption. These economies perform many of the same tasks; yet there are many differences beneath this surface of similarity that cause energy consumption patterns to vary. While there were obvious differences among industrialized economies, they were probably minor as regards achievable energy consumption per unit of output.

Changes in the E/GNP ratio and elasticity are a reflection of numerous underlying factors, such as the state of technology, the price of energy, environmental constraints, the level of activity in individual energy-using sectors, the composition of GNP, and demographic and sociological factors. Neither of these concepts, however, is a forecasting tool. Rather, attention to them following forecasting indicates the net effect of such factors as change in energy mix, conservation, and changing industrial emphasis.

Inexplicably, the E/GNP ratio was often characterized as an unchanging relationship by analysts working in the 1960s and early 1970s. The implication was that every percentage increase in GNP was met by an equal percentage increase in energy consumption—the E/GNP elasticity was one. This rule was based on observations of highly aggregated data.

As the 1970s progressed, and data for the post–oil embargo era became available, it became clear that the one-to-one relationship was not the norm of energy use and economic growth. However, the popular conception of the 1970s was that the period represented an unprecedented break with the past. The historical data examined in this chapter strongly question the validity of the one-to-one rule, even in the pre–oil embargo period.[12]

In a related strain of the literature on energy consumption and economic growth, the one-to-one relationship was viewed as holding in the case of the developed (industrialized) economies. The developing economies were viewed as countries with low E/GNP ratios, which, as development proceeded, would rise to the level of developed countries. Thus, a low E/GNP ratio, with an elasticity greater than one, is an essential characteristic of the early stage of economic development. More recent studies in literature have examined the cross-country evidence in support of such a relationship, but their empirical tests have been something less than convincing in establishing the relationship.[13]

The problem lies in deciding upon the degree of disaggregation into sectors and subsectors. The varying patterns within a sector reflect consumer preferences in goods and services and also follow established, historical patterns of international trade which, of course, are dynamic and change when comparative advantages in production change.

Historical Perspectives

The relation between energy resources and economic well-being was first examined in detail by Schurr, Netschart, Eliasberg, Lerner, and Landsberg[14] some 27 years ago in their book *Energy in the American Economy 1850–1975*. Their analysis showed that there was a strong positive correlation between per capita energy consumption and per capita GNP for the U.S. economy during the 1850–1975 period and their predictions about the aggregate energy demand for 1975 using the qualitative methods were quite remarkably close to the actual trend.

The historical association between economic growth and increasing energy consumption was also examined by Darmstadter[15] who analyzed the changes in energy consumption and GNP rates over time. According to this analysis, between 1880 and 1920, energy consumption in the United States increased one-and-a-half times faster than GNP growth rates. Between 1920 and 1960, however, it grew more slowly, only three-quarters of the rate of GNP.[16] The faster growth before 1920 reflected primarily the disproportionately fast growth of manufacturing in the economy—a sector requiring far higher energy input per unit of activity than the agricultural component that had dominated the economy in the past. The slower growth over the 1920–60 period was due to fuel efficiency as a result of (a) the rapid rise of electrification which greatly enhanced the efficiency of factory operations, (b) a doubling of thermal efficiency improvements, and (c) the replacement of railroad diesel engines—with their greater efficiency—for steam locomotives.

After 1965, the trends of the relative GNP and energy growth rates reversed. The rate of growth in energy consumption was 1.4 percent higher in the second half of the 1960s compared to the first half, and was much higher than the growth rate in GNP. This change was attributed, according to the study, primarily to "electricity conversion losses,"[17] rising petroleum consumption by automobiles and planes, and increasing nonenergy uses. Over the twentieth century, Darmstadter showed that the growth rates of energy consumption and economic growth were almost similar, with 3.2 percent per annum in energy consumption and 3.3 percent in constant GNP.

This observation of historical trends led Darmstadter to argue that it would be difficult to break the association between GNP and energy growth, barring a major technological breakthrough or the imposition of substantial disincentives to demand. Several reasons were given. These included (a) the close link between productivity increases and energy use, (b) the dominance of electricity in consumption increases, (c) the use in the service sector of energy-intensive technologies and the effect of computerization, and (d) the impact of changing tastes and life-styles on increased leisure and recreation.[18]

Broadly speaking, energy use has tended to show a rather strong, positive correlation with overall economic activity—judging both from the historical experience of different countries as well as from multi-country, cross-sectional circumstances at a point in time. However, there are numerous exceptions to the general relationship. Specifically, per capita consumption of energy resources in the United States is considerably higher than it is in a number of other industrial countries, such as France, Germany, and Sweden, whose per capita income or output levels cluster within a range not appreciably different from the United States. Not surprisingly, then, the U.S. energy/output ratio exceeds by a considerable margin the ratio in numerous other countries.[19]

Examining the historical data for the OECD countries as a whole, in the 1960–73 period every 1 percent increase in energy usage was associated with a 1 percent increase in GDP. Between 1973 and 1981, when GDP grew at an average rate of 2.3 percent annually, the consumption of total primary energy (TPE) grew by a mere 0.2 percent per year, suggesting that the association of energy and economic growth had fallen from unity in the 1960–73 period to less than 0.1 percent in the 1973–81 period. This dramatic decline in the energy intensity of the OECD economy reflects primarily the structural changes in the use of energy in the economy, responses to policies and prices, and cyclical effects. As these factors are likely to vary through time and between countries, it is clear that the association between percent changes in energy consumption and percent changes in GDP offer little help in projecting future energy demand.[20]

The wide fluctuations of the energy/GDP growth relationship are also accentuated by the fact that oil price–induced economic recessions usually have a more serious impact on energy-intensive industries than on other industries, strongly dampening energy demand and disproportionately impacting on the overall energy/output relationship. This means then that in periods of prolonged economic slowdown energy consumption per unit of GDP will be lower than underlying trends would suggest.

Relying merely on historical experience, however, seems to be too simplistic to assume an inevitable link between growth rates in GNP and the energy consumption, because no conscious attempt has been made in the past to conserve energy, at least in the context of national energy policy. Often, international comparisons are used to support the view that per capita energy consumption and the level of economic development are inextricably linked. However, the generalization can be overstressed. For instance, in Sweden and Canada—countries with similar living standards and climatic conditions—energy consumption per capita in the former is only about one-and-a-half the level of the latter. The consumption level in the United States is more than twice that of West Germany and three times as much as in Switzerland. In particular, as shown in Table 6.1, the ratio of energy consumption to GDP growth rates has been found to vary widely even among industrial countries, because of differences in industrial and social structures and in rates of economic growth.[21]

Moreover, a country-by-country comparison is weak in the sense that one country is being compared with another whose energy consumption is lower, but which may itself have considerable potential for energy conservation. The comparative approach gives only a partial indication of the potential for energy conservation.

Indeed, the problem of comparing countries and their respective energy use is a complex one, and simple E/GNP ratio comparisons can lead to the wrong conclusions. As has been pointed out, this is, of course, misleading.

Significantly, a survey of energy literature shows that most of the projected E/GNP elasticities fall within a fairly narrow range from 0.40 to 0.80 for developed countries and from 0.9 to 1.3 for developing country regions, as shown in Table 6.2. They tend to echo the historical experience, with developing country regions showing higher elasticities than developed country regions.[22]

Table 6.1
Energy/GDP Ratios in Selected Years

Country	1973 Primary Energy/GDP (10^3 Btu/\$)	1975 Primary Energy/GDP (10^3 Btu/\$)
Canada	81.4	80.5
United Kingdom	68.2	62.8
United States	64.6	64.6
Netherlands	57.0	53.7
Belgium	54.9	49.1
Sweden	48.4	44.8
Italy	47.3	45.4
Germany	43.3	40.9
Japan	41.5	39.9
Switzerland	36.8	38.1

Source: International Energy Agency, OECD/U.N. Paris, 1976.

Table 6.2
Projected E/GNP Elasticities of Major Energy Studies by Regions

Regions	EXXON 1979–2000	IIASA 1975–2000	RFF 1972–2000	OECD 1975–2000	LOVINS 1975–2000	St'd Oil 1980–2000	WEC 1972–2000	DOE 1979–1995	HK 1985–2005	WAES 1972–2000
United States	0.19	0.42	0.63	0.75	-0.60	0.64	0.60	0.45	1.45	0.77
Other OECDs	0.37	0.69	0.71	0.96	-0.50	0.64	0.70	0.43	1.24	0.80
CPE	0.75	0.74	0.98	0.88	0.05	1.12	0.84	n.a.	n.a.	n.a.
Nonoil LDCs	0.92	1.08	1.16	1.33	0.40	1.04	0.76	1.28	1.98	1.05
Oil LDCs	1.02	1.84	1.16	1.13	0.40	1.04	0.93	0.68	1.82	0.86
Non-Communist World	0.66	0.72	0.89	0.90	-0.18	0.76	0.79	0.54	1.70	0.85
World	0.66	0.74	0.93	0.92	-0.11	0.87	0.81	n.a.	n.a.	n.a.

Sources: (1) Exxon: Exxon Corporation, *World Energy Outlook* (December 1980); (2) IIASA: Wolf Hafele, Project Leader, *Energy in a Finite World: A Global Systems Analysis,* Report by the Energy Program Group of the International Institute for Applied Systems Analysis (Cambridge, MA.: Ballinger, 1981), table 7.2, p. 208; (3) RFF: Ronald G. Ridker and William D. Watson, *To Choose a Future* (Baltimore & London: The Johns Hopkins University Press published for Resources for the Future, 1980); (4) OECD: Organization for Economic Co-operation and Development, *Interfutures, Facing the Future* (Paris: OECD, 1979); (5) Lovins: Amory B. Lovins, L. Hunter Lovins, Florentin Krause, and Wilfred Bach, *Energy Strategy for Low Climatic Risks.* Prepared for the German Federal Environmental Agency (San Francisco, CA.: International Project for Soft Energy Paths, June 1981); (6) St'd Oil: Standard Oil Company of California, *World Energy Outlook 1981–2000* (San Francisco, California, 1981); (7) WEC: The Full Report to the Conservation Commission of the World Energy Conference, *World Energy Demand* (New York: IPC Science and Technology Press, 1978); (8) DOE: U.S. Department of Energy, *1981 Annual Report to Congress,* Report #DOE/EIA-0173 (81)/3 (Washington, DC: U.S. Government Printing Office, 1982); (9) HK: Hendrik S. Houthakker and Michael Kennedy, "Long-Range Energy Prospects," *Journal of Energy and Development* (Autumn 1978); (10) WAES: Carroll L. Wilson, Project Director, *Energy: Global Prospects 1985–2000.* Report of the Workshop on Alternative Energy Strategies (New York: McGraw-Hill, 1977).

The predicted level of growth in energy use between 1979–2000 is generally lower than that between 1973 and 1979. It reflects less energy-intensive economic activity and the growing importance of conservation measures and more efficient use of energy. This reduction in energy consumption per unit of GNP will be in the industrialized countries that have been lowering the energy intensity of their industry since the early 1970s.

Indeed, conservation measures will continue the trend towards less energy intensity in the industrialized countries. Some recent studies on the subject of the energy economic growth linkage suggest that, if high energy prices were maintained and conservation encouraged, the breaking of the link between economic growth and the consumption of energy may be easier than has previously been thought. The reason is that a great deal of energy use is only indirectly related to economic growth. Clearly there is abundant scope for improved efficiency which could reduce energy use without damaging economic growth prospects.

THEORETICAL CONSIDERATIONS

Energy-economy interactions and the impacts of energy price on the economy can be analyzed with the use of a simple supply-and-demand framework. Given certain assumptions about economic behavior, the theoretical foundations can be summarized below.

Impact on Output and Employment Levels of a Supply Shock

The relationship between supply shocks and overall output, price, and employment levels is modeled in the studies by Gordon,[23] Findlay and Rodriguez,[24] and Phelps.[25] Gordon performed a study of supply shocks in the form of a two-sector (food and nonfood) model. Findlay and Rodriguez have produced an international model to much the same end. In these models, output is exogenous in one sector called the ''farm'' sector. Prices are set to equilibrate demand and supply; and overall price and output are then determined by the degree of accommodation implicit in the macro policy responses.[26]

Phelps, on the other hand, analyzes a closed economy producing a single final good with attention to traditional matters of capital, inflation, and interest. The exogenous supply of raw materials is considered as one component of an aggregate production function that has the properties of concavity and linear homogeneity.[27] Nonetheless, all of these models allow for some upward adjustment in aggregate price levels as output and employment increase.

Hence, as shown in Figure 6.1 below, the aggregate supply curve, AS, is upward sloping. In the Gordon model, it is assumed that at any level of real aggregate employment, the exogenous decline in farm supplies raises farm and overall prices, hence shifting up the aggregate supply schedule to AS_1. In the

Figure 6.1
Impact on Output and Employment of a Supply Shock

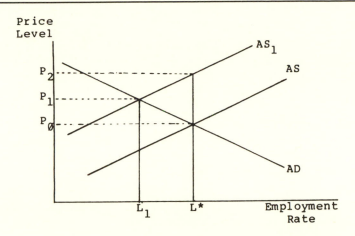

Phelps model, the scarcity of materials lowers labor's marginal product and, with a fixed money wage, shifts up marginal costs and prices to AS_1.

The aggregate demand schedule is shown as the downward sloping curve AD in the diagram. This curve represents the solution of the IS and LM equations. The rationale for the downward sloping of the aggregate demand curve is that the quantity of nominal money stock is fixed along the aggregate demand schedule and will support a higher level of aggregate demand for labor when prices, P, are lower, the real money stock is greater, the IS curve is downward sloping, and the LM curve upward sloping.

The impact on output and employment of a supply shock in these models is found by shifting the aggregate supply curve leftward as shown, yielding temporarily a positive correlation between inflation (dP/P>0) and unemployment ($L_1 < L^*$, where L^* is the natural rate of employment). The new short-run equilibrium is at (P_1, L_1) unless there are an endogenous shift in the aggregate demand schedule, policy change to accommodate the shocks, and rational expectation reaction.[28]

Impact of Higher Oil Prices on Economic Growth

The large increases in the price of imported oil and the cost of domestic energy sources raise the general price level and simultaneously transfer real wealth and income from users to owners of energy resources. Such increases in energy prices relative to others precipitate ''a decline in the goods and services supplied by the economy at any given level of prices.''[29] They tend to reduce real disposable income and the real value of consumer wealth, thereby depressing consumption expenditures and aggregate demand.

To this extent, the real oil price increases imposed by the oil-exporting country have similar effects to that of an excise tax imposed on crude oil in the typical oil-importing country by an external authority that does not inject the tax revenues back into the economy through transfers or additional expenditures. In this case, real income and wealth are transferred from the oil-importing country to the oil-exporting country.[30]

Price increases in domestic energy sources, on the other hand, will create expanded investment opportunities, but the reduction in aggregate demand is inevitable, if the additional profits realized by the domestic energy sector were not injected back into the economy. Under such circumstances, the levels of real GNP will be reduced in the long run with continuing loss of investment expenditures. Some sectors of the economy will contract, while others will expand, as relative prices change, discouraging investment in the contracting sectors and encouraging it in the expanding ones. These adjustments will tend to make real GNP lower than it otherwise would have been in terms of the price structure that prevailed before the real price of imported oil rises.

Effect on Output and the Price Level

The effect of a higher relative price of energy on output and the price level may be examined using a simple aggregate supply-and-demand model, as shown in Figure 6.2.

The aggregate demand curve is represented by the downward sloping curve AD, given levels of current and past monetary and fiscal actions. The aggregate

Figure 6.2
Impact on Output and the Price Level of a Higher Relative Energy Price

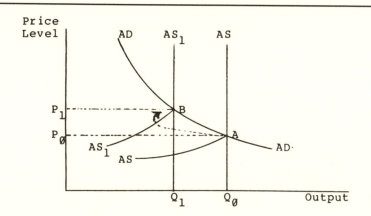

supply curve, on the other hand, is represented by the upward sloping curve AS, given expected nominal wages, the size of the labor force, the existing capital stock, the relative price of energy, and technology. It shows the amount of output that producers are willing to supply at various price levels. This is significantly affected by the supply and demand for labor.

Initially, the economy is in equilibrium with price level, P_0, and real GNP, Q_0, at point A. When the aggregate supply curve slopes upward to the point where labor is "fully employed," at that point, Q_0, it becomes vertical. The vertical portion of the supply curve reflects the assumption that "attempts to expand output beyond levels commensurate with fully employed labor merely bid up the nominal prices of full employed labor, capital, and energy."[31] In other words, it becomes difficult to increase real output despite increases in the general price levels. At this output level, the economy achieves full employment, utilizing available capital and labor resources.

Under such full-employment conditions, shifts in aggregate supply over time occur because of changes in the capital stock and technology, but these factors seldom change abruptly over short periods of time. The price of labor and the price of energy, however, can change dramatically in a short period of time. Movements in the price of labor will, of course, reflect productivity trends as well as past and expected price levels. The price of energy is determined by the interplay of supply and demand in world market.[32]

When the relative price of energy resources increases, the aggregate supply curve, AS, shifts to AS_1. The effect of this change is similar to that for a higher nominal wage. The difference is that full-employment output is reduced to Q_1, as shown in Figure 6.2 by an increase in the price of energy, as producers reduce their use of relatively more expensive energy resources and as plant and equipment become economically obsolete. The reason for this reduction is that the reduction in energy use as a third factor of production lowers the productivity of labor and capital in the short run.[33] Consequently, full-employment output will be less, but the amount of labor employment consistent with that reduced output will be the same as before the increase in the price of energy, provided that real wages decline sufficiently to match the decline in productivity. This, in turn, happens only if the general price level rises sufficiently (to P_1), given the nominal wage rate.[34]

The new equilibrium for the economy is achieved at point B. Even though a rise in the relative price of energy reduces potential output immediately, the effect of this reduction on the price level occurs more slowly. Therefore, the economy may not adjust instantaneously to the new equilibrium B. The immediate incentive to cut production and employment indicated by the leftward shift in the aggregate supply curve need not be accompanied immediately by the adjustment of the price level sufficient to ensure the maintenance of full employment. In this event, disequilibrium GNP will be dominated by the reduction in output before the equilibrium B (and full employment) is achieved. Consequently, output and prices can move along an adjustment path such as that indicated by the arrow in Figure 6.2. Once the adjustment is completed, however, GNP is independent of energy price changes.[35]

Welfare Effects of a Cartel Price

Assuming full employment and external equilibrium, the net welfare loss and the real GNP reduction caused by higher energy prices may be examined with the aid of the standard supply and demand framework used to evaluate the impact of a tariff.[36] Figure 6.3 illustrates this approach.

The diagram shows the domestic supply and demand for energy in a typical oil-importing economy. Without loss of generality, the supply-and-demand curves are assumed all linear, and all other things remain equal. The assumption of a fixed exchange rate permits the conversion of prices in foreign currency to the currency of the oil-importing country.

In this analysis, the economy is assumed to face a fixed import price expressed in terms of other goods. At the precartel world energy price, P_0, the economy produces Q_0 amount of energy and imports Q_0Q_1. Figure 6.3 shows how the effect of a cartel price is spread among consumers, domestic producers, and the government. The total welfare that consumers derive from any given commodity can be measured by what they would pay rather than do without the good entirely. This is approximated by the area under the demand curve and above the market price line. In Figure 6.3 this ''consumers' surplus''

Figure 6.3
Welfare Effects of a Cartel Price

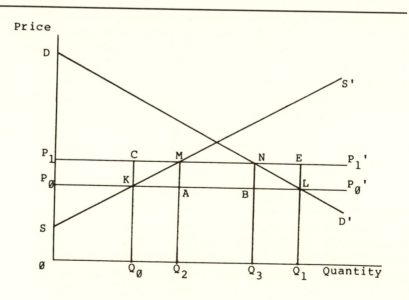

at the precartel price is measured by the triangular area under the demand curve but above P_0L. When the cartel price is imposed at P_1, the economy expands production to Q_2, total consumption reduces to Q_3, and imports decrease to Q_2Q_3. Consumers' surplus shrinks to the area above P_1N, and consumers lose an amount of welfare measured by the trapezoidal area P_0LNP_1, because of the increase in the world energy price. The area KLNM is the net welfare loss to society, because P_0KMP_1 is a transfer from energy consumers to domestic energy producers.

The increase in the world energy price likewise affects domestic producers' welfare. The opportunity cost of factors of production is depicted in the area under the supply curve. Sometimes, increases in output encounter diminishing returns, and, as in Figure 6.3, the supply curve acquires an upward slope. A ''producers' surplus,'' measured by the area above the supply curve, results when some factors employed in the industry earn more than the opportunity cost of their services. Thus, at the precartel price, P_0, domestic producers enjoy the surplus triangular area SKP_0, and total domestic welfare in the oil-importing country is, by definition, the sum of consumers' surplus and producers' surplus. When the cartel price is imposed, the producers' surplus rises to SMP_1, and domestic producers gain from the imposition of the cartel price an amount measured by the area P_0KMP_1.

At the cartel price, the cost of resources used to produce Q_0Q_2 amount of energy instead of importing it at precartel prices is shown by area KAM, which represents the increased cost of resources used in extracting energy from a fixed supply of land. Diverting these resources from the production of other goods lowers real GNP.

The higher cartel price will require an additional cost, as shown by the area ABNM, of importing Q_2Q_3 energy, which is the ''terms-of-trade'' loss in the narrow sense. This cost is necessitated by the change in the terms of trade and does not reduce the production of final goods and services. Therefore, this additional cost as shown by area ABMN, does not represent a reduction in real GNP. The area BLN, on the other hand, reflects the utility losses experienced by households because of the reduction in energy consumption and the efficiency loss incurred by firms because of the substitution of other inputs for energy in production processes. That is, area BLN represents the consumption cost of conserving energy and area (KAM + BLN) the ''inefficiency cost'' in production of area KAM and in consumption of area BLN.

That part of the economic loss representing the utility losses experienced by households that reduce energy consumption does not show up in the statistical measures of GNP, because the GNP cannot measure satisfaction forgone. Therefore, such utility losses can not lower real GNP.

On the other hand, the efficiency losses attributable to the higher cost in resources of domestic production will lower productivity and real GNP, ceteris paribus. At precartel prices, for example, Q_0Q_2MK resources are required to produce Q_0Q_2 amount of energy, whereas Q_0Q_2AK resources are required to produce the other goods necessary to trade for the same amount of energy. Real GNP is reduced by the difference, area KAM, when domestic energy is substituted for imported energy. This is due to the fact that each additional unit of energy from domestic sources that is substituted for imports will require more resources (capital, labor, and materials) than the same unit of energy would have cost if purchased abroad at precartel prices. At cartel prices, Q_0Q_2MK resources are required to produce Q_0Q_2 energy domestically, while Q_0Q_2MC resources are required to produce the other goods necessary to trade for the same amount of energy. Specifically, the additional resources have to be diverted from the production of other goods and services, thereby lowering total real GNP. Hence, instead of trading for it, producing an amount of Q_0Q_2 energy domestically would result in a real GNP gain.[37]

A similar approach can also be applied to the case where the supply curves of both the oil-importing and the oil-exporting country are upward sloping, but the diagram and explanation both become extremely complex since the surpluses of individual producers and consumers will change, thus adding to the complexity of the geometry and the explanation.

This type of analysis, though suffering from neglecting the effects on other markets of the cartel price through the terms of trade, shows clearly the distribution of welfare effects of a cartel price. It, however, is subject to a serious effect, because to add the surpluses of individual producers and consumers requires that utility be measurable.

Moreover, the partial equilibrium approach used in Figure 6.3 has serious limitations in analyzing the effects of higher oil prices on economic growth, because there are likely to be large and numerous changes in prices. Such changes would undoubtedly cause shifts in the supply-and-demand curves for an individual product, thus violating the ceteris paribus assumptions that underlie the supply-and-demand curves for an individual product.

Even so, partial equilibrium has great appeal because it neatly illustrates many effects of the higher oil prices on economic growth. It provides a theoretical foundation for an understanding of the energy-economy interactions, but we must rely upon the concept of the production function and the elasticity of substitution in order to analyze the forces underlying the growth of output potential. This will be the topic of discussion in the next chapter.

NOTES

1. J. M. Keynes, *General Theory* (London: Macmillan, 1936).

2. R. F. Harrod, *Towards a Dynamic Economics* (London: Macmillan, 1949).

3. James Duesenberry, *Business Cycles and Economic Growth* (McGraw-Hill, 1958).

4. Gardner Ackley, *Macroeconomic Theory* (New York: Macmillan Company, 1961), p. 535.

5. Joe Darmstadter, "Energy," in Ronald G. Ridker, ed., *Population, Resources, and The Environment*, vol. III, U.S. Commission on Population Growth and the Amer-

ican Future Research Reports (Washington, DC: Government Printing Office, 1972), p. 107.

6. Harry W. Richardson, *Economic Aspects of the Energy Crisis* (Lexington, MA: Lexington Book/Saxon House, 1975).

7. See the comments of J. A. Strahon, in Energy Policy Project of the Ford Foundation, *A Time to Choose* (Cambridge, MA: Ballinger, 1974), pp. 354–55.

8. The Ford Foundation's *A Time to Choose* accepts this view advocating primary reliance on energy conservation.

9. Richardson, op. cit.

10. See, for example, D. B. Brunham's comments in Energy Policy Project of the Ford Foundation, op. cit.

11. James M. Griffin and Henry B. Steele, *Energy Economics and Policy* (New York: Academic Press, 1980), pp. 214–19.

12. Jae Edmonds and John M. Reilly, *Global Energy, Assessing the Future,* Institute for Energy Analysis, Oak Ridge Associated Universities (Oxford: Oxford University Press, 1985), p. 47.

13. Ibid., pp. 47–48.

14. Sam H. Schurr, Bruce C. Netschart, Vera F. Eliasberg, Joseph Lerner, and Hans H. Landsberg, *Energy in the American Economy 1850–1975,* Resources for the Future (Baltimore, MD: The Johns Hopkins University Press, 1960).

15. Darmstadter, op. cit., pp. 105–49; idem, *Regional Energy Consumption* (Washington, DC: Resources for the Future and Regional Plan Association, 1973); idem, et al., *Energy in the World Economy* (Baltimore, MD: The Johns Hopkins University Press, 1972); idem, J. Dunkerly, and J. Alterman, *How Industrial Societies Use Energy: A Comparative Analysis* (Baltimore, MD: The Johns Hopkins University Press for Resources for the Future, 1977).

16. Between 1880 and 1920, yearly energy consumption growth averaged 5.6 percent, compared to annual GNP growth of 3.4 percent. The annual figures for the period 1920–60 average out to 2.1 percent and 3.2 percent, respectively.

17. The thermal losses associated with electricity conversion at power plants.

18. Darmstadter, "Energy," op. cit., pp. 105–49.

19. Joe Darmstadter, "International Comparisons of Energy Use—Findings from a Recently Completed RFF Report: Summary," in Joy Dunkerley, ed., *International Comparisons of Energy Consumption* (Washington, DC: Resources for the Future, 1978), p. 43.

20. International Energy Agency, *World Energy Outlook,* OECD/IEA (1982), p. 69.

21. Richardson, op. cit., p. 5.

22. Edmonds and Reilly, op. cit., pp. 55–56.

23. Robert J. Gordon, "Alternative Responses of Policy to External Supply Shocks," *Brookings Papers on Economic Activity* 1:1975 (Washington, DC: The Brookings Institution), pp. 183–204.

24. Ronald Findlay and Carlos A. Rodriguez, "Intermediate Imports and Macroeconomic Policy under Flexible Exchange Rates," *Canadian Journal of Economics* 10 (May 1977), pp. 208–17.

25. Edmund S. Phelps, "Commodity-Supply Shock and Full-Employment Monetary Policy," *Journal of Money, Credit, and Banking* 10, no. 2 (May 1978), pp. 206–21.

26. Gordon, op. cit., pp. 183–204.

27. Phelps, op. cit., pp. 207–08.

28. Edward M. Gramlich, "Macro Policy Responses to Price Shocks," *Brookings Papers on Economic Activity* 1:1979 (Washington, DC: The Brookings Institution), pp. 128–29.

29. Tatom, "Energy Prices and Short-Run Economic Performance," op. cit., pp. 3–17; see also, R. W. Hafer, "The Impact of Energy Prices and Money Growth on Five Industrial Countries," *Review,* Federal Reserve Bank of St. Louis 63, no. 3 (March 1981), pp. 19–26.

30. Peter Morici, Jr., "The Impact of Higher Oil Prices on Economic Growth in the Industrial Economies," in A. Bradley Askin, ed., *How Energy Affects the Economy* (Lexington, MA: Lexington Books, 1978), p. 36.

31. Keith M. Carlson, "Explaining the Economic Slowdown of 1979: A Supply and Demand Approach," *Review,* Federal Reserve Bank of St. Louis (October 1979), p. 18.

32. Carlson, op. cit., p. 18.

33. Carlson, op. cit., p. 19; also see Robert H. Rasche and John A. Tatom, "The Effects of the New Energy Regime on Economic Capacity, Production, and Prices," *Review,* Federal Reserve Bank of St. Louis (May 1977), pp. 2–12.

34. John A. Tatom, "Energy Price and Short-Run Economic Performance," *Review,* Federal Reserve Bank of St. Louis 63, no. 1 (January 1981), p. 4.

35. Ibid., p. 4.

36. This discussion draws on Peter Morici, Jr., op. cit., pp. 35–39; and Richard E. Caves and Ronald W. Jones, *World Trade and Payments* (Boston, MA: Little, Brown and Company, 1981), pp. 233–36. Theoretical discussion of this problem can also be found in Giorgio Basvi, "Western Europe," in Edward R. Fried and Charles L. Schultze, eds., *Higher Oil Prices and the World Economy: The Adjustment Problem* (Washington, DC: The Brookings Institution, 1975), pp. 105–42; Edward R. Fried and Charles L. Schultze, "Overview," in Fried and Schultz, eds., supra, pp. 1–69; and J. W. Gunning, J. Osterrieth, and J. Waelbroeck, "The Price of Energy and the Potential Growth of Developed Countries," *European Economic Review* 7 (1976), pp. 35–62.

37. Morici, op. cit., pp. 38–39.

7

Modeling Energy-Economy Interactions

The theory of energy-economy interactions is one of enormous complexity, due to the fundamental role of energy in everyday activities. Though much of the debate on the energy–GNP linkage may be summarized in terms of different views on the elasticity of substitution between energy and other factor inputs to the economy, the methods of analysis available for studying these interactions leave a great deal to be desired.

Prior to the energy crisis in early 1970s, the energy models generally consisted of either a direct energy–GNP link or a partial equilibrium model with demand as a function of energy price, income, and the price of substitutes. To such extent, most of the empirical results obtained by these models have implicitly deduced that energy use will continue to increase as rapidly in the future as it did in the past and price increases will have little effect on energy demand. In the aftermath of the first energy crisis in 1973/74, however, the emphasis shifted to econometric studies of energy demand and supply, institutional analysis of competition in the world petroleum market, derivations of optimal control rules for depleting nonrenewable resources, and evaluations of vertical divestiture in the domestic oil industry.

Since the second oil price crisis in the late 1970s, energy modeling has become much more sophisticated. There have been more systematic analyses of energy-economy interactions, with the greater emphasis placed on the sensitivity of oil price rises, supply strategy, and demand conservation. The relationship between energy availability and economic activity has become an issue of fundamental interest. Even though the energy–GNP feedback has often been neglected, models of the new generation have produced a much more sophisticated picture of the role of energy supply shift and energy-economy interactions.

In view of this evolution of energy modeling, it, therefore, may be useful to review, briefly, the theoretical and empirical underpinnings of energy-economy interactions, as well as different modeling approaches that focus on an ideal, hypothetical economy based on the basic neoclassical model of production. Also reviewed is the alternative approach developed by Kannan (1979) who uses the system-dynamic method to model the energy-economy interactions, with emphasis placed on the disequilibrium paths, rather than the equilibrium points.

THEORETICAL FOUNDATIONS

Most of the empirical studies of the energy-economy interactions are based on the neoclassical model of production.[1] Though the static neoclassical approach casts considerable light on the energy-economy interactions that may take place in an ideal, hypothetical economy, it is far from being adequate to deal with the essentially dynamic character of adjustment processes in the real world of the industrial economy.[2] Even so, a brief review of the basic assumptions and problems of the neoclassical model would facilitate a clear understanding of the inner working of energy-economy interactions.

Basic Assumptions of the Neoclassical Model

The neoclassical model[3] is based on the following assumptions:

1. The market economy consists of rational firms that always strive to maximize their profits in delivering goods and services to consumers.
2. Prices of factors of production (e.g., capital, labor, etc.) are determined solely by the free market forces of supply and demand.
3. The supply of factors of production is dependent on the market price of factors and the utility function of the owners of the factors.

These three assumptions are generally referred to as perfect competition and profit maximization assumptions. Based upon these assumptions, energy is viewed as an input factor, just as are capital and labor, in the production of goods and services. As a response to rising costs and scarcity of the energy factor, the firms will substitute for energy the less expensive factor inputs such as capital, labor, and other resources in optimizing the mix of factors in production processes so as to maximize profits. The degree of such substitutions can be measured by the value share and the elasticity of substitution in assessing the impact of energy scarcity on the rest of the economy.

Efficient Solutions and the Value Share

The energy-economy interactions can be interpreted in the context of value shares. For simplicity, we assume that there are only two types of economic inputs—energy, denoted by E with the unit price P_E, and all other nonenergy inputs such as capital, labor, and other resources lumped together, denoted by R with the unit price P_R. Energy is treated as an intermediate product contributing to the ultimate production of goods and services for final demand. The gross output of the nonenergy sector, denoted by Y and measured in the same units as GNP, can be related to the inputs of energy (E) and all other factors (R) in a simple aggregate production as follows:

$$Y = F(E, R) \qquad E \geqslant 0,\ R \geqslant 0 \tag{1}$$

Equation (1) is linear homogeneous; hence,

$$\lambda Y = F(\lambda E, \lambda R) \qquad \text{for every } \lambda > 0;\ E,\ R \geqslant 0 \tag{2}$$

In turn, equation (2) implies Euler's theorem:

$$Y = (F_E \cdot E) + (F_R \cdot R) \tag{3}$$

where F_E and F_R are marginal products of energy input E and nonenergy input R, respectively; that is

$$F_E = \frac{\partial F}{\partial E} = \frac{\partial Y}{\partial E} \text{ and } F_R = \frac{\partial F}{\partial R} = \frac{\partial Y}{\partial R} \tag{4}$$

The production function F is assumed to be continuous and differentiable for all E and R. The first-order partial derivatives of F with respect to E and R are assumed to be greater than zero and the second-order partial derivatives are assumed to be less than zero. Thus, the production function assumes that the law of diminishing marginal returns is satisfied.

On the basis of the neoclassical assumptions of perfect competition in the product and the factor markets and profit maximization by firms, it follows that

$$F_E = P_E \text{ and } F_R = P_R \tag{5}$$

which provides an economically efficient solution to the problem of profit maximization by firms

$$\text{Max } F(E, R) - P_E E - P_R R \tag{6}$$

If for some reason the price of energy rises, the firms will change the factor mix in such a manner as to achieve a new optimal combination of E and R. Thus, the production technique will assume that the factor prices are always equal to their marginal products.

From equation (5), it follows that

$$\frac{\partial F}{\partial E} \times \frac{\partial E}{\partial Y} = \frac{P_E E}{Y} \tag{7}$$

The left-hand side of equation (7) represents the output elasticity as the input of E varies, assuming that R is held constant, while the value share of the energy input as a proportion of total output is shown on the right-hand side of (7). With equation (7), the importance of the relative size of the energy sector can easily be shown by assuming $(P_E E/Y) = s$. By so defining, then, it becomes clear that a 1 percent change in the energy input will cause an s percent change in gross output. If we further assume that the value share s remains approximately constant over a wide range of E, then

$$\frac{Y}{Y_0} \approx \left(\frac{E}{E_0}\right)^s \tag{8}$$

Implicitly, equation (8) states that major changes in energy inputs could be accommodated over the long run with a small effect on output. However, whether the value share s is constant depends crucially upon the degree of potential substitution between energy and other factor inputs. If the substitution possibilities are quite limited, a change in energy availability will give rise to an increase in energy value share, which could exert significant impacts on the economy.[4]

Further analysis of energy-economic interactions can be based upon a two-factor model and a unique view of reality in the neoclassical approach on the basis of different elasticities of substitution, without assuming a constant value share.

Elasticity of Substitution[5]

The elasticity of substitution is a technical coefficient that measures the degree of substitutability between the two factor inputs, depending upon the state of the technology of production. It provides a dimensionless index of the relationship between the relative use of the two factor inputs and their relative marginal productivities. Therefore, it is extremely important in determining the impact of the energy sector on the rest of the economy. Formally, the elasticity of substitution, σ, is defined as

$$\sigma = \frac{d\ln(R/E)}{d\ln(F_E/F_R)} \qquad (9)$$

which determines the mix of R and E that will be used for factor inputs by the firms.

This technical coefficient ranges from zero to positive infinity. If the elasticity is close to zero, it will be extremely difficult to substitute other inputs for energy. Thus, if energy resources become scarce, the economy suffers in terms of reduced output. On the other hand, if the elasticity of substitution is a high positive number, it will be relatively easy to substitute nonenergy factors such as capital and labor for energy, and the effect on output of energy scarcity will be minimal.

The elasticity of substitution plays another important role in affecting relative income shares. For other things held constant, a rise in the R/E ratio, for example, will be associated with a rise (constancy) or a decline in nonenergy's relative income share (and therefore a fall, constancy, or rise in energy's relative share), depending upon the elasticity of substitution which is either greater than (equal to) or less than unity. Similarly, a decline in the R/E ratio will have the opposite effects on relative income shares under the same conditions.

Assuming the aggregate production function has a constant elasticity of substitution (i.e., excluding three special cases such as $\sigma = 0, 1, \infty$), equation (1) becomes

$$Y^{\frac{\sigma-1}{\sigma}} = aE^{\frac{\sigma-1}{\sigma}} + bR^{\frac{\sigma-1}{\sigma}} \qquad (10)$$

where a and b are the parameters specifying the distributive shares of the output Y among the factors E and R, respectively.

For given prices, the equilibrium mix of factor inputs must satisfy the first-order optimality condition in (5) above (i.e., differentiate equation [10] with respect to E), we obtain[6]

$$P_Y \cdot \left(\frac{\partial Y}{\partial E}\right) = P_Y \cdot a \cdot \left(\frac{Y}{E}\right)^{\frac{1}{\sigma}} = P_E \qquad (11)$$

where P_Y is the unit price of output.

At constant prices, equation (11) implies that the ratio E/Y will be approximately a constant energy/GNP ratio. From equation (11), the demand for energy E can be written as

$$E = Ya^{\sigma}\left(\frac{P_E}{P_Y}\right)^{-\sigma} \qquad (12)$$

which represents energy demand as a function of output and prices. Thus, if Y is approximately independent of energy demand, the price elasticity of energy demand is likely to remain nearly constant and is virtually identical to the elasticity of substitution.

The importance of the elasticity-of-substitution parameter can be interpreted in the context of value shares. Analogous to the discussion of the previous section, equation (7) can be restated as

$$s = \frac{P_E E}{P_Y Y} = a^\sigma \left(\frac{P_E}{P_Y}\right)^{1-\sigma} \tag{13}$$

which shows that the value share of energy, s, is a function of the real price of energy relative to the price of output. If the elasticity of substitution, σ, is one, the value share is constant and equal to the distributive share of the output in the energy factor input E. If $\sigma = 0$, the value share is equal to the real price of energy. However, if σ is less than one but greater than zero, an increasing real price of energy implies an increasing value share associated with a reduced availability of energy. Within this range, the smaller the values of σ, the larger will the value share s be and reductions in energy input will produce large reduction in GNP.

In any case, the concept of elasticity of substitution is useful in analyzing the response of firms in the nonenergy sector of the economy to a rise in energy price and in identifying an important element of the energy-economic interactions. It, however, does not consider the time rate at which substitution occurs, but only the equilibrium mix of factor inputs after all transients involved in changing the production process have passed. In fact, most neoclassical models implicitly assume instantaneous substitution processes. This is clearly a drawback when one is interested in the time rate of the adjustment process of the factor mix.[7]

Moreover, unlike labor factor inputs, it may not be reasonable, as a first approximation, to assume that capital inputs are undiminished by the changed availability of energy factor inputs, even though their productivity declines. Reduced energy inputs will lower the marginal productivity of capital, which, in turn, may depress the rate of saving and the level of investment and will further reduce the level of output and GNP. To such extent, such indirect effects may be the most important component of the economic impact of energy scarcity.[8]

Having observed the energy-economic interactions under the rather specialized assumption of a two-factor production function, we may now proceed to generalize these results to a three-factor linear homogeneous production function. All standard neoclassical assumptions, such as fully variable factor prices, competitive factor and product markets, and the sufficiency of investment to match full-employment saving, are retained.

In the previous analysis, we have examined relevant features of energy-economic interactions by way of introduction to the value share concept and the two-factor production function. It may be useful to examine some relevant properties of linear homogeneous production functions in general prior to coming to grips with the important elements of energy-economic interactions.

Higher Energy Costs: The Long Run and the Short Run[9]

Within the neoclassical framework, a simple model of aggregate supply and resource markets, with an aggregate, three-factor linear-homogeneous production function, can be described as follows:

Aggregate Linear Homogeneous Production Function:	$Y = F(K, L, E)$
First-Order Conditions for Profit Maximization:	$P_L = F_L$ $P_K = F_K$ $P_E = F_E$
Short-Run Resource Supply Assumptions:	$L = L^0$ $K = K^0$ $P_E = P^0_E$
Long-Run Resource Supply Assumptions:	$L = L^0$ $P_K = P^0$ $P_E = P^0_E$

where Y = output P_L = wage of labor relative to the price of output
       L = labor P_E = price of energy relative to the price of output
       E = energy P_K = rental price of capital relative to the price of output
       K = capital

The short run is characterized by fixed supplies of capital and labor resources (K^0, L^0) and by a given relative price of energy resource, P^0_E, determined in the world market. In the long run, however, the supply of capital is variable as firms can increase or decrease the capital stock depending upon their incentives. The relative price of capital, P_K, is assumed to be given in the long run. The long-run supply of labor and relative price of energy are assumed to be the same as the short run (L^0, P^0_E).

The profit-maximizing choice of an input is determined by equating the marginal cost of the resource to the value of its marginal product, $F_i = P_i$, where $F_i = (\partial Y / \partial i)$ is the marginal productivity of resource i, i = K, L, E. By differentiating each system of equations in the model, the short-run and long-run response to a rise in the relative price of energy may be found to be those indicated below:

	Short Run	**Long Run**
Output	$\dfrac{dY}{dP_E} = \dfrac{F_E}{F_{EE}} < 0$	$\dfrac{-(F_E F_{KK} - F_K F_{KE})}{|D|} < 0$
Labor Employment	$\dfrac{dL}{dP_E} = 0$	0
Capital Employment	$\dfrac{dK}{dP_E} = 0$	$\dfrac{F_{KE}}{|D|} < 0$
Energy Employment	$\dfrac{dE}{dP_E} = \dfrac{1}{F_{EE}} < 0$	$\dfrac{-F_{KK}}{|D|} < 0$
Relative Price of Labor	$\dfrac{dP_L}{dP_E} = \dfrac{F_{LE}}{F_{EE}} < 0$	$\dfrac{(F_{LK}F_{KE} - F_{KK}F_{LE})}{|D|} < 0$
Relative Price of Captial Services	$\dfrac{dP_K}{dP_E} = \dfrac{F_{KE}}{F_{EE}} < 0$	0

where the signs of F_{LL}, F_{KK} and F_{EE} are assumed to be negative, indicating the diminishing returns to the employment of each resource, F_{KE} and F_{LE} are positive, and $|D| = -(F_{KK}F_{EE} - F^2_{KE}) < 0$.

The sign of F_{ij}, i, j = K, L, E, indicates the effect of an increase in the usage of factor j on the marginal productivity of a resource i. If F_{ij} is positive, utilization of more of one resource in the production process is generally responsible for increases in marginal productivity of the other resources. Hence, in the short run, the effect on output of a rise in the relative price of energy rests primarily upon the assumptions of a positive marginal productivity of energy and diminishing returns to the utilization of energy resources, given the supply of capital and labor. If the marginal productivity of capital and labor is augmented by energy resources, the real cost of capital and labor must fall to maintain their usage. However, if the marginal productivity of capital and labor is not affected by energy resource utilization, shifts in demand for capital and labor will not occur. The demand price of the factor would rise, only if the marginal productivity of labor or capital decreases as a result of increases in energy usage.[10]

In contrast, in the long run, given that $F_{KE} > 0$, not only are output and energy usage reduced as in the short run, the employment of capital is also reduced. This result arises from a temporary reduction in investment to achieve the smaller amount of capital desired, as capital becomes more expensive in relation to the productivity of such goods.[11] A comparison of the long-run and the short-run effects can be made by subtracting the long-run effect from the short-run effect. These results are:

Output
$$\frac{F_{KE}(F_E F_{KE} - F_K F_{EE})}{F_{EE}\,|D|} > 0$$

Capital Employment	$\dfrac{F_{KE}}{|D|} < 0$
Energy Employment	$\dfrac{-F^2_{KE}}{F_{EE}|D|} > 0$
Relative Price of Labor	$\dfrac{F_{KE}(F_{LE}F_{KE} - F_{EE}F_{LK})}{F_{EE}|D|} > 0$

indicating that the long-run effect on output of the rise in the relative cost of energy, the long-run reduction in energy usage, and the decline in the real wage rate of labor are all larger than in the short run. The reduction of capital employment through a temporary reduction in investment will result in the increased size of the long-run effects.

The Problem of Neoclassical Equilibrium Growth

Discussion in the previous section shows that there is one feature common to neoclassical growth equilibrium, both the presence and absence of technical change. By way of shedding further light, we reexamine the conditions of the existence and stability of equilibrium growth with the focus of the prerequisites of the equilibrium energy-output ratio.

To begin with, let the aggregate production function be

$$Y(t) = F[K(t), L(t), E(t), A(t)] \qquad (14)$$

where $Y(t)$ denotes gross output, $K(t)$ capital input, $L(t)$ labor input, $E(t)$ energy factor input, and $A(t)$ the technology index.

If we assume that the function F is linear homogeneous in its arguments $K(t)$, $L(t)$, and $E(t)$ at each level of the technology index, $A(t)$, then

$$1 = f[v(t), u(t), e(t), A(t)] \qquad (15)$$

where

$$v(t) = K(t)/Y(t)$$
$$u(t) = L(t)/Y(t)$$
$$e(t) = E(t)/Y(t)$$

Equation (15) may be interpreted as showing the different values of the unit isoquant for different values of A. We further assume that F_A (and $f_A) > 0$, where $F_A = \partial F/\partial A$, $f_A = \partial f/\partial A$, and

$$F[K(t), 0, E(t), A(t)] = F[0, L(t), E(t), A(t)]$$
$$= F[K(t), L(t), 0, A(t)]$$
$$= 0$$

Euler's theorem states that

$$Y = F_K K + F_L L + F_E E \tag{16}$$

or
$$1 = vF_K + uF_L + eF_E \quad \text{for all A} \tag{17}$$

where $F_X = (\partial Y/\partial X)$, $X = K, L, E$

Equation (17) states that the relative income shares of capital (vF_K), labor (uF_L), and energy (eF_E) add up to unity. Since $v = K/Y$, $u = L/Y$, and $e = E/Y$, we have, by logarithmic differentiation with respect to time, $\dot{X} = dX/dt$

$$\frac{\dot{v}}{v} = \frac{\dot{K}}{K} - \frac{\dot{Y}}{Y}$$

$$\frac{\dot{u}}{u} = \frac{\dot{L}}{L} - \frac{\dot{Y}}{Y}$$

$$\frac{\dot{e}}{e} = \frac{\dot{E}}{E} - \frac{\dot{Y}}{Y}$$

whence

$$\frac{\dot{e}}{e} - \frac{\dot{v}}{v} - \frac{\dot{u}}{u} = \frac{\dot{E}}{E} - \frac{\dot{K}}{K} - \frac{\dot{L}}{L} + \frac{\dot{Y}}{Y}$$

or

$$\frac{\dot{e}}{e} - \frac{\dot{v}}{v} - \frac{\dot{u}}{u} = \left(\frac{\dot{E}}{E} - \frac{\dot{L}}{L}\right) - \left(\frac{\dot{K}}{K} - \frac{\dot{Y}}{Y}\right) \tag{18}$$

If $\dot{e} = 0$, equation (18) becomes

$$-\frac{\dot{v}}{v} - \frac{\dot{u}}{u} = -\left(\frac{\dot{K}}{K} - \frac{\dot{Y}}{Y}\right) + \left(\frac{\dot{E}}{E} - \frac{\dot{L}}{L}\right) \tag{19}$$

That is, the equilibrium growth rate of output is given by

$$\frac{\dot{v}}{v} = -\left(\frac{\dot{E}}{E} - \frac{\dot{K}}{K}\right) \qquad \frac{\dot{u}}{u} = -\left(\frac{\dot{E}}{E} - \frac{\dot{L}}{L}\right) \tag{20}$$

The general equilibrium condition for energy-output ratio can be derived by differentiating (14) with respect to time, t.

$$\frac{\dot{Y}}{Y} = \frac{KF_K}{Y}\frac{\dot{K}}{K} + \frac{LF_L}{Y}\frac{\dot{L}}{L} + \frac{EF_E}{Y}\frac{\dot{E}}{E} + \frac{AF_A}{Y}\frac{\dot{A}}{A} \tag{21}$$

or

$$\frac{\dot{Y}}{Y} = vF_K \frac{\dot{K}}{K} + uF_L \frac{\dot{L}}{L} + eF_E \frac{\dot{E}}{E} + F_A \frac{\dot{A}}{Y} \qquad (22)$$

Then

$$\frac{\dot{e}}{e} = vF_K \left(\frac{\dot{E}}{E} - \frac{\dot{K}}{K}\right) - uF_L \left(\frac{\dot{E}}{E} - \frac{\dot{L}}{L}\right) - F_A \frac{\dot{A}}{Y} \qquad (23)$$

That is,

$$\dot{e} = -eF_K [\dot{v} + u(F_L/F_K) + F_A \dot{A}/KF_K)v] \qquad (24)$$

Given the time paths of labor supply, energy factor, capital investment, and technology, the differential equation (24) determines the time path of the energy-output ratio, e, and hence the time paths of energy and output that must be followed as a condition of full employment of capital and labor.

Equation (24) provides us with general statements of the problem of neoclassical equilibrium growth, given the energy factor variable. It implies that the input factors of energy and capital in the production process are complementary in the long run and their relationship is rigid in the short run and changes slowly over time as responses to rising energy costs. As energy becomes scarce and costly, less expensive resources are substituted for the energy input in optimizing production process.

Whether capital and energy are substitutes or complements is a continuing controversy, nonetheless. Fortunately, the issue does not affect the result of the energy adjustment, but it is important for such questions as short-run output supply effects and changes in the amount of energy use per unit of capital.

DIFFERENT MODELING APPROACHES

Different models with different scenarios provide information that can be extremely helpful in answering questions about our energy future, and especially in attempting to formulate energy policy, though they aren't predictions of what will happen. It, therefore, may be useful to consider, briefly, the major studies that attempt to analyze the energy interactions and predict the impact of rising energy costs on economic growth. A comparison of projections on U.S. energy consumption and energy/GNP ratios obtained by these studies are provided in Tables 7.1 and 7.2.

The Hudson-Jorgenson Study

The Hudson-Jorgenson study[12] employs an extremely sophisticated macroeconometric model of U.S. energy growth, based on nine production sectors, to

Table 7.1
Comparison of Recent U.S. Energy Consumption Projections (quads)

Source	1980	1985	1990	2000	2010	2020	2025	2030
SFAS/RFF, Base Case[1]								
Gross	86.6	93.0	100.1	114.2	138.9		171.2	
Net	68.2	70.5	75.4	85.2	105.2		128.4	
Brookhaven DESOM-LITM[2]								
Base Case, Gross		100.0	115.3	156.2				
Energy Tax Case, Gross		93.5	97.8	117.9				
Ford-Energy Policy Project (EPP)[3]								
Historical Growth, Gross		116.1		186.7				
Technical Fix, Gross		91.3		124.0				
FEA Project Independence Blueprint[4]								
$13 a barrel, oil								
Gross		91.3	102.8					
Net		69.6	78.0					
Institute for Energy Analysis (IEA)[5]								
Gross								
Low Case		82.1		101.4	118.3			
High Case		88.0		125.9	158.8			
ETA-MACRO[6]								
Base Case		84.9	98.0	126.2	158.1	192.3		232.0
Base Case but No Nuclear		84.1	96.7	118.1	134.4	165.4		198.5
ECONOMY1-Kannan[7]								
Low Price Case		72.5		84.6		52.6		
High Price Case		72.0		75.7		92.0		
Accelerated-Conservation		66.0		71.4		77.2		

128

Sources: (1) Ronald G. Ridker and William D. Watson, *To Choose a Future* (Baltimore & London: The Johns Hopkins University Press published for Resources for the Future, 1980); (2) Brookhaven National Laboratory and Data Resources, Inc., *The Relationship of Energy Growth to Economic Growth under Alternative Energy Policies.* Report prepared for the U.S. Energy Research and Development Administration (Washington, D.C.: U.S. Government Printing Office, 1976); (3) Ford Foundation, *A Time to Choose.* Final Report of the Ford Foundation Energy Policy Project (Cambridge, Mass.: Ballinger, 1974); (4) U.S. Federal Energy Administration, *Project Independence Blueprint.* (Washington, D.C.: U.S. Government Printing Office, 1977), Appendix A1, pp. 37 and 38; (5) Institute for Energy Analysis, *Economic and Environmental Implications of a U.S. Nuclear Moratorium, 1985–2010* (Oak Ridge, Tennessee, IEA-Oak Ridge Associated Univerities, 1976); (6) Alan S. Manne, "A Model of Energy-Economy Interaction," in Charles J. Hitch, ed., *Modeling Energy-Economy Interaction: Five Approaches* (Washington, D.C.: Resources for the Future, 1977), pp. 40–41; (7) Narasimhan P. Kannan, *Energy, Economic Growth and Equity in the United States* (New York: Praeger, 1979), p. 174, table 5.3.

Table 7.2
Comparison of Recent Projections on U.S. Energy/GNP Ratio (10^3 Btu/1971 U.S.$)

Source	1980	1985	1990	2000	2010	2020	2025	2030
SEAS/RFF, Base Case[1]								
Gross	62.0	59.0	55.0	47.0	44.0		40.0	
Net	49.0	45.0	41.0	36.0	34.0		31.0	
Brookhaven DESOM-LITM[2]								
Base Case, Gross		50.0		44.0				
Energy Tax Case, Gross		49.0		39.0				
Ford-Energy Policy Project (EPP)[3]								
Historical Growth, Gross		56.0		55.0				
Technical Fix, Gross		47.0		36.0				
FEA Project Independence Blueprint[4]								
$13 a barrel, oil								
Gross		55.0	54.0					
Net		42.0	41.0					
Institute for Energy Analysis (IEA)[5]								
Gross								
Low Case		51.0		42.0	38.0			
High Case		54.0		50.0	47.0			
ECONOMY1-Kannan[6]								
Low Case		37.4		36.6		24.7		
High Case		38.3		29.1		27.9		
Accelerated-Conservation		35.7		29.3		24.9		

Sources: (1) Ronald G. Ridker and William D. Watson, *To Choose a Future* (Baltimore & London: The Johns Hopkins University Press published for Resources for the Future, 1980); (2) Brookhaven National Laboratory and Data Resources, Inc., *The Relationship of Energy Growth to Economic Growth under Alternative Energy Policies.* Report prepared for the U.S. Energy Research and Development Administration (Washington, D.C.: U.S. Government Printing Office, 1976); (3) Ford Foundation, *A Time to Choose.* Final Report of the Ford Foundation Energy Policy Project (Cambridge, Mass.: Ballinger, 1974); (4) U.S. Federal Energy Administration, *Project Independence Blueprint.* (Washington, D.C.: U.S. Government Printing Office, 1977), Appendix A1, pp. 37 and 38; (5) Institute for Energy Analysis, *Economic and Environmental Implications of a U.S. Nuclear Moratorium, 1985–2010* (Oak Ridge, Tennessee, IEA-Oak Ridge Associated Universities, 1976); (6) Computed by the author based on projected GNP and net energy demand provided in Narasimhan P. Kannan, *Energy, Economic Growth and Equity in the United States* (New York: Praeger, 1979), p. 174, table 5.3.

analyze the energy-economic interactions. The model is a dynamic, two-sector neoclassical model with capital goods and consumption goods as the two basic segments and is linked to an interindustry input-output model in which the technical coefficients were assumed responsive to price changes. It is designed to assess the impact on the outputs and prices of nine major nonenergy sectors of the U.S. economy of alternate energy conservation measures such as energy taxes and technical-fix policies.

Despite its complexity, the model is based on the simple neoclassical assumptions of perfect competition and profit and utility maximization. It is used by the authors to generate equilibrium prices of capital and labor services, the volume of gross private domestic investment, and the value of personal consumption expenditures, which, in turn, are used as inputs to the interindustry model.

The interindustry model consists of nine major sectors, five of which represent the energy sectors (coal mining, crude petroleum and natural gas, petroleum refining, electric utilities, and gas utilities) and the rest represent the four nonenergy sectors (agriculture, nonfuel mining, and construction; manufacturing, excluding petroleum refining; transportation; communications, trade, and services). These nine sectors are set in an input-output framework and the coefficients of the input-output matrix are determined endogenously as a function of four input factor prices: the price of capital services, the price of labor services, the price of energy (both domestic and imports), and the price of nonenergy materials.

The gross private investment generated as an output of the macroeconomic growth model is allocated exogenously among the nine sectors of the interindustry input-output model. Most of these exogenous variables are assumed to continue to be in historical proportions. Inexplicably, the interactive model does not address either the institutional constraints involved in the substitution of labor for energy or the issue of domestic oil and gas production; that is, the model does not explicitly include a resource sector.

Even so, the Hudson-Jorgenson model is by far the most elaborate of the energy models in the literature today. It replicates each of the components of the overall transactions—purchases of primary inputs, sales of goods and services between sectors, formation of product prices, and purchase of output by final users. These aspects of economic activity are brought into consistency by means of simulated market processes. The decision functions that represent the behavior of the household and production sectors are based on the neoclassical assumptions of profit and utility maximization. To the extent that all household and production decision units react to the same set of prices and that prices and quantities adjust so that all markets are cleared and each production sector covers its costs, the heart of the model lies in a series of submodels of production behavior, one for each of the nine domestic producing sectors. This set of production relationships provides the basic information used to determine relative output prices and the corresponding set of input pattern.[13]

The fundamental advantage of the Hudson-Jorgenson approach is that, rather than viewing energy in isolation, it views energy as one of the many interacting parts that make up the economic system. This perspective permits the systematic analysis of all the factors that influence energy on both demand and supply sides and, equally important, it permits the explicit linkage of energy developments to those variables—such as employment, income, and consumption—that are the ultimate ends to which energy use is only a means.

Specifically, the model incorporates the influence of fuel prices on the level and composition of energy use; the effects of the level and pattern of nonenergy activity on energy use; and the reverse linkage of energy prices and supplies to nonenergy price input, output, and consumption patterns. These interrelationships, according to the authors, Hudson and Jorgenson, are "critical" for both forecasting and policy purposes.[14]

The Hudson-Jorgenson model, however, suffers from two major shortcomings. First, there is no feedback from the interindustry model to the macroeconomic growth model. Thus, the model could not be consistently used to assess the impact on economic growth of alternate energy availability or price scenarios. Second, in the interindustry model the substitutions among factors are assumed to occur with no time lags. Implicitly, the Hudson-Jorgenson model assumes that, in the future, other factors can be substituted for energy with the same ease with which energy was substituted for other factors during the three decades prior to the oil embargo in 1973. These shortcomings and unduly optimistic assumptions have led the authors to reach a set of highly optimistic conclusions regarding the potential for substitution of other factors for energy in the future.[15]

As the authors state succinctly, "the flexibility of the economy in adapting to changing resource availabilities, and the power of the price system in securing this adaptation, mean that substantial reductions in energy use can be achieved without major economic cost."[16] The implication is that significant reductions in energy consumption could be realized through a tax on energy use, without loss in real income. In fact, this implication is the single major conclusion of the study.

The Ford Foundation Energy Policy Project (EPP)

The Ford Foundation Energy Policy Project (EPP)[17] study uses the Hudson-Jorgenson model to analyze the relationships between energy consumption and economic growth. In this study, however, energy is linked to economic growth in another way—the share of energy-related sectors in total output and employment.

Different Growth Patterns

In the analysis of energy choices, the EPP study has constructed three different versions of possible energy futures for the United States through the year

2000. These three alternate futures, or scenarios, are based upon differing assumptions about growth in energy use. In many ways, they are quite dissimilar, but each scenario is consistent with what they knew about physical resources and economic effects.

The three scenarios, or growth patterns, are: "Historical Growth," where past energy supply and demand patterns are assumed to continue into the future; "Technical Fix Growth," where energy conservation practices and known energy-saving technologies are incorporated into production and consumption patterns to the extent possible within existing life-styles and economic organization; and "Zero Energy Growth (ZEG)," where, in addition to the technical fix measures, changes in life-styles and economic structure are introduced in order to move toward a situation of constant per capita energy consumption. Simulations of economic growth paths under each of these three scenarios were conducted by Edward A. Hudson and Dale W. Jorgenson using the DRI energy model. A report of these simulations was provided in Appendix F of *A Time to Choose.*[18]

The scenarios are offered not as predictions, but as illustrations to help test and compare the consequences of different policy choices. The most important similarity among these scenarios is that all are based on full employment and steady growth in gross national product and personal incomes. The scenarios of lower energy growth provide major savings in energy with small differences in the GNP from historical growth trends.

Rationale for Energy Conservation

The study assumes that energy supplies would not be a difficult problem at any level of demand. It estimates that the energy industry itself and energy-intensive industries[19] consume about one-third of total energy use, and account for 45 percent of industrial production, 15 percent of GNP, but only 10 percent of employment. It contends that "energy growth could be reduced while growth continues in the output of goods and services—without sacrificing national economic goals," and without drastic changes in the structure of the economy, even to the extent of more than halving the rate of growth of energy inputs. The fear of the ripple effect of economic disruption and lost jobs, if we do not continue high rates of energy growth, therefore, is unfounded.

These contentions led the EPP study to conclude that the future rate of growth in the GNP is not tied to energy growth rates and that "energy conservation should be a central element of any sensible energy policy." Such a conservation-oriented energy policy, according to the study, will provide benefits in every major area of concern—avoiding shortages, protecting the environment, avoiding problems with other nations, and keeping real social costs as low as possible.

The central message is that the United States could and should get along with less energy than historic patterns of growth suggest, and that the transition to "Technical Fix Growth," or even to "Zero Energy Growth," can indeed be accomplished without major economic cost or upheaval. Through available conservation techniques, U.S. energy demand in the year 2000 could be reduced from an estimated 187 quads (the "high" scenario) to 124 quads (the "Technical Fix" scenario), a reduction of one-third; and such a reduction would have little effect on the growth of per capita income. More significantly, it is economically efficient, as well as technically feasible, over the period from 1975 to 2000, to cut rates of energy growth at least in half.[20]

The Project Independence Blueprint (PIB) Study

The Project Independence Blueprint (PIB) study[21] used an economic-impact forecasting methodology composed of two linked models: a price-sensitive input-output table to relate energy prices to other industrial prices and to provide sectoral output predictions; and a long-run macroeconomic forecasting model to link production activity to income, the capital market, and the labor market.

The PIB study examined the implications for growth of an accelerated supply strategy, of demand conservation, and of variations in the world oil price. It concluded that accelerated supply would have different short- and long-run effects and that conservation would reduce the demand for energy, without adverse effects on real economic growth and employment. In the short run, the net impact of an accelerated supply strategy would depend on the state of the economy. In an overheated economy, it could raise inflation with no adverse effects on unemployment. If the economy was sluggish, on the other hand, it would reduce unemployment and also lower inflation via relieving shortages. In the long run, accelerated supply would raise the growth rate to the extent that investment in energy supply was more productive than average investment elsewhere in the economy.[22]

Furthermore, the PIB study holds that high world oil prices would stimulate investment in energy production, but this would be more than offset by dampening effects of high fuel prices on growth elsewhere in the economy. Therefore, the choice of energy policies will not have detrimental effects on the GNP, according to the PIB study. It, however, admitted that there are other more serious economic and social impacts that are related to the balance of payments, inflation, regional growth, housing, and income distribution.

Significantly, both the Project Independence Blueprint study and the Ford Foundation Energy Policy Project study came up with compatible results: Reductions in energy consumption due to energy conservation would have non-negligible effects on economic growth, but the costs would be small enough to warrant the conclusion that a slowing down in the growth rate of energy consumption is compatible with the maintenance of economy growth.

The Institute for Energy Analysis (IEA) Study

The initial IEA study[23] of 1976 addressed the issue of potential decline in national factor productivity due to a decline in the productivity in the energy sector. The authors presented a simple scheme through which the magnitude of decline in aggregate productivity can be computed, given a certain decline in energy sector productivity.

This initial study assumes that the labor force, productivity, energy costs, savings rate, and depreciation rate are exogenous variables. It further assumes that the influence of the energy sector on aggregate productivity is a function of the energy sector's factor share of national product, and that the historical factor share of the energy sector is 1.5 percent of the gross national product. With these assumptions, the authors contended that even if energy costs triple over the next three decades, the impact on economic growth would be minimal, since the energy sector's share of output would still only be 4.5 percent of total output. This conclusion, however, is highly sensitive to the assumption of share values and does not consider the substitution processes by which energy demand could be reduced.

Since the IEA released its initial report on U.S. energy and economic growth in 1976, a number of supplementary reports have been published. These reports incorporated a more general functional form and gave more detailed attention to demographic aspects of the problem. To analyze the relation between energy and economic well-being, for example, Edward L. Allen (1979)[24] uses the methods which are much closer to those used in the early study of Schurr et al. than they are to, say, the very elaborate econometric modeling of the Project Independence Blueprint (PIB) study. The key finding of this new IEA study is that energy demand for the 1975–2000 period is likely to grow more slowly than in the past. The study also finds that the ratio is energy use to the GNP will be improved, and that the demand for electricity is likely to rise faster than the total demand for energy.[25]

In terms of total energy requirements needed to sustain economic growth and employment, the totals given in the low-scenario (101 quads by 2000) obtained by this study are not very different from those given in the "Zero Energy Growth" scenario of the Ford Foundation Energy Policy Project study. However, the low projection was obtained not by imposing changes in life-style as was the case in the Ford Foundation study, but by calculating technically feasible potential of energy requirements per unit of output and by using lower rates of future economic growth than those used in the Ford Foundation study.[26]

Although the IEA approach to energy-demand modeling is basically noneconometric, there are imbedded in the approach a set of implicit price-quantity relationships. These relationships between prices and energy demands are based not on the unwavering assumption that the future will be identical to the past, but on the assumption that there is a reasonable historical precedent for the conservation scenarios developed in this report.

In sum, one of the major conclusions of the IEA studies is that, although there is a serious energy problem, it can be eased by conservation efforts and by the stimulation of new sources of energy supply. However, the study, according to the author, has not been able to identify an inevitable supply/demand "crunch" that will produce economic disruption and record high unemployment in this century.[27]

The Energy Modeling Forum (EMF) Study

The Energy Modeling Forum (EMF) study[28] by Hogan and Manne employs the comparative statics approach to study the sensitivity of the equilibrium value of the gross national product to a change in the availability of energy in the year 2010. It focuses on the criticality of the elasticity-of-substitution parameter between energy and other inputs to production. The authors of the study first use a static production function model and then a consumer surplus model and arrive at the same conclusions.

For simplicity, the study assumes that the economy is represented in terms of just two inputs—energy and all other nonenergy factors of production lumped together. In this analysis, the authors assume a base case consisting of a set of equilibrium values of energy consumption, price of energy, and gross national product at a point in the future. They compute the change in the assumed gross national product for a given change in energy consumption for various values of the elasticity of substitution. Using this method, the authors demonstrate that the elasticity-of-substitution parameter is highly sensitive in determining the future course of the economy and that accurate measurement of this parameter is a matter of great importance.

In other words, the study holds that the future level of the gross national product is dependent on the value of the elasticity-of-substitution parameter. For small changes in energy availability, there need not be a proportional impact upon the economy as a whole; and for large reductions in the availability of energy, there need not be a constant value share. If the value share rises, the GNP effects may become more pronounced.

Using a one-sector model to examine the Btu/GNP ratio as a function of the elasticity of substitution, the study finds that if the elasticity is 0.3 or higher, there is little effect over the range investigated. However, as the elasticity decreases below 0.3, the effect grows large in a nonlinear fashion. If energy is curtailed only slightly (e.g., from 220 to 190 quads), GNP will be curtailed 0.6 percent or less, whatever the elasticity of substitution is, as long as it is 0.1 or larger.

As the extent of curtailment grows, however, the elasticity of substitution becomes progressively more important. This is especially true when energy use is reduced from 220 to 70 quads; even an elasticity of 0.3 will result in a 14.3 percent reduction in GNP. The implication is that the size of the effect is significant for the economy-economic interface. It depends on both the elasticity of substitution and the extent to which energy is curtailed. If there is no substitution, reductions in energy use produce corresponding reductions in economic activity. But if the higher estimates of the elasticity of energy demand are accepted, it follows that major changes in energy utilization can be achieved without corresponding changes in total economic activity.

Despite the limited scope of the EMF study, the authors conclude that the energy sector may not adversely affect future economic growth. They reach this conclusion by suggesting that the elasticity of substitution between energy and other input factors is fairly high. The EMF study, however, does not report any empirical verification of the claim of the authors. In particular, though the study uses a static equilibrium analysis of the energy-economy interaction, it does not address the issues of time lags involved in the factor substitution process.

ETA-MACRO Model

The ETA-MACRO[29] is a general equilibrium model designed to estimate the extent of a two-way linkage between the energy sector and the balance of the U.S. economy. It is a single integrated model that incorporates the following principal features:

1. the impending exhaustion of petroleum resources and a transition to new supply technologies over the next 20–50 years;
2. price-induced conservation with the possibility of substituting other economic inputs in place of energy; and
3. the effects of rising energy costs on the accumulation of physical capital in future time periods.

The model focuses on just one specific policy option which bans the introduction of additional civilian nuclear power plants in the United States. Under the assumptions of the base-case scenario, it argues that a "no nuclear" policy would have negligible macroeconomic impacts prior to the year 2000, but that it could lead to an annual loss on the order of $100 billion by the year 2000. This is a large absolute number of dollars, but would still be a small percentage (about 3%) of the GNP. However, like most other models, ETA-MACRO will lead to very different quantitative results, depending upon the assumptions of the specific numerical input.

While small and comparatively simple, the ETA-MACRO is nonetheless an elegant model capable of providing many insights to the issues of the energy–GNP feedback. Even when the energy–GNP feedback is neglected, a model such as ETA-MACRO produces a much more sophisticated picture of the role of energy supply.

Brookhaven DESOM–LITM Model

The Brookhaven DESOM–LITM[30] developed by Behling, Marcuse, Lukachinski, and Dullienis is a more imaginative and complicated type of model which focuses on the end-use demands for energy and attempts to find the cheapest way of meeting them. It offers only limited ability to substitute other inputs for energy, but gives a detailed picture of the appropriate fuel mix for a given level of end-use demands. In this study, the DESOM model is linked to the LITM model of Data Resources, Inc., which, in turn, models the substitution that occurs between energy, capital, labor, and four types of materials as a result of changes in relative input prices.

The DESOM allows the micro-model to predominate with the macro-model which determines investment and GNP. The macro-model is run through the year 2000 and provides forecasts to the year 2020 using simulations with various assumptions. However, there are many assumptions that are required to produce a forecast, and so there is necessarily an idiosyncratic element in each run due to the actual person making it. Another aspect of the model is that a small macro-model of four sectors and six energy sectors is used to drive a larger interindustry model, which in turn determines the many end-use demands in DESOM. There is necessarily a large component of arbitrariness in this process, since assumptions have to be made in the disaggregation.[31]

The authors have used their model to address a large number of questions. The static part of the model provides an excellent method for finding the cheapest way of meeting a set of detailed end-use demands.

SEAS/RFF System

The Strategic Environmental Assessment System/Resources for the Future (SEAS/RFF)[32] developed by Ridker, Watson, and Shapanka is a series of interdependent models developed for assessing future economic, resource, and environmental consequences for the United States of alternate assumptions about population growth, economic growth, technological changes, environmental policy, prices and supply of energy, and minerals policy. Structurally, the system consists of a number of special purpose models linked to INFORUM, the University of Maryland's 185-sector, dynamic, macroeconomic-cum-input-output model of the U.S. economy.

The SEAS/RFF system focuses primarily on environmental aspects of the problem. It uses the input-output framework to incorporate the many aspects of energy, the economy, and the environment. It also includes other components that involve physical and monetary variables associated with energy, nonfuel minerals, transportation, and the environment at both the national and regional levels.

Ridker, Watson, and Shapanka used the SEAS/RFF system to develop U.S. national economic forecasts through 2025 based on an exogenously specified set of demographic, macroeconomic, energy price, environmental policy, and resource policy assumptions. The scenarios were so chosen as to explore the way the economy might behave in cases where energy requirements are not easily satisfied. For this purpose, four basic scenarios were developed. Two involve cases that incorporate substantial increases in energy prices but in which capacity to satisfy demands at those prices is relatively unconstrained. The other two add stringent restrictions on the use of coal, oil shale, imported oil, and nuclear power, the last being phased out completely by the year 2010. These two assume that the price for new energy systems would be substantially higher than in the first two scenarios. The runs for each scenario differ only with respect to the degree to which the economy can substitute other inputs for energy, assuming a long-run price elasticity of energy demand of -0.25 for the low-substitution scenarios and -0.75 for the high-substitution scenarios.

SEAS/RFF projections of total demand are shown in Tables 7.1 and 7.2. In general, they are lower than most others, but the difference is explained largely by differences in GNP projections rather than in energy/output ratios, at least before the year 2000.

Since the focus of the SEAS/RFF system is the environment, it produces estimates of environmental quality for each year. Using some crude, but not implausible techniques, Ridker, Watson, and Shapanka evaluate the degradation in environmental quality in monetary terms and then calculate the sum of abatement costs and environmental degradation, as well as the losses in productivity due to high energy prices or constraints in supply. They are able to calculate consumption per capita corrected for environmental quality and for the labor productivity losses. According to their calculation, in constant dollars, per capita consumption will more than double between 1975 and 2000, and more than triple between 1975 and 2020. There are only minor variations in the index from scenario to scenario: $6090 to $6136 in 2000 and $9027 to $9557 in 2020. The implication is that consumption per capita is not sensitive to the scenarios, as long as the proportion of GNP saved and put into capital formation is not considered.

Despite its complexity with about 185 sectors, the SEAS/RFF system is quite flexible and capable of more detailed outputs. However, it requires the modeler to make numerous subjective judgments during the run of their scenarios due, in part, from the large size of the model.

ECONOMY1 Model

In contrast to the neoclassical approach described above, Kannan uses the system dynamics method to model the energy-economy interactions with emphasis placed on the disequilibrium paths, rather than the equilibrium points.[33]

Kannan proposes an alternate set of hypotheses that emphasize the dynamics of social conflict over the distributive shares in the economy with "the object of assessing the impact on the economy due to alternate possible contingencies of energy availability and energy prices in the future." With the aid of two computer simulation models, FOSSIL1 and ECONOMY1, Kannan analyzes a selected set of energy policies and their impacts on economic growth, energy imports, and shortages. The study, however, does not address short-term issues such as inflation, unemployment, and interest rate fluctuations.[34]

There are five basic assumptions that govern the behavior of the ECONOMY1 model:

—The energy sector affects the rest of the economy through shortages and/or income transfers from rising energy prices.

—Capital investment in the economy is primarily governed by the realized returns on capital.

—Substitution of capital for labor and energy is governed by the goal of firms to retain the relative share of income to capital at a desired level.

—Capital and energy are complementary factors and the relationship between capital used per year and the energy required to operate the capital is rigid in the short run and changes slowly over time as a response to rising energy prices.

—The increase in total factor productivity obeys the law of diminishing returns to cumulative investments in research and development.[35]

With these five basic assumptions, four scenarios are developed. The first scenario represents the reference case and is called the "business-as-usual" scenario, in which no new energy policies are implemented. This scenario essentially portrays the evolution of the present system with the continuation of existing regulations on energy production.

The second scenario is termed the "low-price" scenario, which represents what would be generally considered ideal by consumer groups. It is based on an assumption of altruism on the part of the OPEC countries, which use a pricing strategy that maintains the current level of oil prices into the future.

The third scenario, the "high-price" scenario, is composed of three major energy policies that are generally considered to be ideal by the energy industries in the United States: deregulation of natural gas prices, deregulation of domestic oil prices beginning in 1980, and imposition of a tariff on imported oil in order to protect domestic suppliers from the vagaries of OPEC pricing policies. It was assumed that a tariff of $9 (1975 dollars) per barrel was to be imposed on imported oil, beginning in 1980.

The fourth scenario represents the ecological viewpoint and is termed the "accelerated-conservation" scenario. In this case, the government plays an active role in promoting, through the use of tax incentives, conservation measures, and energy efficient transportation technologies. The scenario consists of three major tax policies designed to discourage energy consumption: an excise tax on oil, an excise tax on gas, and a tariff on oil imports. It is assumed that revenues from these taxes are passed on to consumers and industries in the nonenergy sector of the economy in order to subsidize the implementation of conservation technologies.

In the "accelerated-conservation" scenario, the average energy price rises until the year 2000, and then reaches a stable level. The energy shortages are less severe than in the case of the "business-as-usual" scenario, according to the study. The imports are reduced to a very low level by the year 2010. In every respect the "accelerated-conservation" case emerges as the most stable of the three scenarios in terms of improvements over the reference case or the "business-as-usual" scenario.

The most important conclusion that emerges from this study is that any conceivable solution to the domestic energy problem of high imports and the possibility of shortages points to severe distributional inequities in the future. The policy analyses of the study indicate that (a) attempts to keep energy prices low in the short term could lead to severe energy shortages in the future; (b) allowing the free market to solve the energy problem (through deregulation) could be highly successful except for its adverse effects on the distribution of income; (c) a program that would accelerate the conservation of energy would not only solve the problem of high imports and shortages but would have less adverse effect on the distribution than the other alternatives; (d) energy conservation alone may be insufficient in the long run in dealing with the distribution problem, and it may require encouragement on the part of government to use more labor and less capital in the domestic production processes; and (e) a labor-intensive economy, in which energy conservation measures are implemented, may be the best course that can be taken to reduce imports, shortages, and inequities, and further, to improve profitability for capital owners.[36]

It should be pointed out that the policy analyses presented in this study are based on a highly aggregated model of the U.S. economy. As the author states correctly, "There is definitely a need for further research in several different areas." However, from a methodological point of view, the ECONOMY1 model provides an alternative to the static neoclassical production models discussed above, and the conclusions reached using ECONOMY1 are considerably different from the ones that emerge from the neoclassical models.

In addition to the aforementioned models of energy-economy interactions, there are 14 other prominent macroeconomic models (BEA, LINK, Chase, FRB-MCM, Claremont, Hickman-Coen, MPS, St. Louis, Wharton, DRI, Hubbard-Fry, Michigan, and Mork) which have been used extensively to analyze a wide range of important economic issues. These models were originally developed to study the economy's response to monetary and fiscal policies. During the 1970s these models were expanded and revised to track the inflationary processes and to incorporate key energy variables so that they could be used to examine the impacts of energy price shocks.

Seeking to improve the usefulness of energy models, the Energy Modeling Forum Working Group conducted a comparison of the responses of these 14 macroeconomic models to supply-side shocks in the form of sudden increases or decreases in energy prices and to policies for lessening the impacts of price jumps. They examined four energy price shock scenarios (oil price increases of 50 and 20%, an oil price reduction of 20%, and an 80% increase in domestic natural gas prices) and considered five policy responses for offsetting the GNP impacts of the larger oil price increase (monetary accommodation, an income tax rate reduction, an increase in the investment tax credit for equipment, a reduction in the employers' payroll tax rate, and an oil stockpile release). Interested readers should refer to *Macroeconomic Impacts of Energy Shocks,* edited by Bert G. Kickman, Hillard G. Huntington, and James L. Sweeney (Amsterdam: North-Holland, 1987) and also *The Macroeconomic Impacts of Energy Shocks: Contributions from Participating Modelers,* edited by Bert G. Kickman and Hillard G. Huntington (The Energy Modeling Forum, Stanford University, 1987).

IMPLICATIONS

A crude correlation between energy consumption and the gross national product can be established if one examines historical data. The past records, however, are not nearly as uniform as often suggested by general comparisons of pre- and post-1973 experiences. It turns out that energy and economic activity need not be closely linked, if there is time to adjust the capital stock and motivation to do so. This means that the nation should focus on a much lower energy future than has been contemplated until recently.

While correlations between energy consumption and economic growth do not prove causality, the possibility exists that energy consumption and economic growth are inextricably intertwined. Even assuming causality, it is not clear if the direction of causality runs from energy to economic growth or vice versa. Energy consumption, however, might be uncomfortable at first, but beneficial in the long run. History tells us that energy consumption is in part a necessary condition for economic growth and in part a consequence of growth.

Various empirical analyses of the energy-economy interactions found in the literature have been based on the neoclassical static equilibrium model, which is far from adequate to represent the essentially dynamic nature of the modern industrial economies. This is due to the fact that the neoclassical model places a greater emphasis on the equilibrium state of the economy rather than the dynamic behavior modes or the adjustment paths. Although time lags can be easily introduced in the neoclassical model, the analysis will become very complex if the profit maximization and perfect competition assumptions are relaxed. To this extent, the static, neoclassical equilibrium analysis does not provide the flexibility needed to test alternate assumptions of imperfect competition and nonmaximizing behavior of economic entities. Thus, there is a need to analyze the energy-economic interactions under an alternate set of assumptions to test the sensitivity of projections of economic variables into the future.

Furthermore, different factors contributing toward energy consumption are important in different countries. Speculation on future trends is meaningful only with the consideration of an individual country's experience. In particular, the varying patterns within a sector in a particular country reflect consumer preferences in goods and services and also follow established, historical patterns of international trade which are dynamic and change when comparative advantages in production change.

Juxtaposed with these factors is the falling productivity in the energy sector which could also adversely affect economic growth by contributing to a decline in overall national productivity. However, this effect could be countered by substitution for energy of capital, labor, and other inputs. Thus, to what degree substitution may offset the effects of falling productivity becomes an important question. Examining the relationship between capital and energy leads to the debate about complementarity versus substitution and the proper measurement of the Allen partial elasticities of substitution.

NOTES

1. For an elementary treatment of the neoclassical theory, see R. G. D. Allen, *Macroeconomic Theory—A Mathematical Treatment* (New York: Macmillan, 1968). For a more general treatment, see Kazuo Sato, *Production Functions and Aggregation* (Amsterdam: North-Holland Publishing Co., 1975); L. Johansen, *Production Functions* (Amsterdam: North-Holland Publishing Co., 1972); and Edwin Burmeister and Rodney A. Dobell, *Mathematical Theories of Economic Growth* (New York: Macmillan, 1970). For an extensive survey of production and cost functions, see A. A. Walters, "Production and Cost Functions," *Econometrica* 31, (April 1963), pp. 1–66. Also see Paul A. Samuelson, *Foundations of Economic Analysis* (Cambridge, MA: Harvard University Press, 1947), Chapters 2 and 4, for a lucid presentation of the neoclassical equilibrium analysis of production.

2. Narasimhan P. Kannan, *Energy, Economic Growth, and Equity in the United States* (New York: Praeger Publishers, 1979), p. 7.

3. Allen, op. cit., pp. 44–55; see also Barry N. Siegel, *Aggregate Economics and Public Policy,* 4th ed. (Homewood, IL: D. Irwin, Inc., 1974), pp. 334–65.

4. William W. Hogan and Alan S. Manne, "Energy-Economy Interactions: The Fable of the Elephant and the Rabbit?" in Charles J. Hitgh, ed., *Modeling Energy-Economy Interactions: Five Approaches* (Washington, DC: Resources for the Future, 1977), pp. 265–66.

5. This discussion draws on Hogan and Manne, op. cit., pp. 266–73; and Kannan, op. cit., pp. 188–91.

6. Hogan and Manne, op. cit., p. 6.

7. Kannan, op. cit., pp. 8, 190.

8. William D. Nordhaus, "The Demand for Energy: An International Perspective," Cowles Foundation Discussion Paper No. 405, Yale University (September 1975); see also, Hogan and Manne, op. cit., p. 272.

9. This discussion draws on John A. Tatom, "Energy Prices and Capital Formation: 1972–1977," *Review,* Federal Reserve Bank of St. Louis (May 1979), pp. 10–11. The model specified below and the comparison of the long-run and short-run effects are taken directly from this paper.

10. Ibid., pp. 10–11.

11. Ibid.

12. Edward A. Hudson and Dale W. Jorgenson, "U.S. Energy Policy and Economic Growth, 1975–2000," *Bell Journal of Economics and Management Science* 5 (Autumn 1974), pp. 461–514.

13. Ibid., p. 509.

14. Ibid., p. 511.

15. Kannan, op. cit., pp. 13–14.

16. Hudson and Jorgenson, op. cit., p. 512.

17. The Ford Foundation, *A Time to Choose: America's Energy Future* (Cambridge, MA: Ballinger Publishing Company, 1974); for a contrary view see the comments of D. C. Burnham on p. 367. Also see, William Tavoulareas, *A Debate on a Time to Choose: A Critique* (Cambridge, MA: Ballinger Publishing Company, 1977).

18. See Hudson and Jorgenson, "Economic Analysis of Alternative Energy Growth Patterns, 1975–2000," a report to the Energy Policy Project of the Ford Foundation, in *A Time to Choose*, Appendix F, pp. 493–511.

19. Energy-intensive industries are those with energy consumption/total output ratios more than four times the national average.

20. The Ford Foundation, op. cit., pp. 45–49.

21. U.S. Federal Energy Administration, *Project Independence Blueprint (PIB) Final Task Force Report,* prepared by the Interagency Task Force on Synthetic Fuels from coal under direction of the U.S. Department of Interior, Washington, DC, U.S. Federal Energy Administration, 1974.

22. Harry W. Richardson, *Economic Aspects of the Energy Crisis* (Lexington, KY: Lexington Books/Saxon House, 1975), p. 7.

23. Edward L. Allen et al., *U.S. Energy and Economic Growth 1975–2010,* Publication ORAU/IEA-76-7, Institute for Energy Analysis, Oak Ridge Associated Universities, Oak Ridge, Tennessee (September 1976). It is a companion to the first volume, *Economic and Environmental Implications of a U.S. Nuclear Moratoriam, 1985–2010* by C. E. Whittle et al., Publication ORAU/IEA-76-4, Institute for Energy Analysis, Oak Ridge Associated Universities, Oak Ridge, Tennessee (1976). A survey of the econometric literature can be found in the IEA study, J. Edmonds, "A Guide to Price Elasticities of Demand for Energy: Studies and Methodologies," Institute for Energy Analysis, Oak Ridge Associated Universities, Oak Ridge, Tennessee (August 1978).

24. Edward L. Allen. *U.S. Energy and Economic Growth.* Institute for Energy Analysis, Oak Ridge Associated Universities, Oak Ridge, Tennessee (Cambridge, MA: The MIT Press, 1979).

25. Ibid., pp. ix–xxxii.

26. Ibid., p. 39.

27. Ibid.

28. Hogan and Manne, op. cit., pp. 247–77.

29. Alan S. Manne. "ETA-MACRO: A Model of Energy-Economy Interactions," in Charles J. Hitgh, ed., *Modeling Energy-Economy Interactions: Five Approaches* (Washington, DC: Resources for the Future, 1977), pp. 1–45.

30. David J. Behling, Jr., William Marcuse, Joan Lukachinski, and Robert Dullien. "The Long-Term Economic and Environmental Consequences of Phasing Out Nuclear Electricity," Brookhaven National Laboratory, in Charles J. Hitgh, ed., *Modeling Energy-Economy Interactions: Five Approaches* (Washington, DC: Resources for the Future, 1977), pp. 46–134.

31. Lester B. Lave. "What Have We Learned from These Scenarios?" in Charles J.

Hitgh, ed., *Modeling Energy-Economy Interactions: Five Approaches* (Washington, DC: Resources for the Future, 1977), p. 285.

32. Ronald G. Ridker, William D. Watson, Jr., and Adele Shapanka, "Economic, Energy and Environmental Consequences of Alternative Energy Regimes: An Application of the RFF/SEAS Modeling System," Resources for the Future, in Charles J. Hitgh, ed., *Modeling Energy-Economy Interactions: Five Approaches* (Washington, DC: Resources for the Future, 1977), pp. 135–98.

33. Kannan, op. cit. The basic concepts of system dynamics are presented in Jay W. Forrester, *Industrial Dynamics* (Cambridge, MA: MIT Press, 1961).

34. Kannan, op. cit., pp. 4–5.

35. These assumptions are taken directly from Kannan, op. cit.

36. Ibid.

8

Energy and Capital: Complements or Substitutes

COMPLEMENTS OR SUBSTITUTES: A CONTINUING CONTROVERSY

Whether capital and energy are substitutes or complements is the subject of a continuing controversy. From the early works of Charles W. Cobb and Paul H. Douglas (1928) and Wassily Leontief (1934, 1941) to the development of the constant elasticity of substitution and the transcendental logarithmic production functions, the literature has tacitly assumed negligible substitution possibilities between energy and materials vis-à-vis capital and labor inputs. Empirical attention has focused on the narrower issues of the homogeneity of the value-added relationship and the elasticity of substitution between capital and labor.[1] The studies since the early 1970s, however, have sought to deal with energy substitutions with other factor inputs, with specific attention directed to substitution possibilities between energy and capital. These typically involve the estimation of a transcendental logarithmic cost function using data from the manufacturing sector. The results are notably contradictory and can be categorized in two major hypotheses.

Energy-Capital Complementarity Hypothesis

Based on the analyses of time-series data on capital, labor, energy, and other nonenergy intermediate goods for U.S. manufacturing, both Berndt-Woods (1975)[2] and Hudson-Jorgenson (1974)[3] find that the cross-price elasticity of factor demand is significantly negative, indicating that energy and capital are complements and not substitutes, while energy and labor are substitutes. This implies that a rise in the energy price (as in late 1973, for example) lowers the use of capital (due to the energy-capital complementarity) and increases the use of labor (due to the energy-labor substitutability). This is often taken as being consistent with a sharp decrease in the growth rate of the U.S. labor productivity after 1973. These analyses inspired studies to empirically ascertain the energy-capital complementarity.

Similar results are obtained by Melvyn A. Fuss (1977)[4] using time-series data for capital, labor, energy and other nonenergy intermediate goods for Canadian manufacturing pooled by region, by Jan R. Magnus (1980)[5] for Dutch manufacturing, and by Paul Swaim and Gerhard Friede (1976)[6] for the West Germany industrial sector. Fuss has found that the cross-price elasticity of factor demand is essentially zero, prompting the author to conclude that, while different energy forms are good substitutes for one another, substitution possibilities between energy and conventional inputs are limited. These results, however, are to be contrasted with those of other studies.

Energy-Capital Substitutability Hypothesis

The conflicting results are found in the studies by James M. Griffin and Paul R. Gregory (1976) and Robert S. Pindyck (1977),[7] utilizing a model developed from time-series data on capital, labor and energy for manufacturing pooled by Organization for Economic Cooperation and Development (OECD) countries. Their empirical estimates show that the cross-price elasticity of factor demand is significantly positive, implying that there are substitution possibilities between energy and capital. Similarly, using cross-section data on capital, two types of labor, and three types of energy by state for eight two-digit SIC manufacturing industries, Robert Halvorson and Jay Ford (1979)[8] have found either significant energy-capital substitutability or insignificant complementarity.

All these econometric studies employ a transcendental logarithmic specification of production function[9] based on either annual or pooled cross-section time-series data not including the post-1973 energy price increases, but different estimation procedures. Many economists, especially Griffin and Gregory, have vigorously expressed the concern that energy-capital complementarity estimates based on annual time-series data actually reflect short-run variation in capacity utilization, and that the "true" long-run relationship is one of energy-capital substitutability; and therefore, pooled cross-section time-series elasticity estimates seem preferable to those based solely on annual time-series data.[10] Besides, the weight of the engineering evidence appears to support energy-capital substitutability hypothesis in production models involving more than two factor inputs.[11]

Although these econometric studies seem to be rather inconclusive, there appears to be a substantial and growing body of econometric evidence supporting the notion of Hicks-Allen energy-capital complementarity. To this extent,

of macro-policies. To some extent, these policy responses reflect different economic, political, and social constraints during the period of economic downturn.

Some economists and policymakers have suggested that the policy response to the supply shock–induced inflation of the 1970s settled too far toward the extinguishing end of the continuum and should have been closer to the accommodative end. They have contended that such policy did not properly enhance aggregate demand in a situation of supply shock–induced recession, thus making the 1973–75 episode less satisfactory than it needed to be.[4] Similarly, non-accommodating monetary policies contained the increase in nominal demand following the second oil shock in 1979, thereby squeezing the growth of real output in the short run as prices accelerated.

There are still many other competing views within realm of aggregate demand management. The "credibility hypothesis," for instance, provides an important objection to adoption of an accommodating policy. It notes that "price expectations have been successfully conditioned to a credible demand management policy." Firmly expecting persistence on the part of authorities, market participants would thereby expect the bulk of the market participants to adjust their cost behavior. To wit, a policy of accommodating supply shock–induced inflation is often perceived as a weakening in the commitment to stand firm against inflationary pressures. Hence, the adoption of such an accommodating policy might have the adverse effect of strengthening inflationary expectations and thereby hindering efforts to stimulate economic growth.[5]

In view of the unpleasant alternatives offered by demand management, many industrial nations have turned to stabilization policies other than aggregate demand management. But such policies, at least those of the wage-price control variety, had proved disappointing.

Indeed, the major schools of macroeconomic thought have been competing in providing a complete treatment of the supply shocks, but there has not been consensus among macroeconomists regarding the right policy mix for sustained recovery and stabilization. For the Keynesians, macroeconomic policy during the decade of oil crises and economic downturn had been too austere, overly directed against fighting inflation. For the monetarists, the case had been almost the opposite. They have contended that "politicians had continued to drive up money growth to fight short-term unemployment, to the sacrifice of longer-term price stability." And for the new classical macroeconomists, the policies were simply too erratic, with policy "surprises" explaining the fluctuations in output growth.[6] Undoubtedly, tight policies can explain high unemployment at certain times and places, but it is doubtful that they provide a general explanation for the experience of the 1970s and early 1980s.[7]

Even so, the key issue in the supply shock literature that developed after the 1973–74 oil price shock has focused attention on the question of appropriate monetary response in the face of supply disturbances. The critical question is whether monetary policy should turn expansionary to accommodate the exogenous shocks from the supply side. Or, should monetary policy turn contractionary to offset the inflationary effects of such disturbances? This issue has occupied the attention of macroeconomists, as well as policymakers, for over a decade now. With oil prices falling in recent years, and most likely continuing to fall in the next few years, the issue promises to be relevant and controversial for some time to come, even though the direction of the shocks has been reversed.

SUPPLY SHOCKS AND MONETARY ACCOMMODATION: DOCTRINAL DEBATES

In their early studies, Gordon,[8] Okun,[9] Logue and Willett,[10] Klein,[11] and Jaffee and Kleiman[12] attempted to fill some of the gaps in our knowledge of inflation's effect on the economy and demonstrated the positive empirical relationship between the inflation rate and its variability or unpredictability. Such heightened uncertainty may produce greater variability of real growth which, in turn, leads to greater uncertainty in production, investment, and marketing decisions.[13]

Blinder,[14] Gordon,[15] Gramlich,[16] Phelps,[17] and Ando,[18] on the other hand, focused on positive aspects of these questions in their studies, leading to the conclusion that "there is an exploitable trade-off between inflation and unemployment in the short run" despite rational expectations. They found empirically "large output effects and small price effects from monetary accommodation in the short run." The implication is that supply shocks should be accommodated.[19]

Nonetheless, the advocates of the rational expectations hypothesis—Lucas,[20] Fischer,[21] Barro,[22] and Sargent-Wallace[23]—questioned the theoretical underpinning and empirical results of the earlier studies on the ground that they had failed to deal properly with inflationary expectation. They contend that "an exploitable trade-off between inflation and unemployment" is a hypothesis of questionable validity and that an accommodative policy is not the optimal response to a supply shock. As Barro wrote, "Adverse shifts like the oil and agricultural crises will reduce output and cause painful relative adjustments no matter what the reaction of the monetary authority. Added monetary noise would only complicate and lengthen the process of adjustments."[24] The implication seems to be that "the authorities should stick to a constant money growth rule and ignore any supply shocks that may occur."[25]

In dealing with the expectionists' arguments, Blinder (1981) extended the analyses of well-known papers by Lucas[26] and Fischer.[27] Into each model, Blinder introduced in the production of domestic output an input such as imported intermediate good as oil, which is neither produced domestically nor consumed directly. The two models were used to address the longstanding issue: "Should the central bank deviate from its constant growth rate rule where there is a supply shock?"[28]

Blinder considers a rule in which the money stock is adjusted in response to anticipated and unanticipated supply shocks and argues that certain types of disturbances may require a monetary contraction. So stated Blinder: "where unanticipated OPEC shocks are concerned, there is always an exploitable inflation-employment trade-off in the short run. . . . Where anticipated OPEC shocks are concerned, conclusions depend more on the specifics of each model." Furthermore, "Accommodation might be optimal . . . if unanticipated OPEC shocks are transitory." In the extended Lucas model, the only potential case for accommodation rests on OPEC's nominal price not adjusting fully to the anticipated U.S. price level. In this case, Blinder argues that "such a situation is likely to prevail in the short run, but not in the long run." In the extended Fischer model, there is "a case for accommodating OPEC shocks that are currently anticipated, but were unanticipated when some existing contracts were struck." With rather mild presumption, Blinder concludes that optimal policy is to contract the money supply after a shock.[29]

By contrast, Fischer (1985) argues that so long as there is no real wage resistance by workers, "supply shocks by themselves are unlikely to lead to unemployment if monetary policy remains passive." Rather, contends Fischer, "it is the aggregate demand effects associated with the supply shocks—including counterinflationary policy responses—that are responsible for unemployment."[30] In his study, Fischer uses a one-sector model to analyze the optimal monetary rule which requires a complete accommodation to the money demand shock. He finds that the price generated by money market equilibrium is precisely the price needed to yield the equilibrium real wage and, therefore, no accommodation is necessary. Under such circumstances, any attempt to alter the money supply in response to the supply shock would result in suboptimal employment and would inflict welfare loss.[31] The implication is that supply shocks by themselves require no monetary response. Fischer's results, however, depend upon very specific assumptions regarding the form of the money demand function. In particular, his analysis, calling for a passive monetary policy, is based on a classical money demand function, with a fixed supply of labor but without wage indexation. As a consequence, if the supply shock is accompanied by an adverse demand shock, according to Fischer, expansionary monetary policy might be used in an attempt to prevent recession.[32]

Aizenman and Frenkel also analyze the case of the optimal monetary rule which requires a complete accommodation to the money demand shock. They attempt to determine the optimal policy rules and to evaluate the welfare consequences and ranking of alternative (suboptimal) rules within a unified, analytical framework for the determination of optimal wage indexation and monetary policy. They first analyze two extreme cases—a rule that stabilizes employment and a rule that stabilizes the real wage.[33] Aizenman and Frenkel's analysis demonstrates that, on the formal level, the various indexation rules bear a dual relation to the various monetary targeting rules. They show that the welfare ranking of the various rules depends on whether the elasticity of the demand for labor exceeds or falls short of the elasticity of labor supply. With such an argument, they contend that "the optimal monetary response to the effective real shock depends positively on the relative share of imported energy in output." In general, however, as long as the interest elasticity of money demand or the elasticity of labor supply differ from zero and the income elasticity of the demand differs from unity, there is room for active monetary policy.[34] Specifically, if the demand for labor is more elastic than the supply, then policy rules that stabilize employment are preferred to policy rules that stabilize the real wage and vice versa.[35]

Although Aizenman-Frenkel allow for supply shocks that are not observed instantaneously, the focus of their analysis is on the tradeoff between wage indexation and monetary policy, rather than on stabilizing for supply shocks themselves. While Aizenman-Frenkel stress how this in turn is important in determining the role of monetary policy, Marston-Turnovsky (1985a)[36] show how the macroeconomic effects of supply disturbances depend crucially upon wages policy. In their later study (1985b),[37] Marston-Turnovsky, however, allow for firm-specific productivity disturbances that may, or may not be observed generally. In contrast, Blinder-Mankiw (1984)[38] show that monetary policy, being an aggregate policy, is not suitable for dealing with sector-specific shocks. Under such circumstances, conclude Aizenman-Frenkel, "optimality calls for sector-specific policies."[39]

In sum, with the exception of the Blinder-Mankiw study, the policy rules typically considered in these studies specify the adjustment of the money stocks to current supply disturbances. With the exception of the studies by Aizenman-Frenkel (1985) and Marston-Turnovsky (1985b), these studies assume that the monetary authorities observe and respond to the current supply disturbance instantaneously.

In his recent study (1987)[40] of supply shocks and optimal monetary policy, Turnovsky attempts to fill the gap in these studies by analyzing those issues not addressed in these studies. He places a greater emphasis on "the distinction between disturbances that are permanent or transitory, on the one hand, and unanticipated or anticipated on the other." From this analysis, Turnovsky draws two main conclusions, subject to the specific assumptions of the model.

First, Turnovsky shows that if current shocks are observed instantaneously, perfect output stabilization can be achieved for any form of supply disturbances with relatively little information about the nature of the disturbances, by using remarkably simple monetary rules. He argues that it is possible and reasonable for the monetary authorities to respond to anticipation of both current and future supply shocks. To such extent, then, the monetary authorities need consider only (a) the current shock, (b) the forecast of the current shock formed in the previous period, and (c) the forecast for just one period ahead. They need not be concerned with "what might occur in subsequent periods beyond, and therefore do not need to determine whether an anticipated shock for the next period is temporary or permanent."[41]

Secondly, Turnovsky shows that if current shocks are inferred from other signals such as the interest rate and price level and are not observed instantaneously, "the optimal rules are of the same form, with the current perceived disturbance replacing the actual," and "perfect stabilization of output may, or may not be possible, both depending upon the information available."[42]

Turnovsky's results are indeed quite significant in our understanding of doctrinal aspects of the monetary accommodation to supply shocks. They are by no means the optimal solution to the longstanding problem. The fact is that at this point there does not seem to be any consensus as to what the appropriate monetary response should be.

These brief remarks on supply shocks and monetary accommodation are all that a wide-ranging survey will permit. The theory warrants the most intensive analysis, both theoretically and empirically. For, though the worst of the post-energy crisis slump has been behind us for the past four years, supply shocks will surely strike again. So the question of their monetary responses and optimal monetary rules will be recurring, whether or not it is in abeyance at this moment. It is to be hoped, therefore, that we will soon be better able to appraise the optimal monetary policy in response to supply disturbances than we have been to date.

Without being embroiled and entangled in further doctrinal debates which is indeed beyond the scope of this book, and to facilitate further understanding of the effect of the money-price-GNP link of higher energy prices, the empirical underpinnings are provided below.

MONEY-ENERGY-PRICE-GNP LINK: EMPIRICAL EVIDENCES

In this section, we explain and assess the magnitude of the energy price effects. Empirical tests are conducted using a modified Blinder's model for nominal GNP, real GNP, and the price level. This model emphasizes the link between money stock growth and economic activity.

The sample period for estimating the relationships is 1951–81. Two subsample periods, 1951–70 and 1971–81, are also considered. This provides an opportunity to test the stability of the relationships over the 31 years, when energy factors were considered to be irrelevant in stabilization policies and when energy prices increased sharply with deleterious macroeconomic effects. An assessment of the size of the effects of energy price increases is obtained from the empirical estimates presented below.

Effect on the Money–GNP Link of Higher Energy Prices

To examine the effect of energy price on the money-GNP link, we consider a variant of the Blinder equation. This equation relates GNP to money stock, velocity of money, and energy prices. It is expressed as:

$$\ln Y = a_0 + a_1 \ln M + a_2 \ln (M/Y)_{-1} + a_4 \ln R + a_3 \ln R_{-1} \qquad (1)$$

and

$$\ln(Y/P) = b_0 + b_1 \ln M + b_2 \ln (M/Y)_{-1} + b_3 \ln R + b_4 \ln R_{-1} \qquad (2)$$

where Y denotes nominal GNP, M nominal money stock, R actual domestic average wholesale price of crude oil per barrel in current dollars. We also consider the equations:

$$\ln Y = c_0 + c_1 \ln M + c_2 \ln w + c_3 \ln k \qquad (3)$$

and

$$\ln Y = d_O + d_1 \ln M + d_2 \ln (M/Y)_{-1} + d_3 \ln w + d_4 \ln k \qquad (4)$$

where w is hourly earning in manufacturing industry, and k denotes the natural rate of output growth.

Estimates of the Real Output

Estimates of the real output are given in Table 9.1. The results obtained are satisfactory in indicating the significance of the money stock—both narrowly and broadly defined. All money elasticities are highly significant at the 0.1 percent level and are less than unity, ranging from 0.5065 (eq. 1.5) to 0.8190 (eq. 1.3). The highest money elasticity occurs in the sub-sample period 1971–81. Most of the Durbin-Watson statistics are within the range for confidently rejecting the hypothesis that there are serial correlations in the residuals. The coefficients of determination (R^2s) for the six equations estimated range from the lowest 0.9827 (eq. 1.1) to the highest 0.9933 (eq. 1.5).

The elasticities of real output with respect to the income velocity of money are highly significant at 1 percent level during the 1951–70 period and also for the entire sample period 1951–81. Nonetheless, the elasticities of the velocity are not significantly different from zero during the 1971–81 period, which is the period of energy crisis.

With the exception of equations 1.4, 1.5, and 1.6, the lagged values of energy prices are not elastic, indicating that the impact of the price of energy on GNP is not significant. We also perform simulation based upon equations 1.1 and 1.2. The real output is underestimated for the cases considered during the subsample period 1971–81 when the broad definition of money (M_2) is used as one of the independent variables. Nonetheless, the standard forecast error (RMSE) is only 0.56 percent of actual ln (Y/P) in eq. 1.2. The standard forecast error is 2.34 percent when equation 1.1 is used.

Table 9.1
Estimates of Real Output

$$\ln (Y/P) = b_0 + b_1 \ln M + b_2 \ln (M/Y)_{-1} + b_3 \ln R + b_4 \ln R_{-1}$$

Sample Period	Eq. No.	M_q	$\overline{R}^2$ / F	DW / SEED	Constant t-Ratios	$\ln M_q$	$\ln (M/Y)_{-1}$	$\ln R$	$\ln R_{-1}$
1951–70	1.1	M_1	0.9827 / 271.3014	2.4084 / 0.0120	1.4609* / 6.6554	0.6113* / 5.1673	- 0.6653* / - 4.9567	- 0.1867 / - 0.8137	- 0.1665 / - 0.7143
	1.2	M_2	0.9870 / 361.0620	2.0771 / 0.0104	1.3756* / 24.6246	0.6692* / 22.6210	- 0.3199* / - 1.8458	- 0.1600 / - 0.7956	- 0.0244 / - 0.1203
1971–81	1.3	M_1	0.9842 / 157.1836	1.9466 / 0.0054	1.3928* / 6.9882	0.8190* / 5.1405	0.2443 / 0.7067	- 0.0338 / - 1.4800	- 0.0324 / - 1.0981
	1.4	M_2	0.9708 / 84.0874	2.0103 / 0.0074	1.6121* / 7.3507	0.6282* / 7.9236	0.2145 / 0.6969	0.0300 / 0.6451	- 0.1172* / - 2.9125
1951–81	1.5	M_1	0.9933 / 1119.2174	2.0167 / 0.0110	1.5837* / 15.7099	0.5065* / 7.8322	- 0.6941* / - 8.8284	- 0.0656 / - 1.5957	- 0.0865* / - 1.8457
	1.6	M_2	0.9932 / 1088.7232	1.5391 / 0.0112	1.4606* / 43.2629	0.6083* / 29.5144	- 0.4442* / - 3.8214	- 0.0711* / - 1.7566	- 0.0860* / - 1.8110

Note: Y = nominal GNP
P = implicit GNP price deflator, 1975 = 100
M = nominal money stock
R = actual domestic average wholesale price of crude oil per bbl. in current dollars.
*indicates significance of the variable at 5% level.

Source: Estimated by the author using Equation (1). Historical data are from International Monetary Fund, *International Financial Statistics,* 1981 Yearbook.

Estimates of the Nominal Output

Estimates of the nominal output are given in Tables 9.2 and 9.3 and are satisfactory from the point of view of the significance of the R^2s. The R^2s for the equations presented in Tables 9.2 and 9.3 seem to enjoy a slight improvement over the equations presented in Table 9.1. All of the money elasticities are highly significant at 1 percent level and are generally higher than those of real output. Nonetheless, all of the current and lagged values of the price of energy shown in these two tables are highly insignificant at 10 percent level.

Substituting the hourly earnings, w, and the natural rate of output growth, k, for the current and lagged values of the energy prices, the R^2s have improved significantly, ranging from the lowest 0.9985 (eq. 3.1) to the highest 0.9993 (eq. 3.5). With the exception of equations 2.3, 2.4, 3.3, and 3.4, for the subsample 1971–81 period the elasticities of nominal output with respect to the nominal money stock and the income velocity of money are consistent with the results obtained in Tables 9.1 and 9.2 for real and nominal output, respectively.

All of the elasticities of the current and lagged values of the energy prices for nominal output, however, are not significantly different from zero for any sample period tested. The significance of the elasticities of the hourly earnings and the natural rate of output growth indicates that the effect of the energy price shock is only a temporary phenomenon. These empirical evidences strongly support the hypothesis that GNP is independent of energy price changes and the shift in aggregate supply due to energy price changes leaves nominal demand unchanged. It should also be mentioned that all of the lagged income velocities of money for the 1971–81 period are highly insignificant at 10 percent level. This might be due to the fact that changes in energy price were rather substantial during the period under study. Moreover, the growth of the money stock was highly erratic during the 1978–81 period. Thus, the ability of equations 2.1, 2.2, 3.1, and 3.2 to simulate (or forecast) the postsample experience is a strong test of effects of energy price shock on nominal output.

Simulation results show that the equations specified track extremely well over the 11-year period from 1971 to 1981. The standard simulation errors (RMSEs) range from 0.87 percent to 3.17 percent of actual nominal output. Despite the accuracy of these simulation results, it must be emphasized that the economy has seldom been forced to adjust to changes in the relative prices of energy.

Effect on the Money-Price Link of Higher Energy Prices

The effect of a change in the energy prices on the general level of prices is examined in the context of a simple equation that focuses on the link between money and prices. Prior studies by Karnosky,[43] Carlson,[44] and Tatom,[45] show that the growth of the money stock over the 1975–80 period is a significant

Table 9.2
Estimates of Nominal Output

$$\ln Y = a_0 + a_1\ln M + a_2\ln (M/Y)_{-1} + a_3\ln R + a_4\ln R_{-1}$$

Sample Period	Eq. No.	M_q	$\bar{R}^2$ / F	DW / SEED	Constant t-Ratios	$\ln M_q$	$\ln (M/Y)_{-1}$	$\ln R$	$\ln R_{-1}$
1951–70	2.1	M_1	0.9894	2.8288	− 0.0646	1.0394*	− 0.9223*	0.0929	− 0.0269
			420.4860	0.0149	− 0.2358	6.8293	− 5.3467	0.3177	− 0.0929
	2.2	M_2	0.9920	2.4843	− 0.0085	1.0397*	− 0.4414*	0.1322	0.1324
			556.4231	0.0130	− 0.1195	26.8265	− 1.8004	0.5247	0.5233
1971–81	2.3	M_1	0.9979	2.2966	− 0.2721	1.2841*	− 0.3542	0.0295	0.0098
			1205.7835	0.0066	− 1.1240	6.6344	− 0.8432	1.0621	0.2727
	2.4	M_2	0.9929	2.1209	− 0.3781	1.2515*	− 0.2571	0.0868	− 0.1051
			351.0020	0.0122	− 1.0441	9.5611	− 0.5058	1.1297	− 1.5816
1951–81	2.5	M_1	0.9983	2.7955	− 0.0475	1.0426*	− 0.9278*	0.0224	− 0.0152
			4185.1619	0.0118	− 0.4240	14.2588	− 9.9539	0.5085	− 0.3034
	2.6	M_2	0.9980	2.0495	0.0553	1.0359*	− 0.5825*	0.0579	− 0.0278
			3656.7056	0.0126	1.3006	43.4898	− 3.6314	1.2483	− 0.5187

Note: Y = nominal GNP

M = nominal money stock

R = actual domestic average wholesale price of crude oil per bbl. in current dollars.

*indicates significance of the variable at 5% level.

Source: Estimated by the author using Equation (2). Historical data are from International Monetary Fund, *International Financial Statistics*, 1981 Yearbook.

Table 9.3
Estimates of Nominal Output

$$\ln Y = d_0 + d_1 \ln M + d_2 \ln (M/Y)_{-1} + d_3 \ln w + d_4 \ln k$$

Sample Period	Eq. No.	M_q	$\overline{R}^2$ / F	DW / SEED	Constant t-Ratios	$\ln M_q$	$\ln (M/Y)_{-1}$	$\ln w$	$\ln k$
1951–70	3.1	M_1	0.9985 / 2957.1230	2.1888 / 0.0056	−0.1695 / −1.6885	0.8016* / 11.5068	−0.5469* / −5.0724	0.5059* / 4.6748	1.0718* / 6.7168
	3.2	M_2	0.9988 / 3646.3279	1.9585 / 0.0051	0.0298 / 1.3176	0.6497* / 10.8610	−0.1318 / −0.9319	0.6646* / 6.1616	0.6959* / 4.2643
1971–81	3.3	M_1	0.9992 / 3198.3250	2.3876 / 0.0040	0.0007 / 0.0035	0.6390* / 3.2663	0.5466 / 1.3581	0.9959* / 3.8152	−0.0191 / −0.1002
	3.4	M_2	0.9980 / 1219.1938	1.4804 / 0.0066	1.1385* / 3.8711	−0.4887 / −1.4332	0.0825 / 0.2754	1.7252* / 4.7771	0.5830 / 1.4616
1951–81	3.5	M_1	0.9993 / 10774.9139	1.9768 / 0.0073	0.0443 / 0.6998	0.8125* / 10.3885	−0.7937* / −12.3430	0.2875* / 3.6118	0.8708* / 5.2781
	3.6	M_2	0.9992 / 8969.7472	1.6507 / 0.0080	0.0839* / 3.0170	0.7459* / 13.3275	−0.4647* / −3.3454	0.4238* / 5.1026	0.7291* / 3.5479

Note: Y = nominal GNP

   M = nominal money stock

   w = hourly earnings in manufacturing industry

   k = natural rate of output growth

   *indicates significance of the variable at 5% level.

Source: Estimated by the author using Equation (3). Historical data are from International Monetary Fund, *International Financial Statistics*, 1981 Yearbook.

determinant of the rate of increase in prices. In this study, we introduce current and lagged values of the energy prices into the money-price equations considered by Karnosky and Carlson. The equation specified is:

$$\ln P = e_0 + e_1 \ln M_q + e_2 \ln P_{-1} + e_3 \ln R + e_4 \ln R_{-1} \qquad (5)$$

where P denotes wholesale price index (1975 = 100), M_q the money stock, $q = 1,2$, and R the price of energy.

Estimates of this equation are presented in Table 9.4. Estimates of the general price level are generally satisfactory. The coefficients of determination are all highly significant at 5 percent level by an F-test. They range from the lowest 0.9666 (eq. 4.2) to the highest 0.9974 (eq. 4.5). Most of the energy elasticities are highly significant at 1 percent level. Nonetheless, the magnitude of the energy elasticities is rather large compared to that of the money elasticities in these equations. The lagged price level seems to have substantial impact on the current general level of prices. During the subsample period 1971–81, the lagged price elasticities are slightly above unity, while those for the subsample 1951–70 period range from 0.6336 to 0.6814.

The most significant result is the insignificance of the money elasticities during the subsample 1971–81 period, when energy prices increased substantially and were dominant. This result might be due to the highly erratic growth of money stock during the second half (1978–81) of this subsample period.

The simulation results indicate that the general levels of prices are mostly underestimated. However, the simulation errors are quite small. As shown in Table 9.5, the RMSEs for the subsample period 1971–81 are 2.05 percent and 2.32 percent using equations (4.1) and (4.2), respectively. These RMSEs are not significantly larger than the standard errors during the sample period.

SUMMARY AND CONCLUSIONS

The new and complex problems as a result of worldwide energy crisis in the 1970s have severely taxed the capacity of traditional economic theory. Monetary accommodation of the 1973–74 oil price increase worked temporarily to offset the output growth-inducing impact of the shock; but, sharply higher energy costs exacerbated world inflation rates and the productivity slowdown. While correlations between energy consumption and economic growth do not prove causality, the possibility exists that energy consumption and economic growth are inextricably interwined. Even assuming causality, it is not clear if the direction of causality runs from energy to economic growth or vice versa. History tells us that energy consumption is in part a necessary condition for economic growth and in part a consequence of growth.

Pellucidly, a sudden large increase in energy prices can have deleterious macroeconomic effects. In situations such as the Arab oil embargo of 1973, there is a tendency for policymakers to adopt restrictive policies to hold down

Table 9.4
Energy Prices and the Money-Price Link

$$\ln Y = e_0 + e_1 \ln M + e_2 \ln P_{-1} + e_3 \ln R + e_4 \ln R_{-1}$$

Sample Period	Eq. No.	M_q	$\bar{R}^2$ / F	DW / SEED	Constant / t-Ratios	$\ln M_q$	$\ln P_{-1}$	$\ln R$	$\ln R_{-1}$
1951–70	4.1	M_1	0.9711	1.9748	0.2615	0.1199*	0.6336*	0.2523*	−0.0060
			152.4378	0.0047	1.7908	3.1618	4.8927	2.7389	−0.0685
	4.2	M_2	0.9666	1.8623	0.2941	0.0620*	0.6814*	0.2763*	−0.0273
			131.3428	0.0051	1.6410	2.6000	4.9774	2.8197	−0.2949
1971–81	4.3	M_1	0.9940	1.5371	−0.3842	0.1481	1.0548*	0.1638*	−0.2518*
			412.3027	0.0105	−1.3374	0.6500	3.5988	3.6889	−2.8821
	4.4	M_2	0.9937	1.7670	−0.3454	0.1123	1.0647*	0.1730*	−0.2644*
			394.4708	0.0108	−1.2001	0.3801	2.5062	3.5264	−2.9555
1951–81	4.5	M_1	0.9974	1.1628	−0.1776	0.1075*	0.9761*	0.1835*	−0.2139*
			2810.7231	0.0081	−1.4918	2.7407	8.0339	5.7340	−4.3501
	4.6	M_2	0.9972	1.2370	−0.1786	0.0528*	1.0463*	0.1865*	−0.2368*
			2588.7213	0.0085	−1.3261	2.2271	8.9640	5.4783	−4.8793

Note: P = wholesale price indejx, 1975 = 100
M = nominal money stock
R = actual domestic average wholesale price of crude oil per bbl. in current dollars.
*indicates significance of the variable at 5% level.

Source: Estimated by the author using Equationn (4). Historical data are from International Monetary Fund, *International Financial Statistics*, 1981 Yearbook.

Table 9.5
Summary of Simulation Errors for the Sub-Sample Period, 1971–81

Equation No.	RMSE %	SPCBAR %
1.1	2.340	0.402
1.2	0.560	0.349
2.1	0.950	0.542
2.2	3.170	0.472
3.1	0.970	0.205
3.2	0.870	0.185
4.1	2.050	0.271
4.2	2.320	0.292

Note: RMSE (root mean square errors) indicates percentage standard error of forecast. SPCBAR denotes SEEB as percent of the average of the dependent variable in regression equation.

inflation. Such policies, however, can contribute to the high unemployment, as both the supply and demand sides of the markets are driving output downward. While monetary policy cannot be expected to alleviate the effects of an exogenous supply shock, if used properly, they can prevent a worsening of the economic situation.

The empirical evidence obtained in this study is consistent with the adjustment process discussed above. It supports the hypothesis that GNP is independent of energy price changes once the adjustment is completed. It also suggests that once energy price effects are taken into account, no significant shift in the relationship between the money stock and major measures of economic performance is evidenced over the sample period 1951–81. The implication is that the exogenous supply shock is a short-run phenomenon and that the shift in aggregate supply due to energy price changes leaves both real and nominal demand unchanged in the long run. A rise in the level of energy prices has no permanent effect on both real and nominal GNP. Antiaccommodative monetary policies are optimal if supply shocks are permanent.

NOTES

1. Jeffrey D. Sachs, "Stabilization Policies in the World Economy: Scope and Skepticism," *AEA Papers and Proceedings* 72, no. 2 (May 1982), pp. 56–57.

2. Franco Modigliani, "The Monetarist Controversy or, Should We Foresake Stabilization Policies," *American Economic Review* 65, no. 2 (March 1977), pp. 15, 17.

3. Edward M. Gramlich, "Macro Policy Responses to Price Shocks," *Brookings Papers on Economic Activity* 1 (1979), p. 126; Robert J. Gordon, *Macroeconomics* (Boston, MA: Little, Brown & Co., 1981), p. 253; Glenn H. Miller, Jr., "Inflation and Recession, 1979–82: Supply Shocks and Economic Policy," Federal Reserve Bank of Kansas City, *Economic Review* (June 1983), pp. 11–12.

4. The preceding analysis draws on Alan S. Blinder, *Economic Policy and the Great Stagflation* (New York: Academic Press, 1979); Robert J. Gordon, *Macroeconomics,* 2d ed. (Boston: Little, Brown & Co., 1981); Otto Eckstein, *The Great Recession* (Amsterdam: North-Holland, 1978); Robert M. Solow, "What to Do (Macroeconomically) When OPEC Comes," in Stanley Fischer, ed., *Rational Expectations and Economic Policy* (Chicago: University of Chicago Press, 1980); see also Glenn H. Miller, Jr., op. cit., pp. 11–12.

5. William Fellner, "The Credibility Effect and Rational Expectations," *Brookings Papers on Economic Activity* 1 (1979), pp. 167–78; William Poole also has criticized what he calls the "activist" policy position with regard to supply shocks. See also, Robert C. Barro, "Rational Expectations and the Role of Monetary Policy," *Journal of Monetary Economics* (January 1976), pp. 1–32; and Miller, op. cit., p. 12.

6. Sachs, op. cit., p. 56.

7. Ibid.

8. Robert J. Gordon, "Steady Anticipated Inflation: Mirage or Oasis?" *Brookings Papers on Economic Activity* 2 (1971), pp. 499–510.

9. Arthur M. Okun, "The Mirage of Steady Inflation," *Brookings Papers on Economic Activity* 2 (1971), pp. 485–98.

10. Dennis E. Logue and Thomas D. Willett, "A Note on the Relation Between the Rate and Variability of Inflation," *Economica* 43 (May 1976), pp. 151–58.

11. Benjamin Klein, "Our New Monetary Standard: The Measurement and Effects of Price Uncertainty, 1880–1973," *Economic Inquiry* 13 (December 1975), pp. 461–84.

12. Dwight E. Jaffee and Edward Kleiman, "The Welfare Implications of Uneven Inflation," I.E.A. Conference on Inflation Theory and Anti-Inflation Policy, Saltsjobaden, Sweden, 1975.

13. Dennis E. Logue and Richard James Sweeney, "Inflation and Real Growth: Some Empirical Results," *Journal of Money, Credit, and Banking* 13, no. 4 (November 1981), pp. 497–501.

14. Alan S. Blinder, op. cit.

15. Robert J. Gordon, "Alternative Responses of Policy to External Supply Shocks," *Brookings Papers on Economic Activity* 1 (1975), pp. 183–204.

16. Edward M. Gramlick, "Macro Policy Responses to Price Shocks," *Brookings Papers on Economic Activity* 1 (1979), pp. 125–66.

17. Edmund S. Phelps, "Commodity-Supply Shocks and Full-Employment Monetary Policy," *Journal of Money, Credit, and Banking* 10 (May 1978), pp. 206–21.

18. Albert K. Ando and Carl Palash, "Some Stabilization Problems of 1971–75, with an Application of Optimal Control Algorithms," in Michael Intriligator, ed., *Frontiers of Quantitative Economics,* vol. 3 (Amsterdam: North-Holland Publishing Company, 1976).

19. Alan S. Blinder, "Monetary Accommodation of Supply Shocks under Rational Expectations," *Journal of Money, Credit, and Banking* 13, no. 4 (November 1981), pp. 425–26.

20. Robert E. Lucas, Jr., "Some International Evidence on Output-Inflation Trade-Offs," *American Economic Review* 63 (June 1973), pp. 326–34; also, idem, "Econometric Policy Evaluation: A Critique," in Karl Brunner and Allan H. Meltzer, eds., *The Phillips Curve and Labor Markets,* The Carnegie-Rochester Conference Series, vol. 1 (Amsterdam: North-Holland Publishing Company, 1976).

21. Stanley Fischer, "Long-Term Contracts, Rational Expectations, and the Optimal Money Supply Rule," *Journal of Political Economy* 85 (February 1977), pp. 191–205.

22. Robert J. Barro, "Rational Expectations and the Role of Monetary Policy," *Journal of Monetary Economics* 2 (January 1976), pp. 1–32.

23. Thomas J. Sargent and Neil Wallace, "Rational Expectations, the Optimal Monetary Instrument, and the Optimal Money Supply Rule," *Journal of Political Economy* 83 (April 1975), pp. 241–54.

24. Barro, op. cit., p. 26.

25. Blinder, "Monetary Accommodation of Supply Shocks under Rational Expectations," p. 426.

26. Lucas, "Some International Evidence on Output-Inflation Trade offs," pp. 326–34.

27. Fischer, op. cit.

28. Blinder, "Monetary Accommodation of Supply Shocks under Rational Expectations," pp. 426–27.

29. Ibid., pp. 436–37.

30. Fischer, "Supply Shocks, Wage Stickiness, and Accommodation," *Journal of Money, Credit, and Banking* 17, no. 1 (February 1985), p. 2.

31. Ibid., pp. 2–12; see also, Joshua A. Aizenman and Jacob A. Frenkel, "Supply Shocks, Wage Indexation and Monetary Accommodation," *Journal of Money, Credit, and Banking* 18, no. 3 (August 1986), p. 319.

32. Fischer, "Supply Shocks, Wage Stickiness, and Accommodation," p. 12.

33. Aizenman and Frenkel, op. cit., p. 304.

34. Ibid., p. 318.

35. Ibid., p. 305.

36. R. C. Marston and Stephen J. Turnovsky, "Imported Material Prices, Wage Policy, and Macroeconomic Stabilization," *Canadian Journal of Economics* 18 (1985a), pp. 273–84.

37. Marston and Turnovsky, "Macroeconomic Stabilization through Taxation and Indexation: The Use of Firm-Specific Information," *Journal of Monetary Economics* 16 (1985b), pp. 375–95.

38. Alan S. Blinder and Gregory N. Mankiw, "Aggregation and Stabilization Policy in a Multi-Contract Economy," *Journal of Monetary Economics* 13 (January 1984), pp. 67–86.

39. Aizenman and Frenkel, "Sectoral Wages, and the Real Exchange Rate," National Bureau of Economic Research Paper No. 1801, February 1986; see also Aizenman and Frenkel, "Supply Shocks, Wage Indexation and Monetary Accommodation," p. 320.

40. Turnovsky, "Supply Shocks and Optimal Monetary Policy," *Oxford Economic Papers* 39 (1987), pp. 20–37.

41. Ibid., pp. 34–35.

42. Ibid.

43. Dennis S. Karnosky, "The Link Between Money and Prices: 1970–76," *Review*, Federal Reserve Bank of St. Louis (June 1976), pp. 17–32.

44. Keith M. Carlson, "The Lag from Money to Prices," *Review*, Federal Reserve Bank of St. Louis (October 1980), pp. 3–10.

45. John A. Tatom, "Energy Prices and Short-Run Economic Performance," *Review*, Federal Reserve Bank of St. Louis (January 1981), pp. 3–17.

Bibliography

Ackely, Gardner. *Macroeconomic Theory*. New York: Macmillan Company, 1961.

Adelman, Morris, A. *The World Petroleum Market*. Baltimore: The Johns Hopkins University Press, 1972.

Aizenman, Joshua A., and Jacob A. Frenkel. "Sectoral Wages, and the Real Exchange Rate," National Bureau of Economic Research Paper No. 1801, February 1986.

———. "Supply Shocks, Wage Indexation and Monetary Accommodation," *Journal of Money, Credit, and Banking* 18, no. 3, August 1986, pp. 304–22.

Allen, Edward L. *U.S. Energy and Economic Growth*. Institute for Energy Analysis, Oak Ridge Associated Universities, Cambridge, MA: The MIT Press, 1979.

Allen, Edward L., et al., *U.S. Energy and Economic Growth 1975–2010*. Publication ORAU/IEA-76-7, Institute for Energy Analysis, Oak Ridge Associated Universities, Oak Ridge, Tennessee, September 1976.

Allen R. G. D. *Macroeconomic Theory—A Mathematical Treatment*. New York: Macmillan Company, 1968.

Almon, Clopper, Jr., Margaret Buckler, Lawrence M. Horowitz, and Thomas C. Reimbold. *1985: Interindustry Forecasts of the American Economy*. Lexington, MA: Heath, 1974.

Anderson, Kent. "Toward Estimation of Industrial Energy Demand: An Experimental Application to the Primary Metals Industry," Rand Corporation Report R-719-N.S.F., Santa Monica, December 1971.

Ando, Albert K, and Carl Palash. "Some Stabilization Problems of 1971–75, with an Application of Optimal Control Algorithms," in Michael Intriligator, ed. *Frontiers of Quantitative Economics*, vol. 3. Amsterdam: North-Holland, 1976.

Askin, A. Bradley, ed. *How Energy Affects the Economy*. Lexington, MA: Lexington Books, 1978.

Barro, Robert J. "Rational Expectations and the Role of Monetary Policy," *Journal of Monetary Economics* 2, January 1976, pp. 1–32.

Basvi, Giorgio. "Western Europe," in Edward R. Fried and Charles L. Schultz, ed., *Higher Oil Prices and the World Economy: The Adjustment Problem.* Washington, DC: The Brookings Institution, 1975.

Bergsten, C. Fred. "The Threat Is Real," *Foreign Policy* 14, Spring 1974, pp. 84–90.

———. "The Threat from the Third World," *Foreign Policy* 11, pp. 102–24.

Behling, David J., Jr., William Marcuse, Joan Lukachinski, and Robert Dullien. "The Long-Term Economic and Environmental Consequences of Phasing Out Nuclear Electricity," Brookhaven National Laboratory, in Charles J. Hitgh, ed., *Modeling Energy-Economy Interactions: Five Approaches.* Washington, DC: Resources for the Future, 1977, pp. 46–134.

Berndt, Ernst R. "Aggregate Energy, Efficiency and Productivity Measurement," *Annual Review of Energy 3,* April 1973, pp. 225–73.

———. "Technology, Prices, and the Derived Demand for Energy," *Review of Economics and Statistics,* August 1975.

———. "Reconciling Alternative Estimates of the Elasticity of Substitition," *Review of Economics and Statistics* 58, February 1976.

Berndt, Ernst R., and Laurits R. Christensen. "The Translog Function and the Substitution of Equipment, Structures, and Labor in U.S. Manufacturing, 1929–68," *Journal of Econometrics* 1, March 1973, pp. 81–114.

Berndt, Ernst R., and Barry C. Field, eds., *Modeling and Measuring Natural Resource Substitution.* Cambridge, MA: The MIT Press, 1981.

Berndt, Ernst R., Melvyn A. Fuss, and Leonard Waverman. "Dynamic Models of the Industrial Demand for Energy," Report EA-500, Electric Power Research Institute, Palo Alto, November 1977.

Berndt, Ernst R., Catherine J. Morrison, and G. Campbell Watkins. "Dynamic Models of Energy Demand: An Assessment and Comparison," in Ernst R. Berndt and Barry C. Field, eds., *Modeling and Measuring Natural Resource Substitution.* Cambridge, MA: The MIT Press, 1981.

Berndt, Ernst R., and David O. Wood. "Technology, Prices, and the Derived Demand for Energy," *Review of Economic Statistics* 57, August, 1975, pp. 259–68.

———. "Engineering and Econometric Interpretations of Energy-Capital Complementarity," *American Economic Review,* June, 1979.

———. "Engineering and Econometric Interpretations of Energy-Capital Complementarity: Reply and Further Reply," *The American Economic Review* 71, December 1981.

Blinder, Alan S. *Economic Policy and the Great Stagflation.* New York: Academic Press, 1979.

———. "Monetary Accommodation of Supply Shocks under Rational Expectations," *Journal of Money, Credit, and Banking* 13, no. 4, November 1981.

Blinder, Alan S., and Gregory N. Mankiw. "Aggregation and Stabilization Policy in a Multi-Contract Economy," *Journal of Monetary Economics* 13, January 1984.

Bohi, D. R., M. Russell, and M. McCarthy Snyder. *The Economics of Energy and Natural Resource Pricing,* A Compilation of Reports and Hearings, 94th Congress, 1st Session, Parts 1 and 2, March 1975.

Bosworth, B. "Capacity Creation in the Basic-Materials Industries," *Brookings Papers on Economic Activity* 2, 1976.

Braff, Allan J. *Microeconomic Analysis*. New York: John Wiley & Sons, Inc., 1969.

Brannon, Gerald M. "U.S. Taxes on Energy Resources," *AEA Papers and Proceedings of the Eighty-Seventh Annual Meeting of the AEA*. May 1975, pp. 397–404.

Brown, Randall, and Laurits Christensen. "Estimating Elasticities of Substitution in a Model of Partial Static Equilibrium: An Application to U.S. Agriculture, 1947 to 1974," in Ernst Berndt and Barry C. Field, eds., *Modeling and Measuring Natural Resource Substitution*. Cambridge, MA: The MIT Press, 1981.

Burmeister, Edwain, and Rodney A. Dobell. *Mathematical Theories of Economic Growth*. New York: The Macmillan Company, 1970.

Burrows, James C., and Thomas A. Domencich. *An Analysis of the United States Oil Import Quota*. Lexington, MA: D.C. Heath and Co., 1970.

Cabinet Task Force on Oil Import Control. *The Oil Import Question*. Washington, DC, 1970.

Carlson, Keith M. "Explaining the Economic Slowdown of 1979: A Supply and Demand Approach," *Review*, Federal Reserve Bank of St. Louis, October 1979, pp. 15–22.

———. "The Lag from Money to Prices," *Review*, Federal Reserve Bank of St. Louis, October 1980, pp. 3–10.

Caves, Richard E., and Ronald W. Jones. *World Trade and Payments*. Boston, MA: Little, Brown and Company, 1981.

Christensen, Laurits R., Dale W. Jorgenson, and Lawrence J. Lau. "Transcendental Logarithmic Production Functions," *Review of Economic Statistics* 55, February 1973, pp. 28–45.

Cline, William E. *International Debt and The Stability of the World Economy*. Institute for International Economics, 1983.

Cline, William E., and Sidney Weintraub. eds., *Economic Stabilization in Developing Countries*. Washington, DC: The Brookings Institution, 1981.

Committee for Economic Development. *International Consequences of High-Priced Energy*. New York: Georgian Press, Inc., September 1975.

The Council of State Governments. *State Responses to the Energy Crisis*. 1974.

Dam, Kenneth W. "Implementation of Import Quotas: The Case of Oil," *The Journal of Law and Economics*, April 1971.

Darmstadter, Joe. "Energy," in Ronald G. Ridker, ed., *Population, Resources, and the Environment*, volume III, U.S. Commission on Population Growth and the American Future Research Reports. Washington, DC: Government Printing Office, 1972.

———. *Regional Energy Consumption*. Washington, DC: Resources for the Future and Regional Plan Association, 1973.

———. "International Comparisons of Energy Use—Findings from a Recently Completed RFF Report: Summary," in Joy Dunkerley, ed., *International Comparisons of Energy Consumption*. Washington, DC: Resources for the Future, 1978.

Darmstadter, Joe, J. Dunkerly, and J. Alterman. *How Industrial Societies Use Energy: A Comparative Analysis*. Resources for the Future. Baltimore, MD: The Johns Hopkins University Press, 1977.

Darmstadter, Joe, et al. *Energy in the World Economy*. Baltimore, MD: The Johns Hopkins University Press, 1972.

Dasgupta, Patha. "Resources Pricing and Technological Innovations under Oligopoly: A Theoretical Exploration," in Lars Matthiessen, ed., *The Impact of Rising Oil*

Prices on the World Economy. London: The Macmillan Press, Ltd., 1982, pp. 149–77.

Davis, David Howard. *Energy Politics.* 3d ed. New York: St. Martin's Press, 1982.

Denny, G. S., and M. Fuss. "The Use of Approximation Analysis to Test for Separability and the Existence of Consistent Aggregates," *The American Economic Review* 67, June 1977, pp. 404–18.

Diaz-Alejandro, Carlos F. "International Markets for LDCs—The Old and New," *American Economic Review Papers and Proceedings,* May 1979.

Doran, Charles F. *Myth, Oil, and Politics.* New York: The Free Press, 1977.

Dorf, Richard C. *Energy, Resources & Policy.* Reading, MA: Addition-Wesley Publishing Company, 1978.

Duchesneau, Thomas D. *Competition in the U.S. Energy Industry.* Cambridge, MA: Ballinger Publishing Company, 1975.

Duesenberry, James. *Business Cycles and Economic Growth.* McGraw-Hill, 1958.

Eckbo, Paul Lee. "OPEC and the Experience of Some Non-Petroleum International Cartels," M.I.T. Energy Lab, Working Paper, June 1975.

Eckstein, Otto. *The Great Recession,* Amsterdam: North-Holland, 1978.

Edmonds, Jae. "A Guide to Price Elasticities of Demand for Energy: Studies and Methodologies," Institute for Energy Analysis, Oak Ridge Associated Universities, Oak Ridge, Tennessee, August 1978.

Edmonds, Jae, and John M. Reilly. *Global Energy, Assessing the Future.* Institute for Energy Analysis, Oak Ridge Associated Universities. Oxford: Oxford University Press, 1985.

Eppen, Gary D., ed. *Energy: The Policy Issues.* Chicago: University of Chicago Press, 1975.

Erickson, E. W., and R. M. Spann. "The U.S. Petroleum Industry," in E. W. Erickson and L. Waverman, eds., *The Energy Questions: An International Failure of Policy,* vol. 2. Toronto: University of Toronto Press, 1974.

Exxon Corporation. *Middle East Oil,* 2d ed. Exxon Background Series, September 1980.

———. *World Oil Inventories.* 1981.

———. *How Much Oil and Gas?* Exxon Background Series, May 1982.

———. *OPEC: Questions and Answers.* Exxon Background Series, 1984.

Ezzati, Ali. *World Energy Markets and OPEC Stability.* Lexington, MA: Lexington Books, 1978.

Fabritius, Jan F. R., and Christian Ettrup Petersen. "OPEC Respending and the Economic Impact of an Increase in the Price of Oil," in Lars Matthiessen, ed., *The Impact of Rising Oil Prices on the World Economy.* London: The Macmillan Press, Ltd., 1982, pp. 80–96.

Federal Trade Commission. Staff Report on Investigation of the Petroleum Industry, July 1973.

Fellner, William. "The Credibility Effect and Rational Expectations," *Brookings Papers and Economic Activity,* 1979:1, pp. 167–78.

Field, Barry C., and Charles Grebenstein. "Capital-Energy Substitution in U.S. Manufacturing," *Review of Economics and Statistics* 62, May 1980.

Filipello, A. N. "A Question of Capacity," *Business and Government Outlook,* Fall 1976.

Findlay, Ronald., and Carlos A. Rodriguez. "Intermediate Imports and Macroeconomic Policy under Flexible Exchange Rates," *Canadian Journal of Economics* 10, May 1977, pp. 208–17.

Fischer, Stanley. "Long-Term Contracts, Rational Expectations, and the Optimal Money Supply Rule," *Journal of Political Economy* 85, February 1977, pp. 191–205.

———. "Supply Shocks, Wage Stickiness, and Accommodation," *Journal of Money, Credit, and Banking* 17, no. 1, February 1985, pp. 1–15.

Fog, Bjarke. "How Are Cartel Prices Determined?" *Journal of Industrial Economics,* November 1976.

The Ford Foundation. *A Time to Choose: America's Energy Future.* Final Report of the Foundation Energy Policy Project. Cambridge, MA: Ballinger, 1974.

Forrester, Jay W. *Industrial Dynamics.* Cambridge, MA: The MIT Press 1961.

Fried, Edmund R., and Charles L. Schultze. "Overview," in Fried and Schultze. eds., *Higher Oil Prices and the World Economy: The Adjustment Problem.* Washington, DC: The Brookings Institution, 1975.

Friedman, Milton. "Subsidizing OPEC Oil," *Newsweek,* June 23, 1975.

Fuss, Melvyn A. "The Demand for Energy in Canadian Manufacturing: An Example of the Estimation of Production Structures with Many Inputs," *Journal of Econometrics* 5 January 1977, pp. 89–116.

Gordon, Robert J. "Steady Anticipated Inflation: Mirage or Oasis?" *Brookings Papers on Economic Activity* 2, 1971, pp. 499–510.

———. "Alternative Responses of Policy to External Supply Shocks," *Brookings Papers on Economic Activity* 1, 1975.

———. *Macroeconomics,* 2d Ed. Boston: Little Brown & Co., 1981.

Gramlick, Edward M. "Macro Policy Responses to Price Shocks," *Brookings Papers on Economic Activity* 1, 1979, pp. 125–66.

Griffin, James M. "Alternative Responses of Policy to External Supply Shocks," *Brookings Papers on Economic Activity* 1, 1975, pp. 183–204.

———. "The Capital-Energy Complementarity Controversy: A Progress Report on Reconciliation Attempts," in Ernst R. Berndt and Barry C. Field, eds., *Modeling and Measuring Natural Resource Substitution.* Cambridge, MA: The MIT Press, 1981.

Griffin, James M., and Henry B. Steele. *Energy Economics and Policy.* New York: Academic Press, 1980.

Griffin, James M., and Paul R. Gregory. "An Intercountry Translog Model of Energy Substitution Responses," *American Economic Review* 66, no. 5, December 1976, pp. 845–57.

Gunning, J. M., M. Osterrieth, and J. Waelbroeck. "The Price of Energy and the Potential Growth of Developed Countries," *European Economic Review,* no. 7, 1976, pp. 35–62.

Hafer, R. W. "The Impact of Energy Prices and Money Growth on Five Industrial Countries," *Review,* Federal Reserve Bank of St. Louis, 63, no. 3, March 1981, pp. 19–26.

Halvorsen, Robert, and Jay Ford. "Substitution Among Energy, Capital, and Labor Inputs in U.S. Manufacturing," in Robert S. Pindyck, ed., *Advances in the Economics of Energy and Resources: Structure of Energy Markets,* 1979.

Harrod, R. F. *Towards a Dynamic Economics.* London: The Macmillan Company, 1949.

Hayashi, Fumio. "Tobin's Marginal q and Average q: A Neoclassical Interpretation," *Econometrica* 50, January 1982.

Hogan, William W., and Alan S. Manne. "Energy-Economy Interactions: The Fable of the Elephant and the Rabbit?" in Charles J. Hitgh, ed., *Modeling Energy-Econ-*

omy Interactions: Five Approaches. Washington, D.C.: Resources for the Future, 1977, pp. 247–277.

Hudson, Edward A. and Dale W. Jorgenson. "U.S. Energy Policy and Economic Growth, 1975–2000," *Bell Journal of Economics and Management Science,* 5, Autumn 1974, pp. 461–514.

International Energy Agency. *World Energy Outlook.* OECD/IEA, 1982.

Jaffee, Dwight E., and Edward Kleiman. "The Welfare Implications of Uneven Inflation." I.E.A. Conference on Inflation Theory and Anti-Inflation Policy, Saltsjobaden, Sweden, 1975.

Johansen, L. *Production Functions.* Amsterdam: North-Holland Publishing Co., 1972.

Johany, Ali D. "OPEC Is Not a Cartel: A Property Rights Explanation of the Rise in Crude Oil Prices." Unpublished doctoral dissertation, University of California–Santa Barbara, June 1978.

Johnson, William A. "The Impact of Price Controls on the Oil Industry: How to Worsen an Energy Crisis," in Gary D. Eppen, ed., *Energy: The Policy Issues.* Chicago: The University of Chicago Press, 1975.

Jorgenson, Dale W., ed. *Econometric Studies of U.S. Energy Policy.* Amsterdam: North-Holland Publishing Co., 1976.

Jorgenson, Dale W., E. R. Berndt, L. R. Christensen, and Edward A. Hudson, eds. *U.S. Energy Resources and Economic Growth.* Final Report to the Ford Foundation Energy Policy Project, Washington, DC, September 1973.

Kannan, Narasimhan P. *Energy, Economic Growth and Equity in the United States.* New York: Praeger Publishers, 1979.

Karnosky, Dennis S. "The Link Between Money and Prices: 1970–76," *Review,* Federal Reserve Bank of St. Louis, June 1976, pp. 17–32.

Kennan, John. "The Estimation of Partial Adjustment Models with Rational Expectations," *Econometrica,* 47, November 1979, pp. 1441–56.

Kennedy, Michael. "A World Oil Model," in Dale W. Jorgenson, ed., *Econometric Studies of U.S. Energy Policy.* Amsterdam: North Holland Publishing Company, 1976.

Keynes, John Maynard. *The General Theory of Employment, Interest and Money.* London: Macmillan Press, 1936.

Kitch, Edmund W. "Regulation of the Field Market for Natural Gas by the Federal Power Commission," *The Journal of Law and Economics,* October 1968, pp. 243–280.

Klein, Benjamin. "Our New Monetary Standard: The Measurement and Effects of Price Uncertainty, 1880–1973." *Economic Inquiry* 13, December 1975, 461–84.

Kopp, Raymond and V. Kerry Smith. "Capital-Energy Complementarity: Further Evidence," mimeo. Resources for the Future, Washington, DC, 1978.

Krasner, Stephen D. "Oil Is the Exception," *Foreign Policy,* no. 14, Spring 1974, pp. 68–84.

Krugman, P. "Real Exchange Rate Adjustment and Welfare Effects of Oil Price Decontrol," Working Paper No. 658, National Bureau of Economic Research, 1981.

Kulatilaka, Nalin. "A Partial Equilibrium Model of Derived Demand for Production Factor Inputs," Working Paper No. 1176–80, Sloan School, MIT, October 1980.

Lave, Lester B. "What Have We Learned from These Scenarios?" in Charles J. Hitgh, ed., *Modeling Energy-Economy Interactions: Five Approaches.* Washington, DC: Resources for the Future, 1977.

Leftwich, Richard H. *The Price System and Resource Allocation,* 3d Ed. New York: Holt, Rinehart and Winston, 1966.

Logue, Dennis E., and Richard James Sweeney. "Inflation and Real Growth: Some Empirical Results," *Journal of Money, Credit, and Banking* 13, no. 4, November 1981, pp. 497–501.

Logue, Dennis E., and Thomas D. Willett. "A Note on the Relation Between the Rate and Variability of Inflation," *Economica* 43, May 1976, pp. 151–58.

Lucas, Robert E., Jr. "Some International Evidence on Output-Inflation Trade-Offs," *American Economic Review* 63, June 1973, pp. 326–34.

———. "Econometric Policy Evaluation: A Critique," in Karl Brunner and Allan H. Meltzer, eds., *The Phillips Curve and Labor Markets.* The Carnegie-Rochester Conference Series, vol. 1. Amsterdam: North-Holland, 1976.

Luttrell, Clifton B. "A Barrel of Oil: Can We Offset OPEC's Gains with a Grain Cartel?" *Review,* Federal Reserve Bank of St. Louis, April 1981.

MacAvoy, Paul W. *Crude Oil Prices: As Determined by OPEC and Market Fundamentals.* Cambridge, MA: Ballinger, 1982.

MacAvoy, Paul W., and R. S. Pindyck. *Price Controls and the Natural Gas Shortage.* Washington, DC: American Enterprise Institute, 1975.

Magnus, Jan R. "Substitution Between Energy and Non-Energy Inputs in the Netherlands, 1950–1974," *International Economic Review,* 1979.

Mancke, Richard B. *The Failure of U.S. Energy Policy.* New York: Columbia University Press, 1974.

Manne, Alan S. "ETA-MACRO: A Model of Energy-Economy Interactions," in Charles J. Hitgh, ed., *Modeling Energy-Economy Interactions: Five Approaches.* Washington, DC: Resources for the Future, 1977, pp. 1–45.

Marston, R. C., and Stephen J. Turnovsky. "Imported Material Prices, Wage Policy, and Macroeconomic Stabilization," *Canadian Journal of Economics* 18, 1985, pp. 273–84.

———. "Macroeconomic Stabilization through Taxation and Indexation: The Use of Firm-Specific Information," *Journal of Monetary Economics* 16, 1985, pp. 375–95.

Matthiesson, Lars, ed. *The Impact of Rising Oil Prices on the World Economy.* London: The Macmillan Press, Ltd., 1980.

McDonald, Stephen L. *Petroleum Conservation in the United States.* Baltimore, MD: The Johns Hopkins University Press, 1971.

Mead, Walter J. *Energy and the Environment Conflict in Public Policy.* Washington, DC: American Enterprise Institute for Public Policy Research, 1978.

———. "The Performance of Government in Energy Regulations," *American Economic Review,* May 1979.

Meese, Richard. "Dynamic Factor Demand Schedules for Labor and Capital Under Rational Expectations," *Journal of Econometrics,* Summer 1980, pp. 141–58.

Mikdashi, Zuhayr. "Collusion Could Work," *Foreign Policy,* no. 14, Spring 1974.

Miller, Glenn H., Jr. "Inflation and Recession, 1979–82: Supply Shocks and Economic Policy," Federal Reserve Bank of Kansas City, *Economic Review,* June 1983.

Mitchell, E. J. *U.S. Energy Policy: A Primer.* Washington, DC: American Enterprise Institute, 1974.

Modigliani, Franco. "The Monetarist Controversy or, Should We Forsake Stabilization Policies," *American Economic Review* 65, no. 2, March 1977.

Morici, Peter, Jr. "The Impact of Higher Oil Prices on Economic Growth in the Industrial Economies," in A. Bradley Askin, ed., *How Energy Affects the Economy.* Lexington, MA: Lexington Books 1978, pp. 35–39.

Morrison, Catherine J., and Ernst R. Berndt, "Short-Run Labor Productivity in a Dynamic Model," *Journal of Econometrics* 16, August 1981, pp. 339–66.

Nordhaus, William D. *The Efficient Use of Energy Resources.* New Haven, CT: Yale University Press, 1979.

———. "Oil and Economic Performance in Industrial Countries," *Brookings Papers on Economic Activity* 2:1980.

Ohta, Makota. "Production Technologies of the U.S. Boiler and Turbogenerator Industries and Hedonic Price Indexes for their Products: A Cost Function Approach," *Journal of Political Economy* 83, February 1975, pp. 1–26.

Okun, Arthur M. "The Mirage of Steady Inflation," *Brookings Papers on Economic Activity* 2, 1971, pp. 485–98.

Osborne, D. K. "Cartel Problem," *American Economic Review* 66, no. 5, December 1976.

Ozatalay, Savas, Stephen Grubaugh, and Thomas Veach Long, II. "Energy Substitution and National Energy Policy," *The American Economic Review* 69, no. 2, May 1979.

Pachauri, Rajendra K. *The Political Economy of Global Energy.* Baltimore & London: The Johns Hopkins University Press, 1985.

Park, Yoon S. *Oil Money and the World Economy.* Boulder, CO: Westview Press, 1976.

Phelps, Edmund S. "Commodity-Supply Shocks and Full-Employment Monetary Policy," *Journal of Money, Credit, and Banking* 10, May 1978, pp. 206–21.

Pindyck, Robert S. "Interfuel Substitution and the Industrial Demand for Energy: An International Comparison," *Review of Economics Statistics* 61, May 1979, pp. 169–79.

———. *Structure of World Energy Demand.* Cambridge, MA: MIT Press, 1979.

———. "The Cartelization of World Commodity Markets," *American Economic Review,* May 1979.

Pindyck, Robert S., and Julio J. Rotemberg. "Dynamic Factor Demands and the Effects of Energy Price Shocks," *The American Economic Review* 73, no. 5, December 1983.

Rasche, R. H., and John A. Tatom. "The Effects of the New Energy Regime on Economic Capacity, Production, and Prices," *Review,* Federal Reserve Bank of St. Louis, May 1977, pp. 2–12.

Richardson, Harry W. *Economic Aspects of the Energy Crisis.* Lexington, MA: Lexington Books/Saxon House, 1975.

Ridker, Ronald G., William D. Watson, Jr., and Adele Shapanka. "Economic, Energy and Environmental Consequences of Alternative Energy Regimes: An Application of the RFF/SEAS Modeling System," Resources for the Future, in Charles J. Hitgh, ed., *Modeling Energy-Economy Interactions: Five Approaches.* Washington, DC: 1977, pp. 135–98.

Rowen, Hobart. "Globally Slow Pace Countries," *The Washington Post,* January 11, 1987.

Sachs, Jeffrey D. "Stabilization Policies in the World Economy: Scope and Skepticism," *AEA Papers and Proceedings* 72, no. 2, May 1982, pp. 56–57.

Sampson, Anthony. "Ten Years of Oil Crisis," *Newsweek*, September 12, 1983.

Samuelson, Paul A. *Foundations of Economic Analysis*. Cambridge, MA: Harvard University Press, 1947.

Sargent, Thomas J., and Neil Wallace, "Rational Expectations, the Optimal Monetary Instrument, and the Optimal Money Supply Rule," *Journal of Political Economy* 83, April 1975, pp. 241–54.

Sato, Kazuo. *Production Functions and Aggregation*. Amsterdam: North-Holland Publishing Co., 1975.

Schurr, Sam H., Bruce C. Netschart, Vera F. Eliasberg, Joseph Lerner, and Hans H. Landsberg. *Energy in the American Economy 1850–1975: Its History and Prospects*. Resources for the Future. Baltimore, MD: Johns Hopkins University Press, 1960.

Siegel, Barry N. *Aggregate Economics and Public Policy*, 4th ed. Homewood, IL: Richard D. Irwin, Inc., 1974.

Solow, Robert M. "What to Do (Macroeconomically) When OPEC Comes," in Stanley Fischer, ed., *Rational Expectations and Economic Policy*. Chicago: University of Chicago Press, 1980.

Spritzer, Ralph S. "Changing Elements in the Natural Gas Picture," in Keith C. Brown, ed., *Regulation of the Natural Gas Producing Industry*. Baltimore, MD: The Johns Hopkins University Press for the Resource for the Future, 1972.

Stapleton, David C. "Inferring Long-Term Substitution Possibilities from Cross-Section and Time-Series," in Ernst R. Berndt and Barry C. Field, eds., *Modeling and Measuring National Resource Substitution*. Cambridge, MA: The MIT Press, 1981.

Stigler, George. "The Theory of Economic Regulation," *The Bell Journal of Economics and Management Science*, Spring 1971.

Summers, Lawrence. "Taxation and Corporate Investment: A q Theory Approach," *Brookings Papers on Economic Activity* 1:1981, pp. 67–140

Swaim, Paul and Gerhard Friede. "Die Entwicklung des Energieverbrauchs der Bundesrepublik Deutschland und der Vereinigten Staaten von Amerika in Abhängigkeit von Preisen and Technologie," Karlsruhe: Inst. für Angewandte Systemanalyse, June 1976.

Tatom, John A. "Energy Prices and Capital Formation, 1972–1977," *Review*, Federal Reserve Bank of St. Louis, May 1979.

———. "Energy Prices and Short-Run Economic Performance," *Review*, Federal Reserve Bank of St. Louis, January 1981, pp. 3–17.

Tavoulareas, William. *A Debate on a Time to Choose: A Critique*. Cambridge, MA: Ballinger Publishing Company, 1977.

Turnovsky, Stephen J. "Supply Shocks and Optimal Monetary Policy," *Oxford Economic Papers* 39, 1987, pp. 20–37.

U.S. Bureau of National Affairs. "Allocations: F.E.A. Adopts Regulations Designed to Equalize Crude, Fuel Oil Costs," in *Energy Users Reports* 69, Washington, DC, December 5, 1974.

U.S. Congressional Budget Office. "The Effect of OPEC Oil Pricing on Output, Prices, and Exchange Rates in the United States and Other Industrialized Countries," CBO Study, February 1981.

U.S. Department of Energy. *Monthly Energy Review*. December 1982.

U.S. Federal Energy Administration. *Project Independence Blueprint*. Final Task Force

Report, prepared by the Interagency Task Force on Synthetic Fuels from coal under direction of the U.S. Department of Interior, Washington, DC, 1974.

Wallich, Henry C. "The Limits to Growth: Revisited," Remarks in the Manville Public Policy Lecture Series, Rockford College, Rockford, Illinois, April 7, 1982.

Walters A. A. "Production and Cost Functions," *Econometrica* 31, April 1963, pp. 1–66.

Weidenbaum, M. I., and Harnish, R. *Government Credit Subsidies for Energy Development*. Washington, DC: American Enterprise Institute, 1975.

Whittle, C. E., et al. *Economic and Environmental Implications of a U.S. Nuclear Moratoriam, 1985–2010*. Publication ORAU/IEA-76-4, Institute for Energy Analysis, Oak Ridge Associated Universities, Oak Ridge, Tennessee, 1976.

Willrich, Mason. *Energy and World Politics*. New York: The Free Press, 1975.

Wood, David O., and Robert B. Hirsch. "Reconciling Econometric Studies of Factor Demand: Data and Measurement Issues," Energy Laboratory Working Papers MIT-EL 81-011WP, MIT, April 1981.

Workshop on Alternative Energy Strategies (WAES). *Energy: Global Prospects 1985–2000*. New York: McGraw-Hill, 1977.

The World Bank. *World Development Report 1982*. 1982.

Yager, Joseph A. *The Energy Balance in Northeast Asia*. Washington, DC: The Brookings Institution, 1984.

Yang, Jai-Hoon. "The Nature and Origins of the U.S. Energy Crisis," *Review*, Federal Reserve Bank of St. Louis, July 1977.

Name Index

Subject Index

ABOUT THE AUTHOR

HUI-LIANG TSAI is Research Associate at the Center for Yugoslav-American Studies, Research, and Exchanges at Florida State University, Tallahassee. He has taught at The Pennsylvania State University Capital College, and Messiah and Lebanon Valley Colleges, both in Pennsylvania. He is a regular contributor to professional journals in economics and statistics and is coauthor (with George Macesich) of *Money in Economic Systems* (Praeger, 1982) and author of *Energy Shocks and the World Economy* (Praeger, 1989).

Dr. Tsai holds an M.S. in economics, an M.S. in statistics, and a Ph.D. in economics from Florida State University.